A CULTURAL HISTORY OF FOOD

VOLUME 6

A Cultural History of Food

General Editors: Fabio Parasecoli and Peter Scholliers

A CULTURAL HISTORY
OF FOOD

IN THE
MODERN AGE

VOLUME 6

Edited by Amy Bentley

Bloomsbury Academic
An imprint of Bloomsbury Publishing Plc

B L O O M S B U R Y
LONDON · OXFORD · NEW YORK · NEW DELHI · SYDNEY

Bloomsbury Academic
An imprint of Bloomsbury Publishing Plc

50 Bedford Square	1385 Broadway
London	New York
WC1B 3DP	NY 10018
UK	USA

www.bloomsbury.com

**BLOOMSBURY and the Diana logo are trademarks of
Bloomsbury Publishing Plc**

Hardback edition first published in 2012 by Berg Publishers,
an imprint of Bloomsbury Academic
Paperback edition first published in 2016 by Bloomsbury Academic

British Library Cataloguing-in-Publication Data
A catalogue record for this book is available from the British Library.

ISBN:	HB:	978-0-8578-5028-7
	HB set:	978-1-8478-8355-1
	PB:	978-1-4742-7004-5
	PB set:	978-1-4742-7075-5

Library of Congress Cataloging-in-Publication Data
A catalog record for this book is available from the Library of Congress.

Typeset by Apex CoVantage, LLC
Printed and bound in Great Britain

CONTENTS

SERIES PREFACE

GENERAL EDITORS, FABIO PARASECOLI
AND PETER SCHOLLIERS

A Cultural History of Food presents an authoritative survey from ancient times to the present. This set of six volumes covers nearly 3,000 years of food and its physical, spiritual, social, and cultural dimensions. Volume editors and authors, representing different nationalities and cultural traditions, constitute the cutting edge in historical research on food and offer an overview of the field that reflects the state of the art of the discipline. While the volumes focus mostly on the West (Europe in its broadest sense and North America), they also draw in comparative material and each volume concludes with a brief final chapter on contemporaneous developments in food ideas and practices outside the West. These works will contribute to the expansion of the food history research in Asia, Africa, Oceania, and South America, which is already growing at an increasingly fast pace.

The six volumes, which follow the traditional approach to examining the past in Western cultures, divide the history of food as follows:

Volume 1: A Cultural History of Food in Antiquity (800 BCE–500 CE)
Volume 2: A Cultural History of Food in the Medieval Age (500–1300)
Volume 3: A Cultural History of Food in the Renaissance (1300–1600)
Volume 4: A Cultural History of Food in the Early Modern Age (1600–1800)
Volume 5: A Cultural History of Food in the Age of Empire (1800–1900)
Volume 6: A Cultural History of Food in the Modern Age (1920–2000)

This periodization does not necessarily reflect the realities and the historical dynamics of non-Western regions, but the relevance of cultural and material exchanges among different civilizations in each period is emphasized.
Each volume discusses the same themes in its chapters:

1. *Food Production.* These chapters examine agriculture, husbandry,
   fishing, hunting, and foraging at any given period, considering the
   environmental impact of technological and social innovations, and
   the adaptation to the climate and environment changes.
2. *Food Systems.* These chapters explore the whole range of the transportation, distribution, marketing, advertising, and retailing of food,
   emphasizing trade, commerce, and the international routes that have
   crisscrossed the world since antiquity.
3. *Food Security, Safety, and Crises.* We cannot have a complete picture
   of the history of food without discussing how societies dealt with
   moments of crisis and disruption of food production and distribution, such as wars, famines, shortages, and epidemics. These essays
   reflect on the cultural, institutional, economic, and social ways of
   coping with such crises.
4. *Food and Politics.* These chapters focus on the political aspects of
   public food consumption: food aspects of public ceremonies and
   feasts, the impact on public life, regulations, controls, and taxation
   over food and alcohol production, exchange, and consumption.
5. *Eating Out.* The communal and public aspects of eating constitute
   the main focus of these essays. Authors consider hospitality for
   guests, at home and in public spaces (banquets and celebrations),
   and discuss public places to eat and drink in urban and rural environments, including street food, marketplaces, and fairs.
6. *Professional Cooking, Kitchens, and Service Work.* These chapters look at the various roles involved in food preparation outside
   the family nucleus: slaves, cooks, servants, waiters, *maitre d'hotel*
   etc., investigating also the most relevant cooking techniques, technologies, and tools for each period, giving special consideration to
   innovations.
7. *Family and Domesticity.* The acquisition, shopping and storage,
   preparation, consumption, and disposal of food in a domestic setting

are among the most important aspects of food culture. These chapters analyze family habits in different periods of time, paying particular attention to gender roles and the material culture of the domestic kitchen.

8. *Body and Soul*. These chapters examine fundamental material aspects such as nutritional patterns, food constituents, and food-related diseases. Furthermore, spiritual and cultural aspects of thinking about and consuming food are highlighted, including religion, philosophy, as well as health and diet theories.

9. *Food Representations*. These essays analyze cultural and discursive reflections about food, which not only contributed to the way people conceive of food, but also to the social and geographical diffusion of techniques and behavior.

10. *World Developments*. These brief chapters overview developments, dynamics, products, food-related behaviors, social structures, and concepts in cultural environments that often found themselves at the margins of Western modernity.

Rather than embracing the encyclopedic model, the authors apply a broad multidisciplinary framework to examine the production, distribution, and consumption of food, as grounded in the cultural experiences of the six historical periods. This structure allows readers to obtain a broad overview of a period by reading a volume, or to follow a theme through history by reading the relevant chapter in each volume.

Highly illustrated, the full six-volume set combines to present the most authoritative and comprehensive survey available on food through history.

Introduction

AMY BENTLEY

Food—not the first subject most people think of to tell the story of history and culture. Upon reflection, however, what better subject could there be? At the base of human existence, food plays a role in virtually every arena that is important to our lives: from the rituals of daily life, leisure activities, and aesthetic pleasure, to politics and government, war, social interchange, and commerce. Food fuels—literally and metaphorically—economic practices (domestic food-relief programs), social movements (lunch counter sit-ins, counter-globalization rallies and protests), business–government relationships (agriculture and farm subsidies), and international policy (famine relief and military alliances). Food not only helps determine both individual and collective identity, but it is also deeply enmeshed in political institutions and economic health. In fact, the consumption of food is an extraordinarily social activity laden with complex and shifting layers of meaning. Not only what we eat, but how and why we eat, tell us much about society, history, cultural change, and humans' views of themselves.

Food has always played a major role, and the ways in which it is produced, processed, distributed, controlled, consumed, and portrayed reveal not only the hierarchies of power, but also the subtle, multi-leveled challenges to that power by groups and individuals in society. Whether minimally processed foods (wheat, cooking oil), industrially manufactured items (instant ramen, Coca-Cola), or hand-made creations (tamales, holi-day sweets), people imbue particular foods with deep-seated meaning and emotion and will go to great lengths to preserve or promote them, regard-less of whether they are involved in their production (farmers, processors) or merely their consumption (tea drinking). Not only is food intimately, and intricately, tied to group image, but it is bound to national identity, and a nation's power or lack thereof. Since food is power—and an abundance of food can mean a surfeit of power—nations have been shaped, blessed, and at times intellectually and socially hindered by the availability of food in the twentieth and early twenty-first centuries, the time period with which this volume of *A Cultural History of Food* is concerned.

Until the last couple of decades many in academia did not view food as a fitting topic in its own right. Prior to this current popularity there were earlier academic studies of food, originating mainly in anthropology, folklore, and the *Annales* school, which regarded the study of food as key to understanding cultures and societies, and individuals' lives within them. Food did not fit a traditional standard of worthiness in most traditional academic disciplines. It was not seen and understood in political or intel-lectual terms, nor was it analyzed aesthetically. And when considered at all, food was often regarded as quotidian, seemingly mundane, and decid-edly female. Frequently, food was employed as an indistinctive backdrop through which to study, for example, labor relations (workers in canning factories and slaughter houses), agrarian political movements (New Deal-era food production), or twentieth-century industrialization (the rise of food-processing conglomerates). However, as social and cultural history combined to explore the intersection of everyday life, especially the ex-periences of women and minorities, with the consumption of all manner of objects, many more topics were deemed worthy of scholarly inquiry, including food. Eating, after all, is much more than ingesting nutrients for biological survival: food plays a significant role in social relationships, is a highly symbolic element in religious and magical rites, aids in developing and maintaining cultural distinctions, and assumes enormous significance in shaping individual identities.

After all, not only does everyone have to eat (and ideally several times daily) to survive, but also all the great civilizations, both ancient and mod-ern, meticulously recorded by historians and philosophers, have essentially risen and fallen according to rulers' abilities to feed their constituents successfully. The salience of recent debates concerning food safety, global environmentalism, and the effect of food production on indigenous peoples and cultures worldwide, and the renewed interest in high-quality, minimally processed food, culinary tourism and fine dining, combined with ever-rising rates of obesity and its adverse consequences, gives this history of food in the modern era rich potential.

This volume examines food from 1920 to the beginning of the twenty-first century: what was produced, processed, distributed, and consumed, under what circumstances and to what end, and how these foods changed over time within a larger framework of society, politics, economics, culture, and important events. Further, it will use the production and consumption of food as a lens to examine the effects of such watershed events as the devastating First and Second World Wars; the emergence of the United States and the Soviet Union as world superpowers; population booms and the shifting landscapes as cities shrank and swelled again with new immigrants; struggles for independence, civil rights, and democracy; and the uncertainty but also creativity of the so-called post-industrial, post-Cold War era of globalization.

A BRIEF SURVEY OF MAJOR EVENTS

It is virtually impossible to summarize accurately the history of the modern era around the globe, and do justice to every nation, every group of people, and every key event across continents—attempting to do so would result more in a list of events than an exploration and interpretation of the role of food in modern history. Despite the challenges, however, it is important and useful to at least point to key events, as the modern era is replete with transformative developments that directly affect the production and consumption of food. To begin, think of the dramatic changes that occurred between the beginning and the end of the twentieth century. Those born in the 1920s whose lives spanned much of the century entered into a markedly different society than the one in which they left. In the 1920s, for example, most farms were devoid of electricity and indoor plumbing, and airplane and automobile travel was unthinkable for most people. By the early twenty-first century, the world was a dramatically

different place. Modes of communication evolved from the radio to the tele-
phone, television, and satellites. Computers and digital media were an integral part of late-twentieth-century society and have continued to rapidly
evolve. Technology, as applied to industrialization and mass production of
goods, similarly fostered dramatic changes in people's lives. While industrialization and mass production of goods had begun prior to the modern
period, they continued to make dramatic inroads with regard to all-important
aspects of life, particularly food production and processing. Industrial processing, the development of plastics, artificial fertilizers, pesticides and herbicides, and refrigeration, for example, all had dramatic effects on food,
culture, and society.

The modern era also experienced dramatic development and change with
regard to political and social institutions, systems of government, and social
movements, including the demise or continuation of colonialism, democracy,
fascism, and communism. *De jure* colonialist regimes were replaced with
de facto colonialism, despots, and corruption. Both the West and East conducted their own evil actions: Jim Crow segregation and other indignities
in the United States, the European Holocaust, as well as Japanese domination and cruel treatment of those in other Asian countries. Yet struggling
independent nations also emerged during this period. Post-colonial independence in the Middle East, Africa, Asia, India/Pakistan, the formation of the
state of Israel and its ensuing Israeli–Palestinian conflict, the emergence of
the European Union—all took their place on the world political stage. Much
of the emergence of more democratic states was a result of those protest-
ing and fighting for equality and human rights: Mohatmas Ghandi, Nelson
Mandela, and Martin Luther King Jr. All took place against the terrible
backdrop of global and regional warfare in the modern era: World War II,
the Cold War, the American wars in Asia (Korea, Vietnam) and the Middle
East (the Gulf Wars), hot and cold wars all over the globe, between industrialized nations, between developing nations, between the mighty (United
States, Soviet Union) and the meager who wore down and outlasted the
superpowers (the Soviet Union and Afghanistan, American wars in Asia and
the Middle East). Further, growing impatience with totalitarianism led to
counter-culture protests around the world, in Europe, the Baltic countries,
the United States, China (Tiananmen Square), and most recently the 2011
social and political protest movements across the Arab world.

THE 1920s THROUGH POST–WORLD WAR II

The early period, the 1920s through to World War II, for many were de-cades of dark, looming uncertainty and destruction. A significant portion of the globe emerged from the Great War battered and despondent, if not devastated by the unprecedented scale of death and destruction. Irish poet William Butler Yeats' famous lines, penned in 1919, embodied an era's pes-simism. "Things fall apart; the centre cannot hold/Mere anarchy is loosed upon the world,/The blood-dimmed tide is loosed, and everywhere/The ceremony of innocence is drowned;/The best lack all conviction, while the worst/Are full of passionate intensity."[1]

The war ushered in economic booms and busts, leading to a sustained global depression in the 1930s. The power vacuums left by the Great War led to totalitarian dictators (Tojo, Hitler, Mussolini, Franco) who quickly capitalized on the political instability to rise to power, control society, and eventually bring the globe to the brink of disaster with World War II. Avant-garde art, philosophy, literature, and film all embodied a pessimism and disillusionment.

In this era there emerged a noticeable shift in food and consumption habits. The industrialization of the food supply allowed greater varia-tion in people's diets and their nutrition subsequently improved, though it can be argued that canned goods and other processed foods diminished taste and nutrients, leading to acclimation to salt and sugar in heavy quantities. To sell these mass-produced items the early twentieth century witnessed the proliferation of communications firms creating increasingly sophisticated advertising. The increased number and circulation of magazines and news-papers, and the growth in population and literacy rates ensured audiences for corporate advertising.[2]

After the worldwide depression of the 1930s, and the destruction from yet another, even more wide-spread and destructive world war, the United States was one of the few to emerge from World War II with its industries and economy thriving, signaling the arrival of what *Time* publisher Henry Luce deemed the American Century. The war had changed, accelerated, and altered the production, manufacturing, and advertising of industrial-ized food, setting the stage for the remainder of the century. During the war North American farmers, with fewer workers, had managed to produce

food at record-breaking levels, in part because of the liberal use of manufactured fertilizers and pesticides, including the new miracle insect killer
DDT. After the war the continued reliance, and increased use, of such elements combined with more and more sophisticated farm equipment and
hybrid seeds led to even greater production (much of which was subsidized
by long-held government parity agreements).

   After the war U.S. farmers, agriculture scientists, and politicians turned
their attention to providing adequate food for the postwar world, ultimately
through famine relief and crop production. Surplus food purchased by the
government was sent abroad to help alleviate and temper the global famine
conditions wrought by drought and wartime destruction. United States'
aid under the auspices of the Marshall Plan pumped in some $12.5 billion
to rebuild European economies and infrastructure, with several billions
going to Asia, particularly Japan, as well. Still, to help answer the demands
of the rapidly growing global population, Rockefeller Foundation scientists engineered new seeds designed to produce significantly more grain
in countries all over the world, and ushered in what was christened the
Green Revolution (discussed in detail in chapter 1). The Green Revolution
seemed to work miracles, vastly increasing the amount of food available
to developing countries. Yet it also put a severe strain on local economies,
endangered subsistence farmers, the environment, and even indigenous cultures, and accelerated the advance toward large, corporate-type farming in
the United States and elsewhere.

   As in farm production, World War II provided the catalyst for the
postwar boom in food processing. Military quartermaster departments
pounded, dried, stretched, and shrunk food in every imaginable way in
order to reduce their bulk and weight to ship them overseas efficiently and
in large quantities. Frozen orange juice, instant coffee and cocoa, cake
mixes, brown-and-serve rolls, dehydrated soups in little plastic bags, instant potatoes, powdered eggs and milk, ready trimmed and packaged
meats, and even the ubiquitous TV dinner all either got their start, or were
perfected with wartime research and technology. After the war the food
industry quickly adopted the knowledge and technology and began producing food items for domestic consumers. Advertisers and enthusiastic
journalists deemed the new preservation techniques "a modern miracle in
the kitchen."[3] The technology so pervasively permeated the global food

supply that eventually high-quality food became synonymous with food capable of a long shelf life and low spoilage. Some of these new food products made their way more quickly into homes than others, of course.

Commercial canning and bottling—well established by the early 1920s and rationed during the war—reached a golden age in the 1950s as new materials, new methods, proliferation of products, and a larger percentage of household budget went to processed foods. Consumers' use in particular of canned foods kept increasing through the postwar years because of their convenience and their ability to remain stable for several years. In many rural areas still lacking in refrigeration and electricity, canned foods were integral to rural long-term food supply.

As food production increased and food costs declined, consumption of food in general went up. The new processing techniques resulted in a phenomenal increase in the number of food products available to consumers, and a corresponding expansion and alteration of grocery stores to accommodate them. Subtly at first, and more dramatically later, there occurred a shift in the seasonal manner of eating experienced by those in developed countries. The increased number of freezers in homes, for example, allowed for the purchase of more frozen items, and also allowed women to buy large quantities of fresh produce and freeze it for later consumption. Further, faster, more efficient methods of shipping (especially reliance on air cargo) allowed fresh fruit and vegetables to be more widely available year round. Similarly, fresh seafood was more frequently available in the land-locked regions.[4]

To keep up with the overwhelming number of new food products, grocery stores also underwent a radical transformation in the postwar era. In the early part of the century most grocery stores were small corner shops, with the grocer standing behind the counter to retrieve items at a shopper's request. Between 1890 and 1950, however, grocery stores became larger and were often supplied by a central warehouse. Chain grocery stores rapidly proliferated, introducing branded food products to consumers. Thus while larger, self-serve supermarkets existed before the war, specifically the A&P, Piggly-Wiggly, and Tesco chains, after World War II they became a permanent fixture on the landscape, eventually swallowing the older style grocery store, as well as contributing to the decline in such specialty stores as butchers, fresh-fruit markets, and bakeries. Supermarkets, as the name implies, expanded in size as well as number to accommodate the plethora of products brought to market with regularity. The new super-markets developed specialized departments, including areas for baby food, gourmet items, self-serve meat departments, baked goods, produce, and dairy. Because such stores allowed customers more freedom to pick up and inspect items, brand names, eye-catching labels, and advertising became more prominent in the hopes of attracting customers.

FOOD AND COLD WAR POLITICS

During World War II, while much of the U.S. food supply was shipped overseas to the military, Allies, and newly liberated countries, consumers received their fair share. United States' food rationing, except for sugar, was quickly dismantled at war's end, largely at food manufacturers' insis-tence. Rationing continued in most European countries for several more years as nations rebuilt farms and transportation systems ravaged by the war. Though Americans made many sacrifices during World War II, includ-ing the mandatory rationing of food and other items, they experienced little (except for those who had fought in the war or who had lost loved ones) of the horrible devastation wrought in other countries. Food, while often in limited supply, was available in sufficient quantities thanks to farmers' and agricultural workers' hard work, as well as a successful rationing program.

By early 1946 international reports revealed the grim details of the world food situation. The war, combined with drought conditions, had threatened crops in Europe, North Africa, India, China, and other parts of Asia, reducing the 1945 total estimated world-food production by 12 per-cent per capita below prewar levels. Further, estimates of the 1946–1947 world harvest, while slightly better, were predicted to come in at below postwar levels as well. European production was 25 percent below normal. In France, when the government's collection of flour ran well below ex-pected levels, citizens staged bread demonstrations. Officials in Italy simi-larly were forced to reduce bread rations and faced similar protest. Even England was short of food and would experience several more years of rationing and shortages.

Outside of Europe the situation was far worse. Australia and parts of South America were hit by drought. Mexicans, experiencing prohibitive inflation, were spending 90 percent of their income on food. India was expecting conditions to worsen quickly. Food shortages in China were acute, particularly in the Hunan province. Korea was running out of food. In Japan people were receiving only 520 calories per day in rations, and the country was hardly in shape to produce sufficient rice. In total, an estimated 500 million people around the world faced famine conditions.[5]

World supplies of food to relieve the famine were limited. The United States, Canada, Great Britain, and a handful of others were the only countries in any kind of position to export grain, and only the United States emerged from the war producing more food than it had before World War II. In fact, American food production maintained record levels, about one-third above the prewar average. Enough food was available for U.S. citizens to consume about 3,300 calories per day, well above the average amount required. In contrast, most in Europe and elsewhere had fewer than 2,000 calories a day, for 28 million the number was 1,500 calories per day, and for some as few as 1,000 calories per day.[6] By contrast, American consumption, even with domestic rationing during the war, had actually increased. Moreover, signs indicated that American postwar-consumption levels would dramatically increase even further.[7]

By 1946, it was clear that the United Nations Relief and Rehabilitation Administration (UNRRA), the organization in charge of famine relief, would not survive the widening rift between the United States and the Soviet Union—former wartime allies and now Cold War rivals. As relations between the East and West became increasingly adversarial, the Soviet Union found itself backing away—as well as being invited to back away—from united nations' relief and turned toward taking care of countries within its own sphere of influence. In 1947, the United States withdrew its support of UNRRA, effectively killing the organization, and practiced what the UNRRA's Director General Fiorello LaGuardia disparagingly called "bread diplomacy," a policy of aiding only those countries whose politics were acceptable to the United States.[8]

In fact, relief efforts directed at the East were never really taken seriously for a variety of reasons, including a strong historical orientation in general to Europe and a view of Asia, especially India and China, as so-called lands of famine that could never be altered. Food aid quickly became tied to politics. Given Truman's policy of containment, American officials deemed it top priority to use food to envelop Western Europe into its sphere of influence while giving up, as it were, on China and to a large extent India, despite pleadings from such well-known Americans as Albert Einstein and Pearl Buck.[9]

The United States limped along in its efforts to meet international food needs until the formulation of the Marshall Plan, which in 1948 finally became a coordinated, government effort to rebuild war-ravaged western European countries. A large percentage of relief was food- and agriculture-related. Of the $4.2 billion in aid furnished during the first year and a half of the Marshall Plan, fully 39 percent consisted of food, feed, and fertilizers. During the entire program, 29 percent of a total aid package of $13.5 billion was committed to these three resources. This was of tremendous benefit not only to Europeans but also to American farmers. Agricultural exports in the 1950s and 1960s remained steady, 22 percent of total exports, worth billions of dollars to American farmers.[10]

Postwar American relief, whether through the auspices of the Marshall Plan or through private organizations, garnered tremendous effect symbolically as well as materially, helping to transmit elements of American culture across the globe. Aid from CARE (Cooperative for American Remittances to Europe) was perhaps most prominent, so much so that the phrase *CARE package* became a generic term. CARE, originally a consortium of private organizations banding together to respond to the postwar famine, shipped thousands of food packages over to war-torn Europe. The first 20,000 packages arrived in 1946 in France, and over the next two decades 100 million more were sent to Europe, and eventually to Asia and other developing countries.

The first packages were US Army surplus 10-in-1 meal packages, so called because they contained 1 meal for 10 soldiers in the field during the anticipated invasion of Japan (never used, of course, because of the atomic bombs dropped on Hiroshima and Nagasaki). Included in the packages were an abundance of meats (beef in broth, steak and kidneys, liver loaf, corned beef, Spam, bacon), fats such as margarine and lard, sweeteners such as honey, sugar, jam, chocolate, and raisins, as well as powdered eggs and milk, and coffee.[11] The tremendous symbolic and cultural effects of the CARE packages were not lost on famine-stricken Europeans, as through them they became acquainted first-hand with the abundances of America,

FIGURE 0.1: 1948 newspaper advertisement of CARE packages. Reproduced with permission.

"an overflowing shop window," one historian has noted, "which displayed the overwhelming achievements of the American economic system."[12]

As farmers continued to produce food at record levels in the postwar era, the U.S. government continued to buy surpluses to distribute as part of foreign-aid packages, a pattern that continued through the latter half of the twentieth century. Public Law 480, Food for Peace, put into effect in 1954, made the practice permanent, as commodity surpluses would be regularly donated to needy countries. "Food can be a powerful instrument for all the free world in building a durable peace," declared President Dwight D. Eisenhower. Yet it was impossible to separate food aid as charitable work to the needy not only from foreign policy, but from disposal of farm surplus as well. Even as people were receiving needed aid, the Foreign Agricultural Service (FAS), an arm of the USDA, referred to the aid as "surplus disposal." "Remember," the Secretary of Agriculture told FAS employees in 1955, "that our own primary mission is to help U.S. farmers. Any unnecessary diversion of our efforts to other enterprises dilutes our effectiveness and runs counter to the expressed wishes of those who gave us our assignments."[13]

Thus in the postwar era the United States hoped to have it all: distribute aid to needy countries, keep farmers contented, and maintain political dominance. It seemed impossible to keep Cold War politics out of even domestic agriculture, processing, and consumption. A 1956 *New York Times* headline demonstrated the political climate with regard to food production. "World Crops 120% of Pre-War Rate: Output Keeping up with Rise in Population, U.S. reports—Free World Lead Reds." "Free world per capita production is 100 percent of pre-war," the article reported, "and the Communist area output is 91 percent."[14] Abundant processed food was similarly held up as a badge of superiority. "State's Canned Food Exceeds All Russia's," read a New York *Times* headline in 1953. "New York State produces two and one-half times more canned goods a year than all of Russia," the *Times* reported the vice president of the American Can Company saying. "The figures clearly indicated," the canning executive went on, "the difference in the energy and know-how between the Soviet Union and the State of New York."[15] Supermarkets began to be hailed as the "shining food palaces of today,"[16] and indeed became a symbol of American political, economic, and cultural dominance in the Cold War era. It became common practice that when foreign dignitaries toured the United States, including the Queen of England and Soviet Premier Nikita Khrushchev, their itinerary would invariably include a typical American supermarket.[17] The press dutifully reported the awestruck visitors' responses to the aisles and aisles of goods. "If Queen Elizabeth is a symbol of Britain," surmised one columnist, "the supermarket is a symbol of the United States."[18]

The overflowing abundance of American supermarkets was difficult to ignore in Cold War politics, which pitted capitalism against communism. Ultimately, the abundance of processed foods exhibited on grocery store shelves became a metaphor for the political, economic, and cultural supremacy of the United States. Indeed, American manufacturers with the help of the U.S. Department of Commerce began to take their wares abroad to world expositions. While industry and government had cooperated to stage a supermarket exhibit in Rome in 1956, it was the *Supermarket USA* display at the 1957 International Trade Fair in Communist Zagreb, Yugoslavia that stirred the most interest—and criticism. Here over 600 American manufacturers supplied more than $200,000 of equipment and merchandise to create a 10,000 square foot modern supermarket stocked to the gills with products. Designed to be viewed as a "dramatic and practical vehicle to demonstrate the American standard of living under 'people's capitalism,'"[19] shelves were laden with all kinds of the latest products. And while Supermarket USA displayed some fresh produce and dairy products, it was the highly processed and packaged items that captured the spotlight: prepared baby foods, soup mixes, canned soups, cake mixes, instant coffee and tea, juice concentrates, prepared meat loaves, cut-up chickens, and a wide range of frozen food. What was intentionally *American* about the display, clearly, in addition to Supermarket USA's large size and overflowing abundance, was the highly processed nature of the food, as well as the individual independence allowed through self-service shopping.

Supermarket USA proved to be a hit with Yugoslavs, so much so that the *Christian Science Monitor* reported that the Soviets, "in the Soviet bid to outdistance the American shopping cart," felt the need to drive attention away from the United States' exhibit by "launch[ing] an air attack on the American supermarket," offering fairgoers helicopter rides from the Soviet pavilion.[20] "The Soviets have only a few consumer goods on display," the newspaper reported, whereas "the American pavilion...is loaded with consumer goods."

FAST FOOD, GLOBAL FOOD

In addition to supermarkets, industrially produced *fast food* became another major export of American culture, with McDonald's being the most prominent brand. Shortly after the end of World War II, the McDonald brothers of San Bernardino, California, set up a bare-bones eatery with the goal of selling hot and tasty, but cheap, food. After realizing that the hamburgers were their biggest sellers, the brothers streamlined their operation, and focused mainly on hamburgers, milkshakes, fries, and coffee. Businessman Ray Kroc, who supplied the milkshake machines the McDonald's brothers were ordering in multiples, visited the McDonald brothers' joint to find out why they needed eight of his machines—each of which mixed five shakes at a time. Upon arrival Kroc witnessed long lines of customers waiting to purchase hamburgers at fifteen cents each, milkshakes for twenty cents, and hot coffee at five cents a cup. Most interestingly to Kroc, the food was being prepared by workers assembly-line style, and people received their orders in record speed. Knowing a good business opportunity when he saw one, Kroc went into partnership with the brothers, and quickly bought them out, though retained the McDonald's name. Kroc refined and popularized the assembly-line food production, calling it the McDonald's *speedee* service system. So popular were the restaurants that the chain quickly developed into the most frequented restaurant in the country. By 1963, fewer than ten years after Kroc took over the operation, McDonald's served its billionth hamburger.[21]

Fast-food chain restaurants could accomplish what locally and individually owned operations had difficulty doing: providing food fast and cheap. Emphasis on economies of scale—purchasing large quantities of supplies, and preparing the food in a centralized kitchen to be warmed and assembled at the chain—led to fast food, even as such cost-saving techniques led to a declining quality. The result, however, was the fast-food taste, and it was appealing to most customers: soft white buns, flat hamburger patties, milkshakes made with increasingly less milk and more added preservatives, flavors, and a uniformity in taste pitched so as to appeal to the broadest customer base possible. The restaurants gained an enormous following, becoming to many a beloved, permanent fixture in mainstream culture. Convenience, then, became the watchword: convenience allowed speedy (*speedee*) delivery, which led to speedy consumption. Fast food was above all convenient, and while some countries, especially in Europe, protested it as an intrusion on national culture and cuisine, others, particularly in Asia, adopted and absorbed the basic concept and menu onto their gustatory landscape.[22]

An abundance of food led to the need, or perceived need, to reduce intake, and the modern era witnessed the full-fledged world of diets and dieting taking hold in the Western world, particularly in the United States. In the 1920s Dr. Lulu Hunt Peters, a Los Angeles physician, published *Diet and Health, with a Key to Counting Calories,* and introduced the idea of counting calories.[23] During the Depression and World War II, dieting understandably declined in popularity as food became less available and the problem for most became getting a well-balanced diet with enough nutrients and calories, instead of too many. However, dieting returned in the postwar period, and by the 1980s, as ideal body sizes grew smaller, and as food became more and more available at all times of the day and night (thanks to twenty-four-hour diners, supermarkets, and fast-food restaurants), dieting, and its accompanying eating disorders, grew prevalent. Fads and dieting advice seemed to change annually: low-carb, low-fat, high-protein, grapefruit only, dieting according to blood type, the Scarsdale Diet, Pritikin, cabbage soup, the list goes on and on. The second wave of Atkins' and other low-carbohydrate diets took the United States by storm in the late-1990s and early 2000s. What remains constant is that Americans, and increasingly, others around the world, will continue to try to suppress their appetites with limited, if any success.

After World War II, and especially toward the end of the twentieth century, there emerged a type of globalization that differed from that of earlier eras both in qualitative and quantitative terms. Technological advances led to lightning-speed communication around the globe, while economic institutions, including the World Bank, the International Monetary Fund, and policy (NAFTA, GATT, WTO agreements) decidedly shaped economics and trade. Populations shifted as immigrants traversed the globe for work, and it became easier than ever to travel long distances for pleasure as well. Global interconnectedness occurred with regard to culture. Western culture disseminated across the globe, as did cultural influences from emanating Asia and Africa, especially beginning in the 1980s–1990s. While food has always functioned as a form of cultural capital—a way of exhibiting one's wealth, status, and savoir-faire—with the rise of late-twentieth-century mass industrialization and globalization this practice only intensified, and in the process, endangered the viability of certain traditional foods and foodways.

Further, the 1990s witnessed increased full-fledged agribusiness and farm consolidation, with farmers increasingly beholden to seed and fertilizer companies. While consumer fears and boycotts challenged biotech production, by the 2000s most of the corn and soybeans planted in the United States were biotech, with increasing percentages in Brazil, Mexico, and elsewhere. Europe, by contrast, resisted to a great extent the production and consumption of biotech crops. The ongoing tensions between the European Union and the United States continue to be played out through politics and trade negotiation. Further, urban sprawl made farmland expensive and farmers found it difficult to resist selling to developers. Environmentalists and farmers (not historically in alliance) began to band together to save farmland as well as wild lands. Thus, by the end of the twentieth century there emerged as a result a counter-movement to big agriculture: organic food production, more emphasis on locally produced, small-scale, seasonal production of food that led to fresher, better tasting products, more inter-action with producers and the consuming public, and in many cases, less damage to the environment.

As a response to what many saw as the worst effects of the industri-alization and globalization of the food supply, there emerged in the late twentieth century small but stubborn efforts to stem the tide. While in the early twenty-first century organic agriculture is still a small percentage of total food production, it has grown at accelerated rates. With conven-tional farming and food corporation profits generally on the flat side, large food conglomerates began to purchase smaller, organic production enter-prises, a phenomenon that has given rise to the dilemma of the so-called Big Organic: a type of agribusiness that, while it eschews petroleum-based products, employs other compromises due to its scale (including exploit-ative use of migrant labor) that the traditionalists regard as counter to the original mission and purpose of *organic*.[24]

A watershed moment occurred in Italy in the 1980s when a McDonald's was about to open near the Spanish Steps in Rome, resulting in the found-ing of Slow Food. The organization, dedicated to combating the erosion of local food and traditional foodways, struck a chord with people around the world. While criticized at times as elitist, the Slow Food organization became a major player in the movement to undo the excesses of cheap, industrialized food. Further, in North America and elsewhere food activists hoped to reconnect citizens with the land and the food they ate through pro-moting farmers' markets, community supported agriculture organizations, urban gardens children's cooking and gardening projects, and other ven-tures designed to support local farmers, promote biodiversity in produce, get people to eat foods in season, and buy organic and environmentally

friendly products. Other events included grassroots Spam festivals, corporate boycotts of Starbucks and McDonald's, and staging subversive food
theater, including throwing pies in the face of Monsanto executives, the
Secretary of Agriculture, and other prominent forces in American, and
global, society.

   As with philosophy or practice, these phenomena also demonstrated a
desire to maintain a cultural distance from mass-produced food for cultural
or aesthetic reasons. Especially for Europeans, for example, such events as
the French farmer who in 1999 ransacked the local McDonald's to protest
the encroachment of the United States into local food cultures, and boy-
cotting Coca-Cola as the symbol of global hegemony, were also largely
about maintaining cultural distinction through food. American foods and
food habits, according to many, have always bordered on the vulgar. Such
American symbols as McDonald's and Coca-Cola that have been marketed
around the world represented touchstones for the growing apprehension
concerning globalization.

THE TWENTY-FIRST-CENTURY LANDSCAPE OF FOOD: SOME OBSERVATIONS

Few would argue with the premise that food has taken on new importance
in recent decades, in large part as a reaction to the industrialization of the
food supply. In the last few decades in many parts of the world, we have
witnessed an emerging food revolution that has attempted to counter (or at
least circumvent) the worst aspects of the industrialization of food. Yet this
recent interest in food has historical roots that reach back centuries, as food
has always been central to the rise and fall of civilizations, even if not overtly
acknowledged by their leaders and chroniclers. In his book *Meals to Come*
Warren Belasco provides an intellectual history of world hunger and the debate
over the ability to provide sufficient food for all. Belasco examines in nuanced
detail how each generation of Western philosophers, economists, politicians,
and fiction writers has framed and evaluated that dilemma, and divides the
discourse into two main camps. On one side are the pessimists (Thomas
Malthus and his intellectual offspring), who argue that there will never be
enough food to feed us all. On the other side are the optimists—Belasco

terms them the *cornucopians*—who see science and human ingenuity as sufficient to meet each generation's challenges and shortcomings. Throw in the egalitarians (William Godwin, Frances Moore Lappé)—those who see the problem as less about quantity than about equal distribution between the haves and have-nots—and you have the basic theoretical positions that keep cropping up over the centuries. What is interesting to note is the culturally bound nature of these debates, especially in terms of writers' definitions of what constitutes *enough* food. Invariably the discussions turn to meat, and it is startling to see successive generations of European and American thinkers worrying about having enough meat, with many fretting that the West will be reduced to so-called coolie (grain-based) diets.[25]

Those involved in the recent food movement have worked to demonstrate the connection between good food and sustainable agricultural practices and to create better-tasting, higher quality food for restaurants and consumption at home. Since the late 1990s, scholarly and political attention to food matters has deepened as the academic field of food studies has emerged, and as popular books by Eric Schlosser (*Fast Food Nation*), Marion Nestle (*Food Politics* and *Safe Food*), and Michael Pollan (*The Omnivore's Dilemma*), as well as films such as *Supersize Me, Food, Inc.*, and *King Corn*, exposed to an interested public the questionable practices of the food industry and the government's willingness to accommodate food-industry demands. The list is long, and the titles themselves revealing: *Stuffed and Starved: The Hidden Battle for the Food System* (Raj Patel), *Food, Inc.: Mendel to Monsanto—The Promises and Perils of the Biotech Harvest* (Peter Pringle), *The End of Food* (Paul Roberts), *Manger: Français, Européens et Américains Face à l'Alimentation* (Claude Fischler with Estelle Masson), *Slow Money: Investing as if Food, Farms, and Fertility Mattered* (Woody Tasch), *The End of Overeating: Taking Control of the Insatiable American Appetite* (David Kessler), *Food Matters: A Guide to Conscious Eating* (Mark Bittman), and *In Defense of Food: An Eater's Manifesto* and *Food Rules: An Eater's Manifesto* (Michael Pollan). Taken together they manifest an awareness of deep problems in the global food supply, problems of all kinds ranging from health and nutrition, to economics and environment, to corporate control of food production, advertising, and consumption, to the peril of people and the planet. What emerges is the realization that seemingly disparate and unrelated topics (obesity, environment, flavor, family meals, hunger) are indeed interconnected. Taken together, a cluster of themes emerges. With various emphases, all address the ethical, health, environmental, and aesthetic issues, as well as the anxieties about cultural and social reproduction that have been central to the discussion about food production and consumption in the last decade.

What cultural and material currents underlie this interest in, and anxiety about food? First is the sheer amount of food that is available, at least in the Global North, with all the ramifications, positive and negative. The United States, as well as other nations, has become particularly adept at producing huge amounts of food, and Americans eat a lot more of it than they used to. The industrialization of agriculture, combined with government policies and politics encouraging the mass production of food, is a double-edged sword, of course. Though it has facilitated better overall nutrition and health, it has also allowed excess and, ironically, poor health. While some critics wonder whether the uproar over rising rates of obesity is fueled less by health concerns and more by superficial cosmetic responses, and by a diet and food industry who benefit from the current landscape of food consumption, there are important health concerns that cannot be dismissed, such as the startling rise in diabetes, especially among children. Combine the sheer abundance with the omnivore's dilemma—the anxiety created by the multitude of food options—and it is easy to understand the well-fed human's predicament in the twenty-first century.

Yet as Chris Otter and Raj Patel each observe, a serious paradox exists in today's world: while approximately 1.6 billion people are suffering from conditions resulting from too much food (obesity, diabetes, atherosclerosis), another billion are suffering from conditions resulting from not enough food (hunger, malnutrition, vitamin-deficiency diseases). Most of the *stuffed* reside in the Global North, while most of the *starved* dwell in the Global South, though there are plenty of people in developing nations suffering from the so-called diseases of affluence. Often the elites of any country, rich or poor, exhibit similar levels of consumption, and generally eat a cosmopolitan cuisine by virtue of their wealth and access to specialty goods from around the globe. The late-2000s' financial crisis coupled with skyrocketing oil prices created severe enough food shortages in some countries to have led to food riots. In fact, notes Otter, more people are hungry today than at any other time in history. [26]

The "stuffed and starved" paradox is directly related to the inequities in the global food supply: "It is part of a single global food crisis, with economic, geopolitical, and environmental dimensions. It is perhaps the starkest, most basic way in which global inequity is manifest," writes Otter.[27] Unfair trade agreements, tariffs, and subsidized agriculture that produce surpluses of grain are then dumped onto developing countries, whose own farmers cannot compete with the cheaper, abundant food on the market. Patel assigns blame to the multinational food and seed corporations who control the food supply with iron fists, strong arming governments to bow to their demands to keep their seeds in production, and the crops in their control. Spiraling grain prices, increased meat consumption, climate change and other types of environmental degradation, combined with market manipulations, together demonstrate "how the basic act of eating a piece of bread or meat binds consumers seamlessly with distant farmers, large corporations, energy systems, economic forces, and international politics."[28] A large portion of the world's population gets too little food (it is too expensive, too scarce, the supply too erratic because of government greed or war which prevents equitable distribution), while an even greater proportion gets too much (too much available, too cheap, too tempting, too few regulations, too unhealthy).

Further, adding to the landscape of anxiety is that we now must reckon with the reality of finite resources: the water, oil, and arable land that have driven the modern agricultural revolution. Paul Roberts, in his ominously titled book *The End of Food,* focuses on the degradation of resources as well as the devastating damage done to land as a result of industrialized farming, especially of livestock. According to the World Wildlife Fund, notes Roberts, "our 'ecological footprint' exceeds the planet's biocapacity by about 25 percent…the largest piece of that footprint…comes from producing food, especially meat."[29] Here we see the convergence of two twentieth-century movements: environmentalism and the delicious revolution begun by California chefs and others, which was among the first to tout local, sustainably produced food as being not only the most healthful and nutritious, but also the best for people and the environment. What Europeans and others knew all along took Americans decades to rediscover.

There are also fears that industrial food culture has damaged the social fabric as well as the environment. The rise of fast food combined with other social and cultural phenomena (more single-parent and two-income families, cars built with cup holders and food trays) have led to changes in domestic food practices, which have, in turn, been viewed as having affected family life and even civil society.[30] Whether this is accurate is unclear but likely more complicated. While I think it is possible (as some do not), for example, to have a meaningful meal prepared from a microwave or around a table of fast food, it is true that by its nature, quickly produced and quickly eaten food changes the qualitative experience of a meal. It makes sense then that food issues are a prominent part of the public discourse in the twenty-first century. For many, careful consideration of the food one eats and serves one's family and friends helps fill a spiritual void. Only a return to more humane, more harmonious methods of growing, cooking, and eating, the thinking goes, will help restore a spiritual connection with the land, with our food, and with each other.

This is not new, of course; thinkers from Thomas Jefferson to Wendell Berry have been preaching these ideas for centuries, but as we have entered the twenty-first century, these notions have taken a qualitatively different turn. As Jackson Lears has demonstrated about mass production in general, in the nineteenth century many people felt alienated by modernism and the industrialization that severed the connection between producer and consumer; that alienation is still palpable in our relationship to mass-produced, industrial food.[31] Seeking local, seasonal food today, then, can be viewed as a version of the early twentieth-century critique of mass society, in which a return to artisanal food functions as a bulwark against the ease and reproducibility of mass-produced, industrial goods—indeed, *pap* and *gruel* were frequently employed metaphors used by critics to describe the fare produced by the media and entertainment industries. For many people, preparing meals from scratch for one's family, using ingredients bought at a local farmer's market, signifies self-reliance, a sense of simplicity, and a voluntary disconnect from the fast pace of our postindustrial, digital era. It can also result in less wastefulness. Many producers and sellers of this alternative vision of food capitalize on and cater to these kinds of desires. Indeed, marketers have learned that while emphasizing the new food culture may not appeal to all (in fact, it may not appeal to the majority), it does appeal to a sizable, influential minority. Supermarkets have become willing to stock their produce section with organic fruits and vegetables, and even if they do not sell readily, they are attractive, powerful loss leaders that may draw customers into stores and bring them back again. Nonindustrial food (and *industrial organic food,* as Michael Pollan terms it)[32] is simply more readily available in most parts of the industrialized world, and that availability is shaping consumption and food habits, at least in certain parts of the globe.

Thus, this recent discourse about food represents a genuine attempt to integrate complex issues linking aesthetics and ethics with health, the environment, family life, social issues, and notions of taste—issues the public might not have recognized as having much in common. Further, today many are more cognizant of the origins of their food, something that became increasingly more difficult in much of the modern era as the connections weakened between producer and consumer. For most of the twentieth century many had little reason to think about and understand the origins of their food: how it was grown or raised, under what conditions, how it was processed, and how it reached the market or the restaurant. If the contemporary conversation about food falls short in any area, it is in addressing the difficult but crucial issue of getting all this healthy, sustainable (more expensive, less widely distributed) food to people of little means. While many applaud the agenda of Slow Food, the work of Alice Waters, or the writings of Carlo Petrini and Michael Pollan, detractors on both the left and the right criticize it as elitist and unrealistic.[33] Finally, many of these writers and activists envisioning this grand theory of food see little difference between science and poetry, between applying rational thought and romantic sentiment to food problems and issues. For them, all knowledge, all emotion leads to the same point: a refashioned food system incorporating sustainable practices, cultural sensitivity, good nutrition, and taste. Such a system, according to this view, in the long run is the most practical and economically viable.

THE CHAPTERS IN THIS VOLUME

A distinguished panel of scholars has taken on the challenge of assessing multiple facets of food in the modern era. In his chapter on production (chapter 1), Jeffrey Pilcher examines agriculture through the lens of industrialization and scientific advancement with its ensuing effects both positive and negative. "The basic trends toward food production over the twentieth century," explains Pilcher, "have been toward greater concentration, standardization, and globalization." Not only grain, but produce, animal livestock, and aquaculture have followed the same trajectory: more food produced, more land or water required to produce the food, more resources devoted to production, greater environmental stress as a result. Thus, while food production has increased exponentially, Pilcher wonders what real cost this has had to the environment, and to human and animal welfare. Complementing Pilcher's assessment, Daniel Block, in his chapter on food systems (chapter 2), details the rise and triumph of the modern food system in the United States and globally. After first defining *food system* and discussing the history of the concept, Block outlines the three major food regimes, resulting in the rise and triumph of the modern food system with its concentration of processing and markets, and the ensuing vulnerabilities of the food system. Peter Atkins, in chapter 3, details food security, safety, and crises in the modern era. Employing a variety of tropes to assess the causes and effects of hunger and famine, and possible solutions, Atkins articulates and sheds light on the complexities of hunger and food security in the twentieth and twenty-first centuries.

In chapter 4, Maya Joseph and Marion Nestle examine the complexities of food and politics. The politics of food, they argue convincingly, is everywhere and in everything—and it invariably boils down to economics. Where there is money to be made, politics enters in, and what gets regulated, what is deemed safe, what is fair, or judged as unfair, is the result of competing interests vying for economic and political advantage. Some of this is played out on the national stage, as they demonstrate with U.S. food policy; others are global in effect, as in food and the international NAFTA, GATT, and WTO agreements.

While chapters 1 through 4 focus more on issues of production, chapters 5 through 7 centre around consumption of food in the modern era. What is *eating out* in the twentieth and twenty-first centuries, asks Priscilla Ferguson in chapter 5? Assuming a structural approach to the topic, Ferguson notes that whereas in previous eras there existed clearer demarcations between domestic meals and meals outside the home, in the modern era those boundaries have softened considerably. Similarly, as rules and structures for fancy dining have relaxed, Ferguson observes, there exists greater space for informality in restaurant dining. In chapter 6, Amy B. Trubek analyses professional cooking, kitchens, and service work in the food industry. Focusing on gender (shifting gender roles and cooking), trends in organized cooking practices (fewer domestic servants, an increase in service workers in professional kitchens), and changing forms and contents of disseminating culinary knowledge (apprenticeship versus culinary school), Trubek traces the history of professional kitchen work in the twentieth century. As she surveys these changes through time, Trubek speculates as to whether a resurgence in interest and emphasis on cooking, such as through the efforts of British chef Jamie Oliver, will reverse these trends and invigorate home cooking. Similarly, asks Alice Julier in chapter 7, how have changes in social and familial relations, combined with changes in the workforce and economic structures changed food at home? Julier describes the structural changes in economics and in the paid workforce, which have a bearing on men's and women's domestic work, especially regarding food procurement and preparation. Further, as families change, notes Julier, and family rhythms of home, school, and work change, so do family meals and the food work of feeding the family. Highlighting such phenomena as the rise of suburbia and the globalization of work and consumption, Julier ultimately concludes that because of the 24/7 nature of today's work obligations, the "family meal is disrupted by global capitalism."

Taking a more emblematic turn, chapters 8 and 9 examine representations of food and the body in modern culture. How might the body be nourished toward loftier, more soulful goals? Warren Belasco asks this in chapter 8, as he explores the landscape of body and soul in the modern era. Seeing twentieth-century food culture as embodied through four tropes (the efficient body, the authentic body, the busy body, and the responsible body), Belasco maps out the moral vicissitudes evident in a world with so much food, yet still replete with problems that require thought and action. Signe Rousseau, in chapter 9, explores the wealth of visual representations of food in the twentieth and twenty-first centuries. The era is rich with food media: books, television, art, online digital works, memoirs, cookbooks, coupled with an "increasingly ambiguous line between public and private" as in "food porn," cooking shows, eating contests, and other food spectacles, and the phenomenon of the celebrity chef. What the future holds, surmises Rousseau, is uncertain, except for one thing: "people will continue to tell stories about—and through—food, because it is a natural conduit for thinking about and negotiating life."

Finally, Fabio Parasecoli, in chapter 10, rounds out the volume by high-lighting events and trends in the non-Western world that may not have been covered in the previous chapters: imperialism and war, post-World War II reconstruction and de-colonialization, simultaneous trends toward collectivization in some countries and modernization in others, and current trends such as the development of food- and agriculture-based tourism in countries in the Global South. Taken together, the chapters provide a win-dow into the story of food in the modern era.

CHAPTER ONE

Food Production

JEFFREY M. PILCHER

In his book *Meals to Come* (2006), historian Warren Belasco identified three basic tropes that have dominated discussions of food supplies for the past two centuries: the pessimistic fears of the Reverend Thomas Malthus that population growth will eventually outstrip agricultural production leading to starvation; the optimistic calculations of the physiocrat Marquis de Condorcet that technological improvement will continue to provide food for the hungering masses; and the redistributionist appeals of William Godwin for a more equitable allocation of limited provisions. The Enlightenment faith in technological progress seemingly triumphed throughout the twentieth century, as scientific advances provided ever-greater harvests, limiting the growth of chronic hunger without actually eliminating it, even as the world population surged from one-and-a-half to six billion. However, Belasco rightly questioned this Panglossian vision, for industrialization has maximized productivity at the expense of resiliency, yielding a food system that may be ill-equipped to respond to future shocks such as global climate change.[1]

Since the 1920s, industrial models have become increasingly common in all areas of food production. Technological breakthroughs have contributed to this productivity growth with biological innovations in breeding, fertilizers, and pesticides, the mechanization of farming and food processing, engineering projects to control land and water, livestock containment and fish farming, and new methods of transportation and preservation. Meanwhile, the so-called Green Revolution began to export this industrial package around the world. Labor practices have been just as important for increased productivity. Although the history of agricultural modernization is often told as the progressive replacement of human and animal labor by machines, the story is perhaps better told as the introduction of factory discipline to farm tasks. Transnational corporations have mobilized vast legions of migrant workers and increasingly sophisticated transportation in search of greater productivity and higher value. As a result, luxury foods, abundant animal protein, and year-round fruits and vegetables, which had once been limited to a small aristocracy, became widely available to the middle classes, at least in the Global North.

The overall sustainability of the industrial food system remains questionable for the twenty-first century. The tremendous gains of the early Green Revolution have already begun to level off as increasing quantities of chemicals yield decreasing productivity gains. Almost a billion hectares of new land went under the plough in the last century and a half, leaving little room for further expansion. And although transnational corporations have proved highly adept at responding to changing consumer preferences and regulatory environments by shuffling production among diverse low-cost sources, the ability of integrated supply chains to withstand systemic shocks remains unproven. Critics warn of the widespread dislocations caused by sudden increases in the price of petroleum and by natural disasters, calling instead for food systems that balance "just in time" with "just in case."[2]

Opponents of industrial farming, who were once dismissed as a countercultural fringe in the developed world and as conservative peasants elsewhere, have begun to gain mainstream legitimacy in their advocacy of alternative agricultural systems. Environmentalists have meanwhile demonstrated the dangers of unsustainable production, particularly as fish populations collapse under current levels of exploitation. This essay seeks to survey twentieth-century developments in industrial farming, husbandry, fishing, and foraging, as well as controversies regarding new technologies of genetically modified organisms (GMOs).

AGRICULTURE

The foundations of industrial farming were already well established by 1920 both in commercial farms of the developed world and in tropical plantations among Europe's colonies. On the eve of World War I, German scientists Fritz Haber and Carl Bosch developed a revolutionary process for synthesizing nitrogen fertilizer.[3] Naturalists also searched the world for diverse plant species that might yield desirable traits through hybrid-crop breeding programs. Mechanization of farm labor was also underway with the development of planting and harvesting equipment, although much of it was still drawn by horsepower at this time. Methods for mobilizing and controlling itinerant farm labor had even deeper roots in early modern systems of indentured servitude and slavery. These technologies were employed with increasing scope throughout the twentieth century.

The gasoline-powered tractor represented a breakthrough in farm mechanization in the years after World War I. Although enormous steam-powered tractors had already been used for wheat farms on the great plains of the United States, Canada, Argentina, and Russia, smaller versions modeled on wartime tanks proved more resilient and maneuverable, plowing muddy hills without bogging down, benefitting farmers in the Midwestern corn belt and Southern cotton country. These tractors performed many tasks, operating ploughs, cultivators, and mowers, and even providing farmers with a convenient power source in the days before rural electrification. Machines initially developed for processing wheat, such as combines, which simultaneously harvested and threshed the grain, were later adapted to other crops, including soybeans, corn, rice, and vegetables. New technology also expanded the reach of irrigation beginning in the 1930s, as turbine pumps and sprinkler systems allowed the cultivation of uneven land unsuitable for flood irrigation. Ultimately, these machines enabled farmers to plant and harvest great acreage without a corresponding growth in labor costs.[4]

Political and economic upheaval of the 1920s and 1930s also contributed to the concentration of agriculture on an industrial scale. The most notorious such program was Josef Stalin's campaign of forced collectivization of the Russian peasantry in the early 1930s. The Bolsheviks saw

industrial agriculture as a means of raising farm productivity while eliminating wealthy peasants, called *kulaks,* but the program proved self-defeat-
ing when the most efficient farmers were denounced as kulaks. Draconian
grain requisitions ultimately led to the famine of 1932–1933, when millions starved to death in the rich farmland of the Ukraine. Although without the extremes of Soviet policy, the fascist states of Germany and Italy
also sought to organize agriculture along national lines to promote self-
sufficiency and population growth.[5]

In the United States, Franklin Delano Roosevelt responded to the
Depression-era collapse of farm incomes by establishing a wide-ranging
system of agricultural price supports beginning in 1933. Intended to assist
small farmers, the New Deal actually concentrated landholding by offering benefits according to production levels instead of need. Government
assistance allowed the wealthiest farmers to mechanize production, while
evicting smallholders, tenants, and sharecroppers from the land. Many of
these displaced farmers migrated to California, where they became known
as Okies and the Arkies, picking cotton and fruit in miserable conditions.[6]
In Mexico, by contrast, the revolutionary government of Lázaro Cárdenas
used the global crisis of overproduction to carry out a program of agrarian
reform in the late 1930s, distributing land to village *ejidos,* which were collectively owned but individually farmed.[7]

Mechanization has transformed the countryside in modern times, but
economic historians Alan Olmstead and Paul Rhode have argued recently
that biological innovation was more important in increasing harvests in
the United States. Ongoing programs of hybrid breeding have yielded more
productive and pest-resistant crops, although such gains are always temporary. The case of wheat breeding illustrates this never-ending struggle
against nature. Beginning in the late seventeenth century, agricultural scientists have travelled the world, seeking out new varieties of wheat that
are resistant to pests including rust fungus and Hessian flies. Of course, the
constant introduction of new grains from around the world inevitably led
to the globalization of plant diseases, such as the Hessian fly, thus spurring
the demand for continued innovation.[8] The primary beneficiaries of this
process were therefore plant-breeding companies, such as Henry Wallace's
Pioneer Hi-bred, which sold the first commercial maize hybrids in the
1920s, and is now second only to Monsanto in international seed markets.[9]

Technology developed for warfare added chemical weapons to the farmer's arsenal, although the benefits of pesticides and herbicides were equally ephemeral. One of the first of these chemicals, the synthetic hormone 2,4-D, upset the internal balance within weeds and caused them literally to grow themselves to death. Midwestern corn farmers in the United States adopted it in the late-1940s, delighted that a single spraying could do the work of three passes through the fields with a cultivator. Unfortunately, the eradication of weeds simply encouraged the proliferation of other natural competitors such as wild grasses, which were not affected by the growth regulator. Nevertheless, many young farmers became so convinced by the future of farm chemicals that they abandoned labor-intensive practices of crop rotation, intercropping, and biological pest control. As weeds and pests began to evolve tolerance, so-called progressive farmers doused their fields with ever-more toxic cocktails of herbicides and pesticides.[10] Again, the profits from this biological arms' race went to companies such as Dow, DuPont, and American Cyanamid, the leading manufacturer of DDT.[11]

The Green Revolution sought to transfer this modern agricultural complex of hybrid seeds, chemical inputs, mechanization, and irrigation to the Global South. This movement began formally in Mexico in 1943, when the Rockefeller Foundation sent a mission to increase agricultural production for the war effort. As hybrids from the United States fared poorly in the different growing conditions of Mexico, scientists initiated a breeding program to improve the yield of native seeds. The project exceeded expectations, and within a few decades, Mexico was exporting surplus wheat. Nevertheless, the importation of U.S.-style capitalist agriculture brought widespread social dislocation in the countryside. The benefits went primarily to wealthy wheat farmers, who could afford the expensive inputs, while millions of poor corn growers migrated to the cities in search of work. The Mexican government, having abandoned the ideals of social justice, exacerbated this inequality by focusing irrigation projects, extension services, and marketing networks on the wealthiest planters.[12]

The Green Revolution spread through large parts of the Global South, with similarly uneven results. The International Rice Research Institute, established in the Philippines in 1960, created strains of high-yielding, so-called miracle rice, while research stations for tropical agriculture in Colombia and Nigeria focused on cassava, beans, and other staples. The

FIGURE 1.1: Dr. Norman Borlaug, father of the Green Revolution, in the field at Chapingo, Mexico, 1965. University of Minnesota Archives. Reproduced with permission.

success of these crops in improving peasant livelihoods varied regionally. In India, for example, market-oriented peasants in the northwestern province of Punjab benefited from improved strains of wheat, imported from Mexico, in part because secure land tenure and few absentee landlords allowed small farmers to compete using family labor rather than mechanization. By contrast, in rice-growing regions such as West Bengal, hybrid seeds proved less adaptable to local microclimates, while areas without irrigation, including Maharashtra, suffered from severe droughts. Food security was a primary goal for agricultural modernizers, but growing reliance on a small number of improved varieties may actually have decreased the resiliency of peasant farming.[13]

The geopolitics of agricultural production and trade were distorted by structural surpluses within the Global North. Following the destruction caused by World War II, European and North American governments established farm incentives to prevent starvation, and although the threat had passed by the 1960s, price supports and protective tariffs were institutionalized to ensure a healthy agricultural sector. The resulting overproduction was dumped on former colonies and Cold War allies through programs such as the U.S. Public Law 480: Food for Peace. Nevertheless, by the 1970s, the European Economic Community had accumulated a veritable mountain of butter, while the United States faced similar unmarketable surpluses. Once again, domestic subsidies favored large landowners, further concentrating the power of industrial agriculture.[14]

These wealthy farmers also benefited from the cheap labor made available by the postwar resurgence of international migration, following half a century of conflict and depression. Migratory circuits ran from Mexico and Central America to the United States and Canada, from Southern and Eastern Europe to their northern and western neighbors, from Africa and the Middle East to Southern Europe, and from Southeast Asia to Australia, New Zealand, and Japan. In a vicious circle of commodity prices and migrant labor, smallholders who could not make a living on the land crossed international borders to harvest crops in the Global North, thereby contributing to surpluses, which were often dumped back in their home countries. Growers sought to reduce their dependence on such labor through continued mechanization, with the development of machinery to pick grapes, tomatoes, lettuce, and other delicate fruits and vegetables, but significant numbers of migrant workers were still needed in the fields at critical times of planting and harvesting.[15]

Of course, producers in the southern hemisphere still possessed some comparative advantages, at least on a seasonal basis. In the 1980s, the neoliberal government of Chile pioneered the marketing of grapes during the northern winter months. These growers soon faced competition from a host of Latin American, African, and Asian countries shipping fresh fruits and vegetables to consumers in Europe and North America. In encouraging these exports, governments often sacrificed the goals of food security for domestic consumers by devoting the best farmland to crops that benefited local elites and foreign shoppers.[16]

Meanwhile, questions began to arise about the environmental consequences of industrial farming. One of the most basic resources needed for farming is water, and supplies have increasingly become at risk, from the Colorado river in the Western United States to the Murray river in Southeastern Australia. Improvements have been made in water conservation through techniques such as drip irrigation, but salinity provides another long-term problem, as salt builds up in the soil after water evaporates, reducing the fertility of the land.[17]

Contamination from farm waste also threatens humans and animals. Significant quantities of pesticides and other chemicals sprayed on fields run off to pollute ground water. DDT, which was used widely in agriculture following World War II, was found to accumulate in the tissue of animals, particularly birds. Global protests led to a ban on its use, beginning in the late 1960s, but opponents of chemical pesticides point out that many dangers remain to consumers and farm workers. Worse still, pests often evolve a resistance to the chemicals used to control them, thereby increasing losses in the fields. Meanwhile, chemical fertilizers can pollute the water in another way, by encouraging the growth of aquatic plants and algae, thus decreasing the available oxygen for fish, a condition called eutrophication. Runoff from Midwestern farms into the Mississippi river has created a giant dead zone in the Gulf of Mexico.[18]

Industrial farming has also increased the prevalence of monocultures, as a small number of high-yield strains replace the diverse varieties that were formerly grown by peasant farmers. This lack of biodiversity increases the risk of catastrophic losses due to the emergence of a new pest or pathogen. Mexico's tequila industry, for example, depended on fields of agaves that were all clones of a single parent plant. When this plant proved vulnerable to a fungus that struck the region in 2000, production collapsed and prices rose. Although tequila drinkers could always find substitutes, the loss of a staple crop, such as happened during the Irish Potato Famine of the 1840s, would have more serious consequences.[19]

Critics of industrial agriculture have increasingly called for alternative forms of organic and local production. The international counterculture of the 1960s rejected capitalism and embraced a more natural way of life, inspired by peasant societies around the world. Groups of young people took up communal farming, recovering the intricacies of crop rotation, recycling nutrients, biodiversity, and integrated pest management. Many of these experimental farms failed miserably, but a handful of successful ones provided the basis for an emerging organic food industry. California first began to certify organic growers in the early 1970s, and demand grew rapidly in the following decades as consumers became aware of the potential dangers of chemicals in their foods.[20]

Yet the development of organic farming as an industry perpetuated many of the same social inequalities that the original counterculture had protested. Unable to use chemicals to control pests, many organic farms relied heavily on the exploitation of migrant laborers. Moreover, as corporations perceived the willingness of consumers to pay more for sustainably grown, organic foods, they lobbied regulatory agencies to change the meaning of these terms so that their own industrial methods would qualify, thus defeating the goals of reformers who sought to challenge the control of big business. Similar patterns of concentration have also been evident in the livestock industry.[21]

LIVESTOCK

The industrial model of meatpacking was already well established in the United States with Chicago as its capital, by the turn of the twentieth century. Beginning in the 1830s, Midwestern packers had already developed an efficient division of labor, breaking down the skills of the master butcher among teams of specialized workers, each of whom performed a single, repetitive task, cutting away a ham or a side of bacon, until the hog vanished completely at the end of this "disassembly line."[22] Fifty years later, refrigerated rail transport allowed the giant packinghouses of Armour and Swift to undersell local butchers throughout the country, while making the bulk of their profits from industrial by-products. Together with Britain's Union Cold Storage and a few other international rivals, these companies came to dominate slaughter in the temperate livestock regions of Canada, Argentina, and Australia. By the end of World War I, producers of refrigerated meat had consolidated their hold on the leading markets of Europe.[23] Following World War II, however, a new round of technological innovation swept the industry, shaking out old market leaders and modes of production.

As a relatively mature industry in the first half of the twentieth century, North American meatpacking fell under stricter government control. The outrage following Upton Sinclair's muck-raking novel, *The Jungle* (1906), led to the enactment of health inspection, and anti-trust regulators kept a vigilant watch for evidence of price-fixing among the so-called Big Four packers. Meanwhile, organizers for the United Packinghouse Workers of America also won better wages and workplace safety standards within the industry.[24]

Industry leaders maintained profits under these circumstances by developing new products for consumers. Advances in processing transformed the sale of pork from brine-cured hunks of meat, sold from a barrel, into packages of sliced bacon, boned ham, and fresh cuts of loin and ribs. The production of sausage meanwhile benefited from the invention of emulsification and artificial casings in the 1930s, which replaced labor-intensive meat chopping and the cleaning and stuffing of intestines. Branded cured and canned meats were available in the early part of the century, and by the 1950s, American consumers embraced such iconic branded products as the Oscar Mayer hotdog.[25]

New systems of livestock production were developed to meet the growing demand for meat following World War II. Confinement feedlots sought to crowd increasing numbers of animals onto smaller amounts of land. In place of grass and forage, the animals received a diet of commercially manufactured bulk feeds, particularly corn. Infectious diseases became a significant problem in the confined herds, and animals were administered antibiotics on a regular basis. When feedlot owners discovered that these drugs caused animals to put on weight more rapidly, they quickly increased the dosages. In the 1970s, the most popular antibiotic, Silbestrol (DEF), was determined to be a carcinogen and banned from use, but the practice of drugging animals remained widespread. Meanwhile, manure from confined animals accumulated in lagoons until bacteria could break down the organic waste. Plumes of methane and carbon dioxide from the lagoons posed hazards to farm workers and contributed to greenhouse gases, while flooding contaminated groundwater. Yet the productivity of these feedlots was unmistakable, and by the end of the century, they had cut in half the average time it took to bring a steer to market, down from three years to one-and-a-half years. Dairy production also expanded dramatically in the postwar era with confinement, automated milking machines, and bovine growth hormones.[26]

Similar practices were common in poultry, which has grown from a regional industry catering largely to ethnic populations into the largest single source of meat consumed in the United States and some parts of Asia, and the second most common type in Europe. Before the mid-twentieth century, most urban Americans ate fowl only rarely, such as a Christmas turkey. Chickens were eaten primarily in the countryside in the form of tough old hens, boiled or stewed when they could no longer produce eggs. Scientific breeding programs sought to transform the chicken, increasing the size of the breast, the most prized meat, while also producing birds that would fatten more quickly. As consumption increased in the postwar era, poultry raising shifted from the Mid-Atlantic states, where farmers had catered largely to the Jewish population of New York City, into depressed regions of the South, particularly Georgia and Arkansas. Industry leaders, Tyson and Perdue, contracted out production to small farmers, who were paid according to a "feed-conversion ratio" intended to bring the animals up to slaughter weight on the least possible feed. Antibiotics were also used widely to control disease in the confined spaces and increase weight more quickly.[27]

Beginning in the 1970s, centralized packinghouses employing stable, unionized workforces faced ruinous competition from a new industrial model. As a result, a new Big Four emerged of Iowa Beef Packers (IBP), Excel/Cargill, Conagra, and Farmland—firms that took advantage of interstate trucking to move production into rural areas, closer to feedlots. But labor rather than transportation costs were the primary motivation for the move, as the companies took advantage of states with anti-union legislation to cut real wages within the industry by a third. The suspension of safety regulations in the 1980s by Ronald Reagan increased profitability still further by speeding up production lines, although at the cost of increasing workplace injuries, especially repetitive-motion disorders. Immigrants soon came to dominate the workforce, and with little recourse to official protection, they faced increasingly hazardous conditions.[28]

Continued globalization of the livestock industry brought similar movement toward low-cost areas of production, along with significant risks to consumers and the environment. Changing balances of wealth created new supply chains, perhaps most prominently, through the growing demand for sheep and goats among the oil-rich Persian Gulf states, and to supply

pilgrims performing the Haj. Australia responded to this demand by imposing Muslim halal practices for all meat slaughtered in the country, except
pork. Meanwhile, an increasing shift from temperate to tropical livestock
raising was stimulated by the growing demand for so-called manufacture
meat used in fast-food hamburgers and other processed food. Tough but
tasty creole cattle in Latin America proved ideal for these industrial applications, although they also contributed to deforestation in Brazil, Costa
Rica, and neighboring countries.[29]

Global trade also prompted recurring outbreaks of foot-and-mouth disease, mostly through imports from South America, where the disease is
endemic. Perhaps the greatest health uproar arose in the 1990s with the
outbreak of bovine spongiform encephalopathy, popularly known as *mad
cow disease*. Consumer fears led to widespread bans on the import of meat
from Britain, Canada, and other countries where the disease was identified.
Nevertheless, regular outbreaks of *E. coli*, a deadly disease caused by fecal
contamination of meat in crowded feedlots, continued to plague consumers
in the rich world.[30] Even greater environmental costs were being incurred
among global fisheries.

FISHERIES

Until the twentieth century, the oceans of the world offered a seemingly lim-
itless bounty of fish, but the techniques of industrial food production have
exhausted even this natural resource. Factory trawlers, using technology
designed for submarine warfare, have harvested some of the most popular varieties of fish almost to the point of extinction. With wild supplies dwindling,
producers increasingly resorted to fish farming, but critics warned that large-
scale confinement would result in the same environmental crises as among
livestock on land. International negotiators have sought to reach agreements
to promote conservation, but politically powerful, national fishing industries
depend on maximizing quotas, and maritime ecosystems hang in the balance.

Anadromous fish, including salmon, shad, and sturgeon, which spawn
in fresh waters and then migrate out to sea, suffered from increasing pollution and the damming of rivers for hydroelectric power. Dams constructed
along the Don and Volga rivers in the 1930s by the Soviet Union, together with massive irrigation projects, lowered water levels and destroyed
spawning grounds. Between habitat loss and overfishing for caviar, Caspian

sturgeon had almost disappeared as a species by the end of the century. Meanwhile, hydroelectric dams destroyed salmon spawning areas in the U.S. Pacific Northwest. Ladders were eventually created to allow migrating fish to return upstream, but the effects of turbines and spillways, along with declining water quality caused a steady decline in fish populations.[31]

At sea, highly efficient factory ships came to dominate the fishing industry in the postwar era. Tuna fishing was transformed in the 1950s with the introduction of purse-seine nets, stretching a mile long and 600-feet deep. Fast motorboats drew the nets around entire schools of tuna, while also trapping large numbers of dolphins, who swam along the surface. By the 1980s, the highly profitable industry was thoroughly globalized; for example, Star Kist, the leading U.S. brand, had cold-storage facilities in Europe, Africa, Puerto Rico, and Samoa. Consumer protests simply led U.S. firms to sell out to Asian competitors, who had lower labor costs and less strict environmental regulations, although nets were altered to reduce the mortality of dolphins.[32] Fishing technology has become so efficient that entire species are identified, popularized, and overfished within the span of a decade. In the 1950s, cod supplied the original source for fish sticks and other fast-food applications, but as catches declined they were replaced by a succession of other species, including whiting, hake, haddock, and most recently, the New Zealand *hoki*. Less appetizing fish, along with the dark meat of tuna, have been used for pet food and fish oil. Shellfish have also been harvested at unsustainable levels. One study found that 85 percent of the world's oyster reefs have been lost over the last century and a half. These bivalves have a critical role in filtering water, so their decline has compounded problems of coastal pollution.[33]

Aquaculture has been touted as a solution to the problem of overfishing and as an abundant potential source of protein. Fish farming in lakes and rivers has been practiced for hundreds of years, and in the 1880s, Norwegian scientists pioneered the use of cod hatcheries to support local fishermen. By the 1950s, hatcheries for trout, carp, and catfish were common in the United States. The contemporary boom in aquaculture began in Norway in the 1970s with the development of giant net-pens for salmon. Within a decade, the practice had spread to Scotland, Chile, and Canada, and was also used for other species, including striped bass, red drum, clams, and shrimp. With selective breeding, salmon gained weight much faster in their cages, and farmed salmon now accounts for more than half of all the salmon consumed globally.[34]

The large-scale confinement of fish, like livestock on land, has produced enormous pollution, making surrounding waters largely uninhabitable. As fish farms are often located near outlets to salmon spawning grounds, environmentalists fear that wild populations will suffer from contamination by lice and even interbreed with escaped farm fish, thus reducing their ability to survive in the wild. Antibiotics are widely used to prevent disease, although such measures have not saved the Chilean salmon industry from devastating outbreaks of infectious salmon anemia. Even the color of farmed fish is artificial, produced by dye, because the fish do not have access to krill, which give salmon their distinctive pink color. Nor do farmed salmon reduce the demands on wild fish populations. According to one estimate, three pounds of feed are needed to produce every pound of farmed salmon, and so factory trawlers continue to sweep the oceans clean of smaller, so-called forage fish. Although often considered unsuitable for human consumption, they provide essential links in the oceanic food chains that support wild salmon, tuna, dolphins, and whales.[35]

In attempting to preserve wild populations, governments have imposed a bewildering maze of restrictions, quotas, and moratoriums. Nevertheless, national regulations have proved less helpful in preserving populations of migratory species, such as tuna. Moreover, modern factory trawlers are capable of filling annual quotas in just a few hours of work. The European Union estimates that as much as 88 percent of European stocks are overfished. Part of the problem is that quotas apply only to the fish that are actually brought to market, and so fishermen dump dead fish that do not fit within their quotas. Reductions in the size of fishing fleets are essential to dealing with the problems, but subsidies continue to support the industry. Yet some local fisheries, such as Alaskan salmon and Icelandic cod, have been maintained at healthy levels. Only the willingness of consumers to pay for sustainable catches will ensure the future health of the seas.[36]

GENETIC MODIFICATION

One of the most controversial aspects of contemporary scientific food production has been the reliance on GMOs. Proponents of this new technology maintain that it simply carries on a millennia-old tradition of plant and animal breeding. Moreover, they believe that genetic advances will benefit

farmers and consumers alike, while helping to offset the risk of future famines. Opponents argue to the contrary that the technology of *gene knock-
out* is vastly different from traditional breeding practices and that the risks
have not been adequately studied. These debates have engaged not only
industry and consumer groups, but also nations in a contemporary version of nineteenth-century imperial rivalries. The United States, the leading
proponent of the technology, has proselytized globally for its introduction,
while Europeans have fought to prevent the spread to the Global South
by banning imports of food from any country that grows such products.[37]

Although the techniques of genetic manipulation were developed in
the 1970s, commercial applications followed from a 1980 decision by the
U.S. Supreme Court that allowed the patenting of new plants, including
their genetic material. With the guarantee of private property rights, companies began to invest vast sums in the expensive technologies needed to
bring products to market. Some of the earliest examples were Monsanto's
Roundup Ready™ complex, which consisted of a powerful herbicide and
soybeans implanted with genetic immunity to the active ingredient, and
Aventis's Starlink™ Bt maize, which was lethal to European corn borers, a
major pest. The companies maintained that GM crops would benefit farmers by allowing them to spray their fields less heavily, although critics argued that savings in pesticides and herbicides would be more than offset by
the increased cost of proprietary seeds. Nevertheless, within a few years,
nearly half the soybeans and a third of the corn grown in the United States
was genetically modified.[38]

Evidence soon discredited industry optimism that GMOs could be kept
under careful control, that productivity gains could be sustained, and that
they did not pose wider risks. Although government regulators in the
United States had approved Bt maize in 1996 only for animal feed, within
five years, genetic analysis revealed that the GM corn had contaminated
human supplies, appearing in taco and tostada shells. A 2001 report indicated, moreover, that GM corn had been discovered growing in Oaxaca,
Mexico, near the original site of maize domestication and one of the regions
of greatest maize diversity in the world. Mexico had banned the planting
of GM corn, although it was imported by Grupo Maseca, a major processor of corn tortillas and partner of the U.S.-based agrifood conglomerate
Archer–Daniels–Midland. The controversy revealed the practical difficulty

of isolating modified from traditional plants. Meanwhile, weeds have already begun to evolve resistance to Roundup herbicide, thus nullifying the advantages to farmers from GM crops. Finally, critics point to early examples of dangerous side effects; for example, Bt maize is believed to kill Monarch butterflies. Nevertheless, the long-term dangers of GMOs are still largely unknown. Some fear that humans could develop allergies to such products. Moreover, modified crops could also become weeds in their own right, as transgenic material that spreads into the environment. However, as these crops are planted ever-more widely, long-term testing will be carried out in farmers' fields and over family dinner tables rather than in carefully controlled laboratory conditions.[39]

FORAGING

Industrialization has not put an end to the oldest forms of human food production—hunting and gathering—although ecological pressures have made such supplies more precarious. Moreover, the privatization of communal lands, particularly in former European colonies, has transformed the nature of foraging. In the Middle Ages, poaching laws were intended to prevent peasants from killing game animals that belonged to feudal lords. With the rise of international conservation in the twentieth century, game laws were introduced to societies ranging from the United States to Sub-Saharan Africa. These laws were largely aimed at indigenous peoples' ancestral hunting practices, which in the U.S. were often protected by treaties, although courts seldom recognized these documents. Even as subsistence practices were outlawed, sport hunting became an increasingly commodified market for middle-class tourists and safari-goers. The loss of wildlife habitat to urban development, along with the spread of livestock onto national parks, put increasing pressure on populations of game animals.[40] Growing demand and environmental degradation have also undermined the gathering of uncultivated foods, whether truffles in France and Italy, or the Brazilian *açaí*, a protein rich berry eaten by Amazonian natives, which is now harvested primarily for juice and smoothies in the Global North.[41]

Another type of foraging, known as *dumpster diving*, became popular around the turn of the millennium among eco-radicals—middle-class youth seeking to take themselves off the grid. Yet for millions of shantytown dwellers in Calcutta, Nairobi, and São Paulo, just as with the homeless of New York, Paris, and Tokyo, urban gleaning has long been an essential means of subsistence. These modern-day hunters and gatherers sift garbage dumps for usable materials to sell, build shelters with, and eat. Ironically, the street foods that emerged from slums in the Global South have recently acquired a measure of gourmet chic among culinary tourists, just as avant-garde galleries have displayed artworks created from found objects. In both cases, the cognoscenti have symbolically rejected the overconsumption of modern industrial society.[42]

PROCESSING AND PRESERVATION

The creation of factory farms and global networks of food production depended on new technologies of processing and preservation. Although salting, chilling, and packaging have long histories, the international food industry has worked methodically to move all forms of cooking from the kitchen to the factory, thereby distancing consumers from living plants and animals.

Transparent cellophane packaging, introduced in the 1920s, set the stage for a revolution in preserved foods. This technology facilitated not only the growth of frozen food products but also self-service refrigerated displays for meat and other foods. With constant improvements, supermarkets could keep meat longer on shelves without either growing mould and bacteria or drying out and becoming discolored. Vacuum packaging, developed in the 1950s, further extended the shelf life of products. Meanwhile, controlled-atmosphere technology, which maintained low temperatures and oxygen levels to inhibit ripening, allowed fresh fruits and vegetables to be transported long distances without spoiling.[43]

The food-processing industry also developed entirely new ranges of products. Some of these were not technological products, but were created via simple marketing creativity, such as the addition of fruit to yogurt in the 1930s, which transformed a medical product into a popular snack food. Frozen orange-juice concentrate was marketed successfully in the late 1940s by mimicking fresh-squeezed taste through the addition of essential citrus oils to a frozen slurry of juice. Other products involved the complete deconstruction and reassembly of foods. Fish sticks, for example, a product of the 1950s, were made by processing low-value white fish into a homogeneous fish meal, then freezing it into slabs that could be conveniently cut into individual pieces, which were battered and fried. A similar approach was later adapted to chicken nuggets. A whole industry of taste additives has grown up to replace the natural flavors lost as a result of food processing.[44]

Even when foods retained their essential form, the labor of preparing them was increasingly moved into a factory setting. Don Tyson, the Arkansas chicken king, was the first to recognize the value of selling parts in different markets, shipping legs and feet to Asia while retaining breast meat and wings for domestic sale. Likewise, the new meatpackers of the 1970s profited from the sale of boxed beef—individual cuts of ribs and loin as well as ground meat that was already packaged for supermarket display cases. Restaurant chains likewise purchased portion-controlled cuts of vacuum-packed meat that was ready for cooking.[45]

CONCLUSION

The basic trends of food production over the twentieth century have been toward greater concentration, standardization, and globalization. In quantitative terms, world food production has increased at a staggering rate, yet these gains have been won at a heavy cost to the environment, and to human and animal welfare. The widespread use of agricultural chemicals, tractors, and irrigation has strip-mined fertility from the soil, while global fisheries have been harvested with similar lack of thought for the future. Large-scale confinement feedlots for all kinds of livestock and fish have resulted in pollution, disease, and antibiotic usage. A final environmental cost of the industrial model has been in biodiversity, as the focus on particular improved varieties has narrowed the genetic base of our food supply. Global supply chains have exploited cheap oil and cheap labor to bring food from around the world to affluent consumers, but the ability to sustain this model seems increasingly questionable.

Yet optimists counter this grim picture pointing alternately to continued industrial technology or to local organic initiatives. Some believe that genetic modification and other biological innovations, including growing animal protein in laboratories, will feed the planet into the foreseeable future.

Others argue that sustainable biodynamic farming using recycled inputs and integrated pest management could replace factory farms. These two trends will likely continue to move in parallel, but whether they will be sufficient to maintain the twentieth-century cornucopia and avoid future famines remains to be seen.

CHAPTER TWO

Food Systems

DANIEL BLOCK

Food-systems research is a rising area of interest for academic researchers, urban planners, public-health practitioners and other government officials, urban farmers and local food activists, and food-policy advocates. Much of this rise in attention comes from a general response to weaknesses in mainstream food systems and the rise of alternative, often local, connections between producer and consumer. A food system, perhaps most simply defined as a network of linkages between food producers, distributors, consumers, and laborers that connects the food humans eat to its sources, is shaped by the society within which it forms. As activist writer Wayne Roberts suggests, a food system "operates in much the same way as the body's circulatory system...where each part is most deeply understood in terms of the whole."[1] Food systems are influenced by not only the economic and political systems and structures under which they form, but also the culture, available technology, and even physical characteristics of the region they serve. While important in itself, food-system research may thus also be a tool that reveals the particular characteristics of a society and economic system.

In this chapter, we will focus on the evolution of the concept of food systems and the historical development of food systems from 1920 to the early twenty-first century. The geographic focus will be primarily on developed countries, and in particular the United States, but will also include a discussion of globalization and its effect on global food systems, and the rise of both local and global niche-market food systems. A particular focus will be on scale. Food systems of global, regional, and local scales have occurred over many centuries. Much of the growth in interest in food systems is around creating more localized food systems as an alternative to the dominant food system, which while producing "the bulk of our food in an incredibly efficient manner," has also "resulted in environmental degradation and economic disaster for scores of small family farmers…and community residents who do not have access to an adequate, healthful food supply."[2] Industrial food systems continue to supply the vast majority of food consumed in the United States and other developed counties.

COMMODITY SYSTEMS, VALUE CHAINS, AND FOOD REGIMES: THE EVOLVING FOOD-SYSTEM CONCEPT

The study of regional food systems predates most disciplinary boundaries and was often concerned with the provision of food for a particular city, such as Dodd's 1856 study of London. Later, agricultural scientists and others completed in-depth studies of the extent of *milksheds*—the area surrounding a particular city with its fresh milk—as well as studies of particular agricultural districts.[3] As regional planning came into being, sociologists, planners, and geographers created reports on agricultural regions in addition to their urban work.[4] While often insightful, these investigations were usually primarily descriptive. This continued into the mid-twentieth century. For instance, mid-twentieth-century geographer Loyal Durand published a variety of articles on milksheds that described most fluid milk-producing areas in the United States.[5] Durand's work is extremely useful historically; however, his focus was mainly upon the basic characteristics of production areas rather than the production–consumption relations that shaped them.

A breakthrough in food-systems studies occurred in 1981 when sociologist William Friedland published *Manufacturing Green Gold,* an investigation of the lettuce industry of California's Salinas Valley that incorporated an analysis of production, labor, politics, ethnicity, and culture, and the way that all of the factors shaped, and were shaped by, the development of iceberg lettuce.[6] Friedland's book promoted the idea that entire food chains, from the point of production to the point of consumption, can be studied through an examination of the political, economic, and cultural structures that constitute them. Friedland named the new approach *commodity systems analysis*.[7] Friedland's commodity systems approach expanded traditional, less analytical, and more descriptive approaches to studying systems such as milksheds, by promoting the intensive study of the political and economic systems in order not to just describe a particular sector or region. As later defined by Buttel and Goodman, the goal of the approach is "to understand agricultural commodity production as a system in which technical and manufactured inputs are incorporated into a labor process in which commodities are produced, processed and marketed in distinctive industrial structures."[8] Through this information, commodity systems analysis strives to conduct a deeper analysis that reveals much about the society that these systems lay within and the connections that make up the backbone of the food system.[9] More recent work based in the commodity systems tradition has studied global commodity systems and competition between multiple systems, including fresh produce in France and the United Kingdom,[10] catfish producers in the Mississippi Delta and the Mekong Delta of Vietnam,[11] and three tomato processors in the Toronto region that differed by size and their use of local produce as examples of so-called systems of provision, processes by which production, distribution, marketing, and consumption are vertically integrated.[12]

A related approach is the study of value chains. This concept, which primarily comes from business literature, has been used in food-systems work particularly by activists and researchers interested in promoting the development of new connections between producers and consumers in which the ethical values of the production techniques are translated through a commodity system to the consumer, inspiring trust and communication of information about the foods back up the chain to the producers.[13] Value chains specifically concentrate on the connections that must be made between actors in order to create a successful product.[14] According to Kaplinsky, a value chain "describes the full range of activities that are required to bring a product or service from conception, through the intermediary phases of production, delivery to final consumers, and final disposal after use."[15]

The commodity systems and value chain frameworks have greatly in-fluenced the study of food systems and connections between producers and consumers, but the product and its production are prioritized over the consumer side of the chain. A competing approach focuses on food regimes, or what rural sociologist Harriet Friedmann called "the rule-governed structure of production and consumption of food on a world scale."[16] Food-regime theorists divide global, modern world food systems into three general regimes. The first food regime was based in colonial trade. Much of food policy was concentrated on the role of food produc-tion in the building of an empire. In the United States this mainly meant a focus on the development of the Western United States, including such pro-grams as the Homestead Act and extensive grazing and grain farming in the Great Plains.[17] During the early twentieth century a transition occurred to the second food regime, characterized by increasing state involvement in agriculture, high tariffs protecting domestic farmers, policies promot-ing cheap food, intensive agricultural development, and standardized and processed foods.[18]

A number of authors have questioned whether we are currently enter-ing a third food regime, characterized by a greater variety of products, global food markets, a new emphasis on freshness, lower tariffs, and gov-ernment deregulation.[19] These articles are particularly notable for the ex-tent to which they discuss the forces behind the rise of this new regime, and their explicit recognition of the relationship between consumer desires, conditions of production, and regulation. The rise of the third food regime is often seen to be consumer-, or at least, retailer-led orientation around freshness and the provision of a wide variety of global produce.

The whole idea of the food regime has been criticized for its generalizing form, its simplification of economic history, and particularly for ignoring the fact that industrialization began in American agriculture long before the New Deal.[20] However, food-regime theory is helpful in three particu-lar ways. First, it is explicit in its focus upon the relationships between government, food production, and food consumption. Second, while the transitions between food regimes are often gradual and differ over space, food-regime theory can be used as a lens to view and contextualize these historical transitions, and specifically to view the interconnectedness of regulation and the conditions of production and consumption.[21]

Two final groups that have recently taken note of food systems are researchers and practitioners in urban planning and public health. The American Planning Association, in particular, has increased its focus on food-systems' planning and regional planning processes may now include a food-systems component. The importance of food-systems' work to planning is strongly stated by Pothukuchi and Kaufman, who argue that food "is unique among human needs in its basic connections...to land; in the centrality of its wholesomeness and nutrition to health; and in the social, economic, ecological, and political implications of the location of its sources."[22] The specific connection to health is at the root of much of the current interest among public-health practitioners and researchers as well, where environmental effects on health, including food availability, is a growing field of interest with its roots in the study of health disparities.[23] A particular growing interest among both is *food deserts*, or areas of low food access, usually in minority, lower income, or geographically isolated rural areas. This interest in food systems among planners and public-health professionals is nothing new. Food safety, particularly milk, was at the heart of the work of public-health departments from their beginning in the nineteenth century and still is a key part of their work today.[24] In the early twentieth century, planning departments and their antecedents placed much attention on the development of more efficient food-distribution systems.[25] Interest, however, waned in the post-World War II period as the systems' approach to both planning and public health were replaced by approaches that tended to focus less on connections between regions and more on particular large-scale projects, such as expressway building and urban renewal (within planning), or specific diseases and nutrients (within public health). The remaining portions of this chapter chart the evolution of global food systems from 1920 to the present.

THE RISE AND TRIUMPH OF THE MODERN FOOD SYSTEM: 1920–1973

In 1959, with the modern food system firmly in place in the United States, the USDA's *Yearbook of Agriculture* was entitled *Food*. The frontispiece of the book shows the evolution of grocery shopping. Below is a well-dressed housewife in a grocery store, kneeling to pick some produce from a low bin, which she gives to a well-dressed grocer to put into her cart, which is filled with other produce and a bag full of what looks like cookies (figure 2.1). The store itself looks clean, modern, and streamlined. Above are depictions of fresh vegetable and fish carts, with litter on the ground. Although it is somewhat difficult to tell who is who, the vendors at the carts appear to be women in babushkas, along with a man in farmer-type suspenders.[26] This depiction illustrates the mainline view of the evolution of the American food system during the first half of the twentieth century. Clean, well-stocked supermarkets had replaced street vendors. Clean-cut grocers had replaced vendors of uncertain ethnicity or farmers. The potential value of such ideas as direct connections between farmers and consumers were nowhere to be seen. The material within the book reflects this modern attitude as well. It devotes chapters to each important nutrient, followed by human food needs organized by age. A rather general section on production and distribution focuses on food quality and grades, as well as the newest USDA and land-grant research, divided by industry. The only mention of government programs is at the very end, focusing on aid to developing countries and school lunches. In this way, the yearbook represents the modernist view of food in the way in which it is broken up into component nutrients, quality is protected by grades and inspectors, and new technologies are created by trusted agricultural scientists.

Dixon shows how the modernist food production was also characterized by modernist eating, or at least modernist eating advice.[27] Diseases were reframed "not as diseases of destitution but as diseases of vitamin deficiency," which "provided food processing corporations with a new platform for profit-taking through food enrichment."[28] Levenstein's book *Revolution at the Table* focuses on the rise of scientific eating during the late nineteenth and early twentieth centuries, including the growth of the "Newer Nutrition" in which food was taken apart, found to have vitamins, then put back together or "enriched."[29] Milk, for instance, was discovered to contain one of the first vitamins to be isolated: vitamin A. It was then heavily promoted by public-health professionals as well as the dairy industry itself for these properties until it was seen as almost magic.[30] A problem with choosing specific foods based on nutrition was safety, particularly during a period in which many staple foods were being produced increasingly further away from the consumer. The increased

FIGURE 2.1: Frontispiece from *Food: The Yearbook of Agriculture* (1959), USDA.

distance also meant that contaminating microbes within foods had longer to multiply. By the 1920s this issue was beginning to be addressed.
Milk, for example, was protected by placing technological barriers such
as pasteurization between the producer and the consumer, as well as tu-
berculin testing and pasteurization ordinances, but it was not until the creation of the U.S. Public Health Service's Grade A milk system, a suggested
municipal ordinance, put into place across many cities and states during
the 1930s and 1940s, that these rules were at all standardized.[31] Similar
grading systems were introduced for meat, vegetables, fruit, eggs, butter,
cheese, and other products. In 1959, the amount of meat coming from
graded plants was still less than fifty percent of all U.S. meat produced,
but the goal of standardization, protecting the consumer through technology and government regulation, was being approached, particularly for
animal-derived products.[32]

On the farm, there was movement from more to less local production, from little to large amounts of government involvement in agricultural pricing and the protection of foodstuffs, and toward larger scale, more industrial agricultural production. As outlined by Cochrane, the percentage of farm inputs coming from capital investments jumped from twenty-four percent in 1900, to forty-one percent in 1940 and fifty-four percent in 1960, while the percent from labor dropped from fifty-seven percent to twenty-seven percent during the same period.[33] These increasing levels of technological investment were paralleled by decreasing farm numbers, increasing farm sizes, and increasing production per unit area and per animal. In the U.S. dairy industry, for instance, the number of commercial dairy farms dropped from 602,000 to 168,000 between 1945 and 1978 while total production per cow more than doubled. The percent of farms with over fifty cows rose from less than one percent in 1949 to more than two percent in 1981.[34] Connections between these patterns are often explained by what Cochrane called the *technological treadmill*. Early adopters of new technology receive increased profits due to the lower input costs following their investment. However, as others adopt the technology, prices drop. In order to keep earning high gross profits, farmers must either adopt additional new technologies or cannibalize weaker neighbors by buying their farms, building the original farm size.

Central to the modern food system was the rise of national-government involvement in the pricing of commodities, particularly during the New Deal and afterwards. In the United States, previous to World War I, food prices remained relatively unregulated. To further combat the crisis, farm interests proposed a broad plan that would dump surplus crops on the export market to maintain a parity price for these crops in the United States, based on the prices between 1910 and 1914, a time of general agricultural prosperity. This plan never was put into place, but the idea of supporting agricultural prices towards parity became an important part of U.S. and world agricultural policy.[35] In 1933, when Franklin D. Roosevelt came to power, the United States implemented a wide variety of agricultural programs, many of which were designed to control prices. While these programs evolved over time, the general idea was "to limit output so as to increase the price per unit and thereby raise the net income of farmers" to the parity price.[36] This was done through a variety of means, most of which focused on the government setting target prices for commodities and paying farmers if the price fell beneath this target, or buying crops until it did. This was done mainly for commodities, including wheat, corn, cotton, rice, peanuts, and tobacco. In addition, prices for other products, including butter and cheese, fresh milk, and sugar were supported through a variety of means including tariffs and so-called marketing orders, setting minimum prices to be paid by processors and distributors.[37] It is obvious from this list of products, in particular the commodities, that farm support and not support of food production was the focus. These commodities, often purchased by the government, became the core of the school lunch program, as well as U.S. foreign-aid packages. In addition, the low prices of what often amounted to industrial inputs (in particular corn and milk powder) promoted the use of these inputs in the development of industrial foods or inputs such as American cheese and corn syrup.

Retail markets completed the modernist American food system. Chain stores and supermarkets increasingly dominated the scene, although nowhere near the levels of later in the century. At the same time, home delivery of products such as milk, which in 1929 accounted for almost ninety-four percent of milk sales in Chicago, declined rapidly.[38] By 1963, grocery-store sales were ninety-two percent of all food-store sales. Chain groceries accounted for forty-seven percent of sales in groceries, rising from thirty-four percent in 1948, while affiliated independent groceries (in such groups as IGA or Certified) accounted for forty-four percent in 1963, rising from thirty-five percent in 1948. Only nine percent of sales were at unaffiliated groceries in 1963, down from thirty percent in 1948. In 1963, thirty-four percent of total grocery-store sales were at stores run by the top twenty companies, up from twenty-seven percent in 1948. Also between 1948 and 1963, the total number of grocery stores declined by one-third. In addition, mergers were common within the industry between chains as a growth strategy.[39] About sixty percent of total grocery sales occurred at supermarkets in 1963, rising quickly from around forty-two percent in 1954—a phenomenon that would later emerge in Europe and elsewhere as well.[40] Trends in food retailing thus paralleled trends on the farm. While chain groceries, as well as large farms, were nothing new, there were increasingly fewer farms and fewer groceries and the ones that remained were increasingly large. In addition, in both cases so-called cannibalism occurred, with buyouts being common. At the consumer level, it seemed as if consumers had accepted a government-controlled, mass-produced, mass-marketed, and branded product that appeared never to vary and came (as far as they knew) from nowhere. A reaction against this, however, was slowly forming.

GLOBAL FOOD-SYSTEM POLICY IN THE MODERN ERA AND BEYOND

In a seminal 1982 paper, sociologist Harriet Friedmann laid out a history of the global food system of the twentieth century to that time, focusing on the post-World War II international food system, which she called the postwar international food order, leading to its demise following the U.S. grain sale to the Soviet Union in 1973.[41] Friedmann argues that this international system was based on American food policy, which "maintained grain surpluses, especially American grain surpluses, well above effective world demand."[42] The United States also gave much of this surplus as aid, which both increased overall American grain exports and depressed world grain prices. This opened new grain markets in the underdeveloped world that took on new cheap-food policies based on the low-priced (or free) imports. This cheap food, and the minimal amount of revenue that could be made from agriculture given the depressed prices, supported urbanization and outmigration from rural areas, first in reconstructing war-ravaged Europe and Japan, and then in underdeveloped countries throughout the world. In the developing world, it was part of specific policies that promoted urban industrial development based on cheap food, following a U.S. model.[43] The policies that helped construct the international food order had their roots both in the New Deal, which promoted raising revenue to American grain farmers while maintaining relatively cheap consumer prices partially by buying surplus grain, and through Cold War political policy, which followed the experience of the Marshall Plan in using food aid both as a development strategy and for specific political goals. The model was followed by other exporting countries and regions, in particular Canada, the European Economic Community, and Argentina, but the United States dominated. As Dickens and Moore stated in 1981, "Canada and the United States rely on global food dependence to maintain domestic agricultural prosperity."[44] "Extension of wheat markets dovetailed with the extension of the free world," writes Friedmann.[45] In addition, these policies were supported by the Bretton Woods monetary system, which in 1944 was set up to support the currencies of the postwar era through tying the U.S. dollar to gold and by limiting the amount that other currencies could fluctuate by in their value against the dollar to one percent. The dollar thus became the base currency for much of the world. This was supported through currency purchases through the International Monetary Fund (IMF), which was also created at Bretton Woods, along with the World Bank.[46]

The ties between domestic U.S. food policy and aid are clear in the section on aid in the 1959 USDA yearbook. It discusses the high levels of 1954 and 1955 following the Korean armistice. "Foreign countries faced serious dollar shortages and our export levels were high. Our consumption at home was already at relatively high levels. There was little hope of any sizable reduction in the rates of government acquisitions."[47] The author explains that the Agricultural Trade Development and Assistance Act of 1954 was conceived as a temporary way out of this dilemma. Following this, "distribution overseas jumped from 184 million pounds in 1954 to 2 billion pounds in 1958."[48] United States food aid amounted to an amazing 31.8 percent of all wheat exports between 1956 and 1960, rising to 35.6 percent between 1961 and 1965.[49] The infusion of this huge amount of low-cost product into the market seems to have had a depressing effect on prices. Prices per bushel of wheat declined during the last half of the 1950s (though they rebounded somewhat in the 1960s), from $1.86 in 1953 to $1.49 in 1959 on the Sydney market, for instance. Prices in the United States were generally higher, although they also declined.[50] Whether these policies actually make up a world food order is somewhat debated, as well as the particular power of the U.S. postwar food policy. However, the patterns of the promotion of agriculture and trade in the core through food aid, a decline in agricultural exports from the periphery, and an accompanying decline in the ability of developing countries to feed themselves, are generally accepted.[51] The postwar food order generally aligns to the second food regime, linking to the mass production of foods based on cheap commodities both in America and worldwide.

The decline of this system was gradual, but a pivotal point was the collapse of the Bretton Woods system in the late 1960s and early 1970s, as the U.S. trade deficit grew too large to continue to support it. The United States decoupled its currency from gold in 1971, and the current era of currency markets began. "In the absence of a stable system of (national/ international) regulation," writes McMichael, "nation-states have been set adrift to negotiate their own competitive position in the world economy."[52] A second key moment was the U.S. sale of grain to the Soviet Union in 1973, beginning the end of the tie of U.S. Cold War political policy directly to aid. This also ushered in an era of rising prices, and the lowering of the focus on controlling surplus with the famous comment of Earl Butz, Nixon's Secretary of Agriculture, to plant "hedgerow to hedgerow."[53] Global competition also greatly increased. Between the early and late 1960s U.S. wheat exports dropped from fifty percent to thirty-four percent of the world total, due largely to increased exports by such countries as Argentina and Chile. The United States' food aid dropped precipitously, from 16.9 percent of all international wheat exports in the late sixties to just 5.2 percent in the early 1970s.[54] Food aid today makes up only around two percent of the total world grain trade.[55] During the previous period, the nationally based agricultural model, where cheap food and agricultural industrialization promoted the development of the entire economy promoted by the United States, had become "a universal idea."[56] The new period transitioned from the Bretton Woods system to international organizations such as GATT (the General Agreement on Tariffs and Trade) and the WTO (World Trade Organization) to generally oversee trade negotiations, often within an overwhelmingly neoliberal economic framework. While such negotiations were rarely successful, and protectionist policies and national-based price supports for agricultural sectors remain in place, the general push is for freer trade. Within this structure, corporations have found it much easier to grow transnationally, building their power often to match or exceed governments. While local and national markets are still very important, agrifood capital is now global, and national policies, while also important, often are related to specific corporate issues, including the famous Chiquita banana incident of the mid-1990s, in which the United States under Clinton argued for the end to protected status connections between European countries and their former colonies.[57] Its decline heralded the beginning of a new system, led by large retailers and transnational corporations, but also allowing more spaces for new transnational trade connections, often stemming from new production areas in the developing or newly developed world serving niche markets within wealthy nations.

RETAIL POWER, GLOBALIZATION, AND TWENTY-FIRST-CENTURY FOOD SYSTEMS: 1973–2010

Since the mid-1990s, it has been posited that a new food regime has appeared, characterized variously by growing retail power, interest in freshness and naturalness of food, restructured global agrifood supply chains, and a growing financialization of the sector.[58] Whether or not this mix of characteristics constitutes a new food regime or an extension of an older one is debated, but there is general agreement that global food systems have greatly evolved during the period following the breakdown of the Bretton Woods system and multinational corporations, many of them retailers with increasingly global scopes that have been leaders in these changes. This global scope was accompanied by the development of new regions of production, such as the Chilean wine region, along with a seeming countermovement in local production seen particularly in many wealthier nations. Burch and Lawrence tie the new developments to the rise of neoliberal economic policy during the 1980s and onward, which "resulted in a food system…characterized by flexible production and the international sourcing of a wide and diverse range of food products on terms set by the international retailers, and increasingly organized around…convenience, choice, health and 'wellness', freshness, and innovation."[59]

The past twenty-five years have seen an increasing concentration in supermarket corporations. Between 1992 and 2005, the market share of five leading retail-food chains in the United States increased from nineteen to forty-six percent.[60] Concentration is even higher elsewhere. In Norway, for example, the top four chains sell almost one-hundred percent of groceries.[61] This trend has, in many cases, been related to the financialization of supermarket capital, as chains are seen as investments and they look to quickly expand through purchasing other companies. While the supermarket business is still largely regionally and nationally based, many of the largest supermarket chains are multinational. Developing and non-Western countries, which are relatively unsaturated with hyper- and supermarkets, represent opportunities for quicker growth than in the home countries of retailers such as Wal-Mart and Carrefour (although this has not stopped the continuing opening of many Wal-Mart Supercenters in the United States, often replacing traditional Wal-Mart stores with little food offerings). Corporate globalization has encountered hurdles. While Wal-Mart international sales were up seventeen percent in 2004, for instance, and the company is doing very well in Mexico and Central America (perhaps somewhat due to the large number of residents with experience of living in the United States), Wal-Mart left Germany and South Korea due to low profits caused in part by local labor laws and an overly simplified attempt to transfer the U.S. model outside the United States.[62] In general, concentration is occurring both within nations and through the arrival of multinationals in new countries.

In the United States, another important and related trend is an overall decline in the number of stores, while the size of individual stores has greatly increased, although this trend has recently moderated. Median store size of U.S. supermarkets increased over 10,000 feet between 1994 and 2006, from 35,100 to 48,750 square feet.[63] In many cases one large store has replaced two or more smaller ones within the same company. Interestingly, in the United States (and France), the trend of increasing store size has since reversed. Median size in the U.S. dropped from 48,750 in 2006 to 46,755 square feet in 2008.[64] In general, the number of traditional supermarkets has decreased, while discount stores such as Aldi, hypermarkets such as Wal-Mart Supercenters, specialty stores such as Whole Foods, and ethnic-oriented supermarkets have increased. In the Chicago area, between 2005 and 2007 the total number of supermarkets remained the same, but traditional models declined in numbers while the numbers hypermarkets, specialty, ethnic, and discount stores increased.[65] These dual patterns of increasing concentration and market differentiation have led retailers to attempt to gain greater control over the production of the foods sold at their stores. In most cases, this has been accompanied by a growing use of private labels, particularly by discount retailers, such as Aldi, which specialize in private-label items, but also by specialty retailers such as Whole Foods and Trader Joe's, and hypermarkets such as Wal-Mart. Even name brands may be pushed to change the properties of their food or their labor practices to fit the standards or price points of a large retailer such as Wal-Mart. Discount retailers such as Aldi or specialty retailers such as Whole Foods may work directly with a food processor to develop a private label (and usually cheaper) version of, say, a Swanson's frozen entrée, or a name brand may develop a version of their product to be sold as a private-store label. Stores setting and controlling standards may not necessarily mean increased overall quality. Retailers may emphasize look over taste, or choose produce that needs to be artificially gassed to ripen.[66] However, this may allow other retailers to find a niche around taste, or even develop social and environmental standards for the products sold at their stores, or some may even try to source food locally.[67]

Retailers may also find a niche by sourcing and offering harder-to-find products, either of local or global origin. As Friedland discussed, often this may involve the increasingly global fresh-food system, including the development of contra-seasonal production, such as Chilean grapes or blueberries, the promotion of new exotic produce, and a search for new value-added products, including organic and fair trade.[68] While Friedland's argument focuses on globalization of such supply sources, local sources, especially with connections to particular farmers, also may fall into this category, especially as smaller stores attempt to find a niche to survive given the appearance of hyper and discount markets in the region.[69] Sources of quality food may also be both tied to specific place-based niches, or, with quality defined differently, industrial production. Mansfield, in an article on global *surimi* (fish paste) commodity chains, discusses the importance of quality in an industrial food product. She states that in an industrial situation quality actually takes on "new meanings, precisely because *surimi* production is highly mechanized…and it is used to make many products that are sold in mass markets."[70] In other words, in order to meet the needs of industrial processes, *surimi* has to meet very specific quality standards. This actually is much like earlier quality standards, such as grading of milk, corn, or wheat, or such products as tomatoes and other produce designed not just for taste, but also for large-scale picking, wheat designed for particular milling processes, or even corn or other grains designed to produce more ethanol. Such new quality standards, which actually may increase in use importance due to the larger amount of uncertainty and risk in global

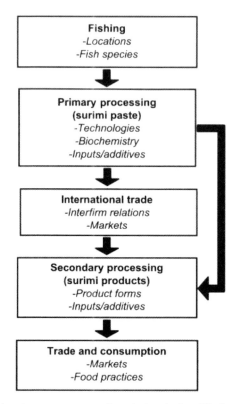

FIGURE 2.2: Generalized *surimi* commodity chain. A simplified version of a chain, including some of the factors at each stage that contribute to quality assemblages. Not all these factors are important in every case, nor are the items listed here exhaustive of all factors that might be important. Reproduced with permission.

markets, show the variety of forms the current global food system takes, and the continued importance of industrial systems and standards.

In many cases, food processors are much more concentrated than retailers. In the United States, for instance, the top five beef packers controlled over eighty-three percent of the market and even in 1992, the top five food processors controlled eighty-five percent of the market. Three companies control eighty-one percent of maize exports from the United States. While other sectors were lower, none were as low as the forty-six percent controlled by the top five retailers.[71] According to an interlocking directorate analysis completed by Schwartz and Lyson, food retailers have a much lower number of ties between the boards of food companies than among similar boards of processors.[72] Food-retailer board members also do not usually have a background in the food industry. In these ways, food retailers seem to see themselves as having more in common with other retail businesses rather than with other agrifood-sector businesses. In actuality, retailers often compete with processors to control a larger share of profits—a situation that does not necessarily lead to increased cooperation.

For smaller and international producers, the effects of the new global food system on suppliers are mixed. Many gain a market, yet they are subject to control by an often foreign-owned company that may understand little about the culture and growing conditions of the production region. Friedberg presents a fascinating comparison of the export markets of Burkina Faso (mainly exporting to France) and Zambia (mainly exporting to the United Kingdom). In Zambia, exporting was limited to two large firms, who contracted with local "outgrowers."[73] These export companies had high standards, pushed by the U.K. supermarket chains they contracted with. These chains would sometimes send buyers to Zambia to inspect not only the processing of the produce, but production practices. Given these pressures, the export companies often reject produce judged to be not up to standard, although growers believe this occurs when the exporters simply are oversupplied with produce. Many growers have gotten out of the business. A former grower quoted by Friedberg concludes "it was never profitable" due to high rejection rates, and according to Friedberg, "the costs of conforming to the food safety, environmental, and social welfare standards of the U.K."[74] Similarly, according to Fuchs, Kalfagianna, and Arentsen, Brazilian research "shows that the new regulatory conditions set by retailers are recreating and reinforcing other forms of economic and social cleavage."[75] Even in upstate New York, small local producers often have difficulty meeting the demands of even fairly small, local green stores. One store representative states about a relatively large producer: "At this point she is distributed through our main supplier, so she's getting into [stores] throughout the northeast…whereas if you're dealing with very small establishments it's 'how come you can't make this work for me?'" Other barriers to small producers included bar coding, marketing, and pricing.[76]

THE WORLD FOOD CRISIS, FOOD DESERTS, AND EGGO WAFFLES: VULNERABILITIES IN THE MODERN WORLD FOOD SYSTEM

The current dominant global food system excels in creating cross-global food linkages, identifying new markets as well as new production regions and products, and, in general, providing a wide variety of foods to upper-class people throughout the world and relatively cheap, processed food to others in developed nations. The system, however, does not always work well. Issues lie at many levels. First, there are a multitude of issues associated with inequities within the mainstream food system itself. Terms of trade as well as subsidies are tipped towards multinationals and wealthier nations, forcing peasants and small producers to lose control (or sovereignty) over their production decisions, as well as their own food sources. An oft-cited example is the undercutting of Mexican corn prices by subsidized U.S. corn, particularly after the passage of NAFTA, making it difficult for small Mexican farmers to survive, particularly without the use of increased chemicals.

A related issue is that when foods become primarily commodities, as Burch and Lawrence (2009) describe, food companies become primarily financial investments, often for organizations with little interest in food production itself, the so-called foodness of the product matters little, and the replacement of production for food ends by production for other industrial ends, such as ethanol and other fuels, becomes simpler.[77] The issues with this came into focus in 2007–2008, when food prices rose worldwide and food riots occurred in cities on multiple continents. The very presence of quickly rising and fluctuating food prices shows a shift from the cheap-food system devised in the 1930s that was the core of the second food regime. The reasons behind the rising prices were complex, but as McMichael describes, key factors put forth were the rising demand for meat (and thus feedstuffs) in middle and growing-income countries, grains being used in the production of ethanol and other fuels at a time of quickly increasing energy prices, and speculation.[78] The role of speculation is still debated but is particularly worrying and interesting. As the financial crisis began and real estate, stocks, and other areas of investment lost money, investment capital flowed into the energy and food sectors, raising demand,

not actually for grains and other commodities, but for the investment opportunity they offered, particularly as prices continued to rise. This rising
demand pushed prices to rise even more. McMichael notes that between
2005 and late 2007, world food prices rose seventy-five percent. At the end
of 2007, the *Economist* food-price index was also at an all-time high (since
its inception in 1845) and world grain stocks were historically low.[79]

While food prices have since dropped, at least somewhat, the basic
reasons for the crisis remain: increasing use of grains in fuel production,
decreased regulation allowing for increased speculation on food commodities, and increased food-based demand. A key issue is that if food prices
are increasingly volatile, a major part of the deal that was at the core of the
development of the modern food system is undermined: the provision of
relatively cheap foods at steady prices to working- and middle-class people
in developed countries. If these foods are no longer reliably cheap, the rest
of the deal—farm subsidies for commodity production, for instance—may
also lose support, although these subsidies have in reality been very politically difficult to remove.

Many writers point to inequities and labor and ecological issues in the
mainstream food system. Even overlooking these major issues, however,
the system does not always work well, not on every occasion, for every
person, nor for every place. One example of this is the existence of areas
of low food access, or food deserts, found in many low-income, minority,
and rural areas of the United States. While evidence from elsewhere in the
world has been mixed, U.S. studies have generally found direct connections between poverty and minority status and poor food access, usually
defined as access to chain supermarkets, in both urban and rural areas.[80] In
general, much of this difference was in the type, rather than the number of
groceries serving the area. In a three-state study of selected census tracts in
North Carolina, Maryland, and New York, Moore and Diez Roux found
that minority and racially mixed neighborhoods had more than twice as
many grocery stores, but half as many supermarkets, than predominantly
white neighborhoods.[81] In Erie County, New York, Raja et al. calculated
that supermarkets and meat and fish markets were much less likely to be
within a five-minute walk in predominantly black neighborhoods than in
predominantly white, while no such relationship was found for smaller
grocery stores and convenience stores. Fruit and vegetable markets were

found to be more likely to be within a five-minute walk for those in pre-dominantly black than white communities.[82] Similar patterns were seen in comparing impoverished to wealthier communities. Morland and Filomena found that in randomly selected census tracts in Brooklyn, no supermarkets were found in predominately African American tracts, while at least one was found in about every third white tract.[83] Finally, in Chicago, Block and Kouba found that while a predominantly lower-middle income, African American neighborhood of the city had many stores, they were almost all small. When fresh produce was available, it was often very sparse and of low quality.[84]

The existence of food deserts strikes a particular chord with both com-munity residents and activists working to uplift impoverished communities and local food activists, since it so clearly defines the geographic conse-quences of unequal retail investment. In many ways, the food-desert issue is a consequence of the evolution of the retail food industry over the past eighty years in the United States. In general, a system of smaller neigh-borhood stores was replaced by larger supermarkets that needed larger footprints and were built for driving rather than walking. Over time, these original supermarkets have often been replaced by even larger markets (often within the same corporation), with somewhat greater distances be-tween them. In inner-city and rural regions, the smaller stores closed, but no larger stores opened, leaving a gap. In urban and suburban predomi-nantly immigrant and ethnic communities, smaller supermarkets still exist, but in African American communities as well as smaller rural towns, these stores have generally closed. More recently, discount stores with smaller footprints, including both food stores such as Aldi and so-called dollar stores, which sell household items at cut-rate prices, have moved in and offer increasing amounts of food, but are generally not focused on being full-service markets.[85]

Both the dependence of U.S. customers on industrial food and its vul-nerability to disruption are highlighted by a late-2009 shortage of Kellogg's Eggo waffles.[86] In September 2009, a state inspection found listeria in a sample of Eggo waffles from a plant in Atlanta. After notifying the U.S. Food and Drug Agency (FDA), FDA inspectors found several violations of safety standards as well as listeria in the plant itself, including on the tires of a forklift, which is worrying due to its ability to spread the virus. While no illnesses are known to have occurred due to the incident, Kellogg closed the plant for a period of intensive "hygienic restoration."[87] Furthermore, in October 2009 a severe flood hit the Atlanta area, inundating the plant just as it was set to re-open. Another cleaning was required. Finally, at the same time, another Eggo plant in Tennessee was undergoing repairs.[88]

The result of this was a severe shortage of Eggo frozen toaster waffles. Late-night comic Steven Colbert called for President Obama to open the "strategic waffle reserves." The vulnerability of such an iconic item to a series of not particularly unusual industrial and natural mishaps, points out the limited backup that the mainstream food system has. The shortage was also somewhat mysterious. It was revealed primarily by the lack of waffles available at supermarkets, rather than any company statement. Despite the possible health issues, internet discussions about the Eggo shortage mainly had to do with how to deal with the shortage (including hoarding, recipes and other suggestions), rather than worries about possible health issues or dunounciations of the Kellogg company. Furthermore, the availability of the remaining waffles is enlightening. Kellogg stated that waffles were supplied based on "historical percentage of business, meaning that generally waffles were supplied more to larger stores, which tend to be in specific types of communities."[89]

The Eggo story indicates both the vulnerability of the mainstream system as well as the possible relationship between this vulnerability and geographic disparities in food access, as well as the intensity of consumer–product relationships. Growing awareness of the ecological and ethical issues in the mainstream system has helped lead to the development of alternative food systems, including the promotion of local food production, organic food production, fair-trade systems, community supported agriculture (CSA), and many other models. These new systems are important and growing. However, as Blay-Palmer, Guthman, and others have pointed out, many of these systems are increasingly industrial themselves, and the fact of being local does not necessarily lead a food system to be ethical.[90] Nonetheless, the very existence and increasing popularity of these alternative systems points towards increasing concerns and fears among many consumers with industrial food. At the same time, as the Eggo shortage and Colbert's tongue-in-cheek call to open the waffle strategic reserves indicates, industrial food, while vulnerable to shortages, is still very much a part of not only American eating, but also American culture.

CHAPTER THREE

Food Security, Safety, and Crises: 1920–2000

PETER J. ATKINS

Famines gather history around them.[1]

A history of the twentieth century is a history of hunger. Although modernity brought with it improved technical and logistical means of eliminating famine, nevertheless the century saw the greatest number of famine deaths in history. Famine-related mortality—not all from starvation—has been variously estimated, but a total of seventy-five million seems very likely (figure 3.1).[2] There has been some improvement. As Devereux points out, famines have now been absent from Europe for sixty years, from East Asia for fifty years (discounting the unique circumstances of North Korea), and from South East Asia in the thirty years since the horrors of Pol Pot's regime in Cambodia.[3] It is Africa where the problem has continued to be most troublesome in a post-colonial era of conflict and poor governance. Yet at the time of writing, among the fabulous wealth that has been created worldwide, there are still 857 million people chronically hungry—about one in seven, and rising.

There are many ways of writing histories in the epistemologically complex field of food insecurity. This chapter is organized as a series of tropes, in

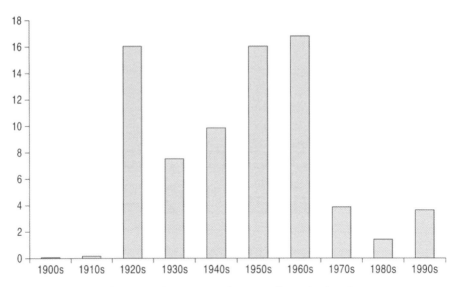

FIGURE 3.1: Twentieth-century famine mortality (in millions) by decade. *Source*: Devereux et al. 2002, 2. Reproduced with permission.

effect figurative distillations that amount to framings of the key actors. This will facilitate a novel cultural history. First, there is a consideration of those pockets of food poverty that persisted throughout the century in Europe and North America. This is followed by the role of conflict in exacerbating malnutrition, along with a discussion of what we may call famine crimes. Next, the mediatization of famine, and the creation of the victimhood of starvation are considered, with a brief theoretical meditation derived from welfare economics. The final trope is that of the administrators of improved food quantity and quality—those representatives of the collective will of us all to see the elimination of food insecurity in all its forms. The irony for them, and for the chapter as a whole, is that new forms of hunger appear with each succeeding decade, so that our history, unfortunately, also has a future.

HUNGRY PEOPLE AMONG PLENTY

It may seem strange to start a cultural history of food insecurity with an account of the Global North in the recent past and present, but it is important at the outset to unsettle any complacency about universal nutritional sufficiency in advanced economies. As early as 1939, John Steinbeck lifted the lid on hunger in America with his novel *The Grapes of Wrath*, which was soon made into a Hollywood film. This novel followed the Joads, a family of poor sharecroppers from Oklahoma forced to start a new life in California. Most novelists can only dream of having such an impact. The conscience of the world's richest nation was touched by the plight of the Joads and the many real-life victims of the 1930s dust bowl. Action was something else, however, and Marion Nestle has shown that, subsequently, attitudes to malnutrition in America have gone through cycles of policy according to prevalent political priorities and ideological shifts.[4]

On the other side of the Atlantic there were similar debates before World War II. The Hungry England controversy was especially lively from 1933 to 1938.[5] A number of prominent nutritionists and social-welfare campaigners argued that the diet of working people was inadequate. This was not just a matter of malnutrition in the sense of an imbalance of vitamins and minerals, but also an insufficiency of calorie intake—in other words, hunger caused by under-nutrition. The landmark assessment made by Sir John Boyd Orr in 1936 was that up to 50 percent of British people were affected, with consequences in terms of ill-health, inefficiency of manual labor, and intellectual under-achievement by school children. The government of the day opposed his interpretation on the grounds that poor diets were often the result of a lack of nutrition education and that each family bore the responsibility for making the best use of their resources, especially when these were meager. According to Mayhew, "officials maintained there was no connection between low income and malnutrition; if sections of the population were malnourished, then the fault lay with individual idiosyncrasies or ignorant housewives."[6] Partly this attitude was to counteract the political impact of the hunger marches made on a regular basis by the unemployed in the 1920s and 1930s.[7]

Even today, thirty-six million Americans live in households that are food insecure.[8] This represents 17 percent of all children, 22 percent of black households, and 38 percent of households whose income is below the official poverty line. The food supply of one-third of these people is so insecure that they suffer malnutrition and severe health consequences, and the other two-thirds employ a wide variety of coping strategies, including participation in Federal food and nutrition assistance programs—National School Lunch Program, the Food Stamp Program, and the Special Supplemental Nutrition Program for Women, Infants, and Children—or attend charitable soup kitchens. The main reasons for hunger in American cities are poverty, un-employment, high food prices, and housing issues such as the foreclosure of sub-prime mortgages during the financial crisis that began in 2007.

There is now a growing literature in various countries demonstrating hunger among marginalized and excluded groups, such as the homeless, runaway adolescents, and failed asylum seekers.[9] Such individuals are most at risk of food insecurity if they have mental-health problems, are infected with tuberculosis or HIV/AIDS, or have a drug habit.[10] There is an increas-ingly rich seam of field research with these people. Amistani and Terrolle, for instance, worked with *gleaners* in Paris, who cannot afford a balanced diet and who have a wide range of practices, legal and illegal, to supple-ment their resources.[11] These include begging, busking, eating while walk-ing round a supermarket, the collection of out-of-date food from retail outlets, or simply theft.[12] Apart from the risk of malnutrition, diabetes and high blood pressure are common health consequences because many rely on energy-dense foods that are poor nutritionally.

Discussions of malnutrition in Western countries require some nuanc-ing. Apart from the homeless, a literature has recently developed on food insecurity in so-called food deserts. These are inner cities and inaccessible rural areas where purchasing a balanced diet is difficult for the most eco-nomically disadvantaged groups in society. The problem may be immobility due to a physical disability or the lack of public transport, or it may be the result of food retailing becoming increasingly concentrated in out-of-town hypermarkets. There may also be a lack of affordable healthy foods, such as fruit and vegetables, by comparison with cheaper, high-energy junk foods.

Food deserts are a problem for marginalized groups in North American cities, but less so in Britain.[13] In both there is an increasing problem of obesity and all of the associated health risks. Researchers are now arguing that there is food insecurity in what they term *obesogenic* environments. These are poor city neighborhoods with a mix of factors that discourage exercise; for instance, where street crime means that residents minimize their outings or where there are few recreational opportunities but many fast-food outlets.[14]

THE RATIONED, THE BESIEGED, THE REFUGEES

War, at both the global and regional scale, had several distorting impacts upon food systems in the twentieth century. The first, which we can term *the act of omission,* resulted from lack of foresight or poor organization by combatant powers unprepared for the modern age of industrial warfare.[15] Under such circumstances of broken or disrupted food chains, people reverted to the wide variety of pre-industrial coping strategies that had been familiar to their nineteenth-century forebears. These ranged from dietary supplementation by foraging for wild or unusual foods, through to the sale of key assets such as livestock or even land. Migration to where there might be food was another option. The hunter–gatherer instinct remained strong throughout the period, as it does today, even in wealthy countries, where it now performs more of a recreational than a nutritional function. In wartime this supplied additional sustenance, such as mushrooms, small mammals, and freshwater fish. In Britain there were a number of schemes organized in World War II for the collection of wild fruits and plants. The fruits included blackberries, bilberries, cranberries, elderberries, rowan berries, and crab apples, all mainly gathered for jam or jelly-making.[16] Rosehips were also popular in syrup form for their vitamin C, and plants collected included foxgloves, sphagnum moss, and stinging nettles for medicinal purposes.

Employing an ethno-literature approach, Alicia Guidonet has analyzed Mercè Rodoreda's novel *The Pigeon Girl.*[17] This is about the Spanish civil war and is a rich source of information about food shortages in the time of civil disturbance. The heroine, Natàlia, loses her husband to the fighting and has to deploy a variety of strategies for survival, mostly through relationships of love and friendship. They are an alternative to collecting famine foods in the hedgerows and closely mirror the shared morality of reciprocity that one often finds among the dispossessed and the hungry. Guidonet has also collected oral testimonies about the civil war in Catalonia.[18] These, again, shed light on the moral economy, but they are stripped of any cozy altruism. Theft, swindling, and the black market all play a part in her stories.

In the first half of the century Europe contained many such vulnerable regions, with agrarian economies that were not self-sufficient in food production. The Tyrolean valleys of Austria may be prosperous today as a result of tourism, but in the early twentieth century they were economically marginal. In 1933, for instance, 50,000 people living there were said to be suffering a state of near-famine. Shortages were exacerbated during World War II and as late as the early 1950s in the Tyrol so that "people could hardly believe that hunger would not return."[19]

Among the unintended consequences of war, one of the most serious is the diversion of resources away from food production toward the war effort. Irrespective of the effect of bombing and invasion, there is often a decline in supplies, along with a diversion of foodstuffs to the armed forces. One estimate suggests that global food availability per head dropped by 12 percent during World War II, with much greater falls in Europe and East Asia.[20] This was despite efforts to restructure productive capacity. The United Kingdom, for instance, quickly geared its agriculture to the war effort and by 1943–1944 was producing 91 percent more in terms of the calorific value of net output than before the war.[21] This was partly due to a shift from livestock-based to arable agriculture and it was also the result of mechanization.

Around the world, in the first half of the twentieth century, two wars and a deep global economic depression left psychological scars and fears of continuing food insecurity. In Austria, Germany, and other war-torn countries in Europe, the return of prosperity meant the onset of what has been called the *1950s syndrome*. This was a compensatory expansion of calorie intake (the *fresswelle* or eating wave) that was a celebration of the possibility of eating. Waistlines expanded, giving the first inkling of the trend toward obesity that has now reached worldwide epidemic proportions.[22] It is important to note that many food and agricultural politics in the second half of the century were a result of the earlier worries. By way of example, the Common Agricultural Policy of the European Union came into being as a means of solidifying peace through the guarantee of sufficient food from its own resources. As a result, consumers had to put up with higher prices to subsidize farmers and the politics of this historical dynamic have rumbled on into the twenty-first century.

More sinister among the consequences of war are the *acts of commission* that caused such great suffering. These fall into several categories. First, there is the deliberate severing of food supplies to a region, as happened in the Dutch hunger winter of 1944, when a strike by railway workers was punished by the German army.[23] Their closure of supply routes caused at least 20,000 deaths. Second, starvation was at times part of a strategic plan to weaken the enemy and undermine morale. Leningrad was blockaded in this way by the Wehrmacht from 1941 to 1944, one of the longest and most destructive sieges in history. Up to one million died of starvation and

there were many others who suffered from long-term mental and physio-
logical damage as a result of malnutrition. The siege of the Warsaw Ghetto
(1940–1942) was even more despicable because it was a racially motivated
attempt to starve over 400,000 people, mainly Jews, who were crammed
into a small neighborhood of the city. At least 100,000 died there of hunger
and disease. Such painful memories explain why hunger and starvation are
not common as autobiographical or even fictional subjects.[24] Nevertheless,
the importance of recording the evil of genocide has at least guaranteed it
a place in the Holocaust literature. One of the most famous examples is
the first-hand account of the ghetto by Emmanuel Ringleblum.[25]

Deprivation during occupation, either deliberately punitive or due to
incompetent administration of scarce resources, is another act of commission. One shocking example was the conquest of Greece (1941–1944) by
Italy, Germany, and Bulgaria, which cost between 250,000 and 450,000
lives by starvation because of a trade blockade by the British and a collapse of the food economy due to low productivity, hyperinflation, and
passive resistance among public servants.[26] Other occupied countries were
actively exploited, for instance, Denmark and France, which between them
supplied over half of Germany's food imports by value from its tributaries
in 1942–1943.[27] The Danes operated this system efficiently themselves,[28]
with minimal interference, but the situation in France was less manageable. The occupation there was complicated by the division of the country
into zones, with the semi-autonomous Vichy administration in the south
and east. Official rations gave working adults at best 1,500 calories per
day, falling to below 1,000 calories in 1944.[29] Supplementing this with officially sanctioned or illegal sources occupied a great deal of people's time
and tested the traditional moral values of French culture. One curious feature was that food parcels of up to 50 kg could be sent through the post,
with the result that family networks in town and country were mobilized,
as never before, to provide mutual support. Nevertheless, naturally rich
agricultural regions were significantly less affected by food insecurity than
their urban and industrial counterparts because farmers dispatched less to
market and fell back on subsistence for self-preservation. What was left of
the prewar integrated food system was tightly controlled by the Germans,
who dictated prices and rations for particular commodities. The dark side
of rationing was the inability of certain isolated and marginalized groups to

fend for themselves, such as the elderly, the sick, and the inmates of mental asylums, 45,000 of whom are thought to have starved to death.[30]

This is not to say that rationing always leads to extreme hardship and malnutrition. Examples of successful policy-making exist, for example in Britain during World War II, where shortages during the U-boat campaign in the Atlantic threatened the survival of a nation that had previously been heavily dependent upon imported foodstuffs. A so-called food front was opened up that included much propaganda and a myth was created of a carefully planned diet that, in reality, was more a matter of muddling through. A key food was the national loaf—wheatmeal bread that was disliked by consumers but had the virtue of a high extraction rate from flour and therefore had improved vitamin and fiber content.[31]

Apart from the stringencies of rationing, wartime can sometimes be an opportunity for innovations. This is particularly the case with policymaking, where peacetime vested interests are temporarily silenced and progressive ideas can be experimented with. Deborah Dwork picked up this idea in her book *War is Good for Babies,* where she argued that welfare foods and mother and baby support services were available during World War I in Britain to a level that politically would otherwise have been impossible.[32] Other innovations have been technical. For instance, the Third Reich placed food research at the heart of its war planning, and achieved much in the fields of frozen, dried, and powdered foods. These were not necessarily new technologies, but the scale of investment and drive of the military–industrial complex meant a more rapid uptake than would otherwise have been the case.

After the conclusion of the war, like many other German cities, Berlin was short of food. Allied commanders had great difficulty in sourcing raw materials, especially during the Soviet blockade of 1948–1949, when they resorted to an airlift on an unprecedented scale. They also found it difficult to control a vigorous black market, which, at one point in 1948 is estimated to have handled between one-fifth and one-third of the food supply. Hunger challenged normal views of morality, and criminality was not only widespread, but at times condoned. Cardinal Frings of Cologne, for instance, in 1946 preached a temporary suspension of the seventh commandment that "thou shalt not steal." His concern was for the welfare of ordinary people but this was misinterpreted by many, to the extent that any act of theft became known as a *Fringsen.*[33] Other antisocial behavior,

Table 3.1: Estimated impacts of African conflicts, 1970–1993

	War Years	Average difference (%) in food production between peaceful and war years
Angola	1975–93	−44.5
Burundi	1972, 1988–93	−5.6
Chad	1980–87	2.2
Ethiopia	1974–92	−10.9
Ghana	1981	−9.5
Kenya	1991–2	−3.4
Liberia	1985–8, 1990–93	−25.5
Mozambique	1981–92	−5.0
Nigeria	1980–81, 1984, 1991–2	−4.3
Somalia	1988–93	−23.1
Sudan	1984–93	−18.5
Uganda	1971–87	10.2
Zambia	1984	−13.7
Zimbabwe	1983–4	−19.8
All		−12.3

Source: Messer et al. 1998.

such as hoarding and foraging, was difficult to control, but far more significant was what Paul Steege calls the *economy of connections* that ensured
better access to food for the articulate middle classes.[34] This networked
dimension of food security in times of crisis is under-researched and opens
out into debates about social capital, everyday collective knowledge, skill
banks, informal circuits of exchange, and a morality that is negotiable according to circumstances.

Official histories of war rarely mention black markets or sharp practices,
such as overcharging or favoritism in situations of shortage.[35] However,
popular oral histories tell a different story. Mark Roodhouse recounts
some stories about Britain during World War II and concludes that there
was plenty of scope for evading the detail of the rationing system.[36] Having
said that, he argues that black markets were deeper and more widespread
in the occupied and liberated countries, and even in the United States, than
in Britain. Attempting to explain this in terms of the cultural context of
private morality is fraught with complexity.

In the second half of the twentieth century the type and location of warfare changed, away from the industrial scale of the European theatre to guerrilla conflicts in Asia, and civil wars and insurgencies in Africa. In the 1970s and 1980s these were ideologically driven, fuelled particularly by the Cold War, and food insecurity was not only a common consequence but also, in many cases, a deliberate policy.[37] The United Nation's estimate is that from 1970 to 1997 $121 billion worth of agricultural production was lost around the world due to armed conflict; this has resulted in the lowered availability of daily energy supplies (table 3.1).[38] Scanlan and Jenkins concur with the scale of these losses in their survey of the experiences of seventy-five less developed countries, but they also find that militarization and military rule are not *always* necessarily bad for food security.[39]

THE FAMINE-STRICKEN

There have been many popular imaginaries of hunger. James Vernon argues that famine was discovered as a humanitarian concern in the nineteenth century and he gives examples of various devastating famines in South Asia that became widely known through journalism.[40] Then, during World War I the trope of victim took on a new power when it was realized that the Entente blockade of Central Power countries was causing near-famine conditions. The Save the Children Fund (SCF) was set up in 1919 to relieve this suffering and was also soon active in the famine that accompanied the civil war in Russia of 1921–1923. The SCF deployed *claims' making* strategies to attract the attention of governments and media, providing them with the motivational frames that they required.[41] There was an emotional element to their campaigning but they also carefully nurtured the notion of so-called deserving victims—a familiar moral stereotype of the day.

Photography also transformed the representation and understanding of food insecurity in the twentieth century. A "spectacle of suffering"[42] was created and gradually absorbed into the general critique of Western hegemony in Asia and Africa. Michael Buerk and Mohamed Amin's BBC/NBC television report from Korem on the Ethiopian famine in 1984 was particularly iconic and was watched by an estimated 470 million people around the world.

Dawn, and as the sun breaks through the piercing chill of night on the plain outside Korem it lights up a biblical famine, now, in the 20th century. This place, say workers here, is the closest thing to hell on earth. Thousands of wasted people are coming here for help. Many find only death.[43]

This generated an immediate response, including the fund-raising concert Band Aid. But imaging hunger can also have negative consequences. Pictures of starving children have become so widely consumed that there is a danger of stereotyping Africa as unproductive, weak, and unable to sustain a modern economy and lifestyle. Such images encourage a reductionism that we, as lazy voyeurs, accept and then fail to look for the tremendous variety of experience and resilience in that continent. Still photography (figure 3.2) and TV news packages come pre-digested and do the work for us. Even the illustrated campaign literature of aid agencies, though well-meaning, is often complicit in this uncritical approach to hunger. The point here is that the visual image is prone to what we might call the inductive fallacy of seeing: that one shot stands in as representative of a wider truth. For our purposes this poses a dilemma. Have journalistic and academic analyses of twentieth-century famines discursively contributed to the construction of a popular impression of passivity and hopelessness in poor countries or have they have shone a light on a problem that would otherwise have been unseen? Either way, David Campbell sees photographic images of war or famine as part of a broader visual economy, and we can add to this that editorial selection of what to publish reifies a set of market forces that filter our knowledge of these events.[44]

The style and content of images has evolved during the twentieth century. The Holocaust was one influence, with its depictions of emaciation, and modern-day photography uses these as reference points, if only subconsciously. But over-familiarity can lead to compassion fatigue and there is no doubt that the media are having to try harder to shock us.[45] In 1994, for instance, the *New York Times* published a picture of a starving child collapsed on the ground with a vulture watching her from a few feet away. The photographer, Kevin Carter, won a Pulitzer prize for this image but he was heavily criticised.[46] This raised the knotty issue of whether a photographer is just a witness or has some responsibility for her/his subject.

FIGURE 3.2: Photographers take pictures of a starving child during the 1992 famine caused by the civil war in Somalia, 1992. © Paul Lowe/Panos Pictures Mogadishu, Somalia, 1992.

The idea of the famine victim has also been developed in various types of literature. Starting in the 1920s, we can see that Walter Mallory's book *China: Land of Famine* demonstrates early sophistication in the depiction and analysis of hunger.[47] As Secretary of the China International Relief Commission, he was in a good position to take an overall view of the country most at risk in that decade, and this enabled him to present a multi-factorial interpretation that included economic, environmental, political, and social causes, along with his suggested cures. China was certainly in the front line of disasters in the interwar years, with major floods in 1924, 1931, 1933, 1935, and 1939, and droughts in 1920 and 1928–1930, with a consequential mortality of eleven million.[48] However, it was not until the 1931 novel, *The Good Earth,* by Pearl S. Buck, that the human element of famine in China was appreciated in the wider world. Buck's was one of the twentieth century's best known books on food insecurity, and it won her the Nobel Prize for Literature.

China continued to feature in the famine imaginaries of the second half of the twentieth century. This was mainly due to the Great Leap Forward famine of 1959–1961, which, it is estimated, claimed thirty million lives, making it the most deadly famine in history. Until the 1980s, relatively little was known about this in the West, hence the subtitle of Jasper Becker's book—*Mao's Secret Famine*.[49] Since then, oral testimony has come forward, as used by Ralph Thaxton in his account of Da Fo village in Henan province, where there was hardship but also a range of coping strategies, such as remittances from relatives, illegal labor migration, begging, and even the theft of crops from neighboring villages.[50]

In the physical sense, hunger was, of course, a driving force behind Mao's revolution, but at the same time in party propaganda it was not rated as highly as the political hunger of the revolutionary spirit. Jung Chang successfully renders the tension between the ideological imperative of the Cultural Revolution and its devastating consequences in her factional family autobiography, *Wild Swans*. This has the primary aim of unmasking the inherent chaos of this period of China's history, but readers all over the world also learned about the widespread hunger in the ten years up to Mao's death in 1976.[51]

Theorizing the structure and causality of such famines and hunger was problematic until recently; one thinks of the many population and resource frameworks rooted in the thinking of Thomas Malthus, for instance. This began to change in the 1980s when Amartya Sen saw that famines can happen where there is no shortage of food.[52] Sen grasped that the *exchange entitlements* of individuals or households—in short their access to food—is the key to whether they starve, and not the amount of food in the local warehouse or shop. This entitlement can be eroded by a loss of bargaining power in the market, for instance, by unemployment or rising prices, or, in the nonmonetary sense, by the denial of traditional community-support mechanisms.

Sen's book received name checks right across the food insecurity literature and his work has influenced international aid thinking over the last thirty years. Despite this, critical scrutiny suggests that his examples work best as particular types of famine in particular socio-economic contexts.[53] These are mostly peasant societies with private property and some engagement with market-based exchange, where a shock to the system has reduced employment opportunities or inflation has made basic foodstuffs unaffordable. Sen's approach is less predictive for pre-capitalist societies dominated by common property resources and in famines under centrally planned socialism.[54] He is least effective in dealing with famines that occur in times of civil conflict and war because his theory makes the assumption of stable, legal-based entitlements. He is also convinced that democratic institutions are a powerful anti-famine tool because political and media debate will hold the state and its agencies to account, but in reality there are many examples of widespread chronic hunger in liberal democracies.[55]

A number of improvements to Sen's original framework have been suggested. One of the most important is the need for a greater awareness of culturally and socially embedded variations in consumption practices. For instance, we know that people often choose to reduce their food intake as a means of minimizing the risk to their family's long-term endowments, such as land or other key assets. This *choosing* to starve is different from the *having* to starve of a famine, but it may not necessarily be altruistic.[56] Weaker and marginal family members usually suffer first and most, with gendered outcomes that favor the interests of productive adult males.

Another crucial extension of Sen is the recognition of non-market methods of getting access to food. These are based on whatever social relations and networks each household can call upon in time of need. They may be far-reaching but there is plenty of evidence that they may be eroded in circumstances of exploitative exchange relations, or insensitive and disruptive political control. Watts' in-depth analysis of the moral economy of Hausaland showed that reciprocity had broken down under colonial rule.[57] To add to this, in the quarter of a century since this pioneering study, there has been a 'network turn' in sociology and human geography, so that now we have a much better understanding of how food-insecure families draw upon their social capital and devise a wide range of coping strategies to maintain themselves in the long-run.

At the beginning of the twenty-first century the humanitarian aspect of food insecurity has been reinvigorated through a debate about the *right to food*. For some time international law has seen this as an inalienable human right, enshrined in the Universal Declaration on Human Rights and the International Covenant on Economic, Social, and Cultural Rights, but implementation has been slow and patchy. Some observers argue that in the case of famine there is always liability, at the very least for negligence or occasionally for genocide, justifying action by the International Criminal Court. This begs a new kind of question: who benefits from famines?

In retrospect, there are many examples of such crimes. In the years 1932–1933 in the Soviet Union, for instance, particularly in the Ukraine and Kazakhstan, there was widespread famine and a total of between five and seven million people died following the forced collectivization of agriculture. Whether this was a deliberate policy to suppress peasant resistance to communism, or the tragic coincidence of a number of unforeseen circumstances is still a matter of bitter controversy.[58] It was impossible in Stalin's time to seek answers because the subject of famine was taboo, to the extent that the population even suppressed their own memories and grief.[59]

One can certainly envisage that famine denial might be a crime. In the Sudan, for instance, the government failed to acknowledge a drought-related famine in 1984–1985—a tragic mistake that cost a quarter of a million people their lives. More recently, in 2004, U.S. Secretary of State Colin Powell stated that "genocide has been committed in Darfur and the government of Sudan and the *janjawiid* [Arab militias] bear responsibility."[60] He was referring to the government's counter-insurgency by proxy, which has used famine as a weapon. Alex de Waal points out that the verb *to starve* is transitive in Sudan and to most outsiders it would certainly appear that crimes have been committed against humanity in this dirty war. However, it is notable that the indictment against Omar Hassan Ahmad Al Bashir, President of Sudan, issued in March 2009 by the International Criminal Court, did not mention the use of famine as a weapon in its listing of war crimes and crimes against humanity.

Recently, famine theorizing has incorporated legal arguments on genocide and negligence. This is constructivist thinking that seeks to identify the human fault of omission or commission and to apply remedies through international courts.[61] In this dark vision, there are *beneficiaries* of famines.[62] Ignoring opportunities to prevent famine is culpable and a number of small acts together may amount to the active manufacture of hunger and starvation.[63] In extreme cases this may amount to genocide and all of these famine-creating and famine-perpetuating activities are crimes against humanity.

THE INTERVENTIONIST AND THE REGULATOR

The Foucaultian perspective of governmentality is appropriate for understanding responses to food insecurity from the nineteenth century onward.[64] Through the medium of state biopolitics, we have become aware of the need to collect data on food production and bodily nutrition. It was in the twentieth century that ministries of food were established in many countries and sample surveys initiated in order to monitor the variety and balance of diets across a suitable demographic range, and to provide a basis for food and public-health policies.

A development in the 1920s and 1930s was the increasingly loud voice of scientists arguing that the newer knowledge of nutrition, especially the role of vitamins in bodily health, should drive policy and underlie the nascent "international food movement."[65] A number of them advised the League of Nations, including Sir John Boyd Orr, who later went on to lead the Food and Agriculture Organization of the United Nations (1945–1948). Orr had a global vision of helping the malnourished but he found neither the British or American governments willing to support his idealistic plan for a World Food Board, and so he resigned. Postwar attitudes to food insecurity instead evolved slowly within a fragile social-welfare consensus. Coupled with decolonization in the 1950s and 1960s, this eventually pulled the center of gravity of famine relief to what by then was known as the *third world* and the modern era of emergency disaster aid and development had begun.

One aspect of development was charitable disaster relief; for instance, the origins of Oxfam in 1942, which was started to help the victims of the famine in Greece. Later known as non-governmental organizations, there has been a proliferation of such humanitarian initiatives. After the war they were joined in the field by international agencies devoted to development and disaster relief, such as those of the United Nations and World Bank, either funding emergency feeding or long-term projects to increase food production. In terms of bilateral relations, America led the way with the postwar Marshall Plan (1947–1952) and Public Law 480 (1954), which was an important foundation stone of international food aid, soon followed in the 1960s by the formation of many national aid agencies. In recent years there has been a widespread recognition of a human *right* to food and the development of a strong literature on the ethical case for assistance.[66]

No history of food in the twentieth century would be complete without a comment on food quality and safety. These concepts changed so fundamentally that, in a way, they are metaphors for the century itself. In

1920 it is probably fair to say that modern consumers were deeply cynical about their food supply, partly because of the disruptions of war, but at a deeper level because there were worries about food poisoning and the adulteration of foodstuffs inherited from the nineteenth century. Many of these were scandals about the manipulation of food composition, by the addition or extraction of ingredients—for instance, the watering of milk[67]—but there were also concerns about the simulation of expensive items by what came to be called the process of *falsification*. In France the main concern was wine. Their law of 1905—which later became the basis of European Union food-standards' legislation—was an outcome of this, and the United States' Food and Drug Act followed in 1906. Both were influential in eliminating the worst abuses. Progress has been slow in the Global South although, encouragingly, in countries such as India and China, the media have played a role in uncovering scandals about poor food quality.

One point to make here is that the branding was introduced to give consumers confidence in their favorite processed foodstuffs. Companies were successful if they could convince the public that such trust was justified, and the manipulation of ingredients that previously might have been thought of as adulteration, was increasingly seen to be a means of creating distinctive products.[68] A second point is to note the rise in the 1920s and 1930s of attentive publics demanding better quality food at an affordable price. Some were activists in consumer organizations, such as cooperative societies; others demanded free trade in the hope of accessing food from all over the world; and still others wanted tariff barriers to protect their jobs.[69]

The period 1920–2000 witnessed several reassessment phases of food quality and therefore food security. Two in recent decades have been the public's wariness about agro-chemical residues and the use of processing additives, which together have encouraged the beginnings of a demand for organic foodstuffs, and also the frenzy associated with mad cow disease (1984 onwards), salmonella in eggs (1988), and many other infective agents.[70] According to Ulrich Beck, these are representative of a new phase of modernity, which he calls the "Risk Society."[71] Food scares, he claims, have undermined public trust in the regulation of quality and purity by the state and in the reliability of scientific expertise.

THE FUTURE

Food is, of course, a cultural marker of great significance, to the extent that it is a contributory factor in identity formation, both individually and collectively. An insecurity of supply may, then, present a fundamental challenge, not just physiologically, but also psychologically. In some societies the presence of hunger today is so uncomfortable that there may be denial, and memories of food insecurity in the past are sometimes deleted.[72] In others, famine is a hitching post of history and a constitutive part of the values and metrics through which the world is understood. Either way, the latest literature demonstrates the complexity of the livelihoods involved and calls for multi-factorial studies of household livelihood dynamics through time and across space.[73] It seems that there is a potentially important research agenda here for historians and geographers.

In future, researchers will need to pay more attention to the new famines that appeared at the end of the twentieth century.[74] These complex emergencies are presently the biggest global risk to food security.[75] They are often conflict-related but the spread of HIV/AIDS has been another major factor.[76] On its own this disease has significantly reduced productive capacity in several African countries; it has also increased dependency ratios and made care of the sick a major burden. Often, family decision makers are affected by the disease but it is their dependents, including a generation of orphans, who are most susceptible to malnutrition. Other new famines include an excess mortality of hundreds of thousands in Iraq during the period of UN trade sanctions, 1990–2003, and as a consequence of other economic crises, such as in Indonesia (1997), Russia (1998), Argentina (2001–2002), and many others in the so-called credit crunch of 2007–2010.[77] Contemporary cultural histories of food insecurity have a profound significance in helping us to understand the perplexing continuation of this fundamental issue, and one way to achieve this is by acknowledging the variety of circumstances in which shortages and poor-quality diets arise.

CHAPTER FOUR

Food and Politics in the Modern Age: 1920–2012

MAYA JOSEPH AND MARION NESTLE

It is unusual to think of food as being political. And yet, it is just as rare for a modern food system *not* to have its origins in national and international politics. Often, the politics of food is most visible in the debates and decisions made within official institutions of government. Farm subsidies, for example, are thrashed out in the halls of national and regional legislatures. Federal, state, and local institutions oversee food safety and food standards. Enormous international agencies structure the loan and trade agreements that govern world commerce. Politics, in the narrowest definition, consists of precisely these institutions, the decisions made within them, and the rules, laws, and norms that govern social and economic interactions.[1] But the politics of food in the modern age is hardly confined to such institutions. Political clashes over food also arise in everyday life.

The inconspicuous and often unrecognized decisions and activities that constitute everyday life also constitute a kind of politics.[2] At times, political differences about food may arise from collisions in values, customs, religious beliefs, and social priorities. Considered in this light, the politics of food is ubiquitous in the modern world.

As has been true throughout history, however, many of the most intense and far-reaching examples of food politics occur because of economic disputes over who benefits financially from the existing structures of food production, distribution, and consumption.[3] To demonstrate how such quarrels have unfolded in the modern age, we present case studies in areas of food politics related to food safety, food biotechnology, agricultural policies, dietary guidelines, health claims on food labels, and international trade. Some of these areas—food biotechnology and agricultural policies, for example—are notoriously political subjects. Others, such as food safety or dietary guidelines, appear to be inoffensive matters of routine inspection or common sense. However, because of their economic implications, even such mundane food matters often give rise to bitter, intractable, and long-standing political debates.

FOOD SAFETY

Food safety would seem to be the least political aspect of production and consumption; everyone wants food to be safe. Instead, this area best illustrates how economic considerations can quickly turn everyday food matters political. Producers want to increase their profit margins by spending as little as they can on the foods they sell. Consumers want to spend as little as possible on the foods that they buy. Economic pressures for lower prices encourage unscrupulous food producers to reduce costs by cutting corners.

Manufacturers can adulterate food by replacing costly ingredients with cheaper and sometimes harmful substitutes. Or, viewing safety procedures as expensive or time-consuming burdens, they ignore them or handle them sloppily.

These temptations and risks are nothing new. Nor is the need for government action to prevent and police them. Indeed, one of the most basic actions required of any government has been to oversee food safety and food quality. Throughout recorded history, codifying and enforcing the rules that specify how food must be produced, measured, and sold has traditionally been among the earliest ways that governments have intervened in the marketplace.[4] Industrialization and globalization, however, have drastically altered the shape and quantity of government action required to keep food free from adulteration and harmful microorganisms.

The imperative to reduce costs, coupled with the complexity of the modern food system, has created greater risks and more opportunities for contamination in food manufacturing. Food is now harder to trace and to keep safe due to the great distances it travels and the number of hands, trucks, warehouses, and processing plants through which it passes. The concentration of production and processing (whether in slaughterhouses, feedlots, factories, or farms) means that pathogens that once may have been isolated in a single product, batch, animal, or locale are now quickly dispersed throughout the food system.

The number of ingredients in many packaged foods, the amount of processing they undergo, and the sheer number of miles travelled by the average food product creates opportunities for innumerable ways to adulterate processed foods, contaminate agricultural commodities, and defraud, dupe, or sicken unsuspecting consumers. From *E. coli*-laced apples to *Salmonella*-ridden peanut butter, the production, transportation, and consumption of food in the modern world remain a risky and potentially lethal business.[5] Meanwhile, the long-distance transportation chain keeps food producers both geographically and temporally separated from their consumers, making it possible for producers to abjure responsibility for ensuring food safety.

While it might seem bad for business to sicken customers, food businesses have responsibilities to shareholders as well as to consumers. The same trust-building, transparency, and prevention measures likely to make for confident eaters may dismay stockholders interested in maximizing short-term profits.[6] As individuals are limited in what they can do to prevent safety problems, political institutions must be responsible for ensuring that safety measures are in place and actually followed.[7]

Strict standards require strict oversight. In the United States, oversight of any private industry is a politically charged issue.[8] Thus, food companies may resist mandatory safety procedures while appealing to the political notion of keeping government out of private business matters.

Distaste for federal oversight of economic actors helps to explain the history of food-safety regulations in the United States. For reasons of history, safety oversight is divided largely between two agencies: the U.S. Department of Agriculture (USDA) and the Food and Drug Administration (FDA). The USDA oversees the safety of meat and poultry, and receives three-fourths of congressional food-safety funding. The FDA regulates the

safety of all other foods—roughly three-fourths of the entire food supply—
but receives only one-fourth of the funding. Although for years food safety
advocates have urged the creation of a single food-safety oversight agency
with authority to order recalls of contaminated products, the U.S. Congress
has consistently failed to act. This intransigence perpetuates a food-safety
regime replete with gaps, loopholes, and errors.

The inadequate funding provided to the FDA, for instance, explains
why an internal investigation found this glaring disparity: from 1970 to
2007, the food industry grew exponentially, but FDA inspections decreased
by 78 percent. Since the early 1990s, Congress had imposed more than one
hundred new tasks on the FDA, but given it little additional funding to
conduct these tasks.[9]

One result of the FDA's weakened condition is that food-safety problems are discovered after contaminated foods are consumed. Just in 2009,
the FDA had to deal with a large number of recalls of foods already on the
market, as a result of discoveries of suspected or proven contamination with
potentially lethal bacteria: E. coli O157:H7 (refrigerated cookie dough);
Bacillus cereus (Slim-Fast drinks); Listeria monocytogenes (bean sprouts,
frozen waffles, smoked salmon, soft cheeses, packaged sandwiches); and
Salmonella in an absurdly long list of foods: alfalfa sprouts, cantaloupes,
chocolate-covered peanuts, cilantro, chai tea, dry milk powder, granola nut
clusters, green onions, ground red pepper, hazelnuts, hot cocoa mix, parsley, peanuts, peanut butter, peanut butter-containing products, pistachios,
romaine lettuce, spinach, tahini, trail mix, yogurt, and watermelons.[10]
These represent only a selection of items recalled in 2009, and do not include the meat and poultry products regulated by the USDA.

In some of these incidents, investigators found evidence of only casual
attention to food safety. Food companies, for example, have strong disin-
centives to test products for harmful bacteria. Products that test positive
must be recalled. The politics of food safety means that food companies
have little incentive to protect consumers beyond lawsuits and class-action
settlements, from which many businesses soon recover. Hence: the need for
independent oversight and authority to impose preventive measures and to
recall contaminated products.

At the international level, the FDA's limited capacities demonstrate how
thinly federal resources are stretched to meet the demands of food imports

to the United States. The number of FDA-inspected imported goods increased from 2.8 million shipments in 1997 to 8.2 million in 2007. Lacking additional resources to keep up with this growth, the FDA managed to inspect less than 1 percent of these shipments in 2007.[11]

The contemporary global food system presents even more opportunities for potential harm. Many food ingredients are untraceable without teams of sleuths. When a mysterious substance in nearly one hundred brands of American pet foods sickened cats and dogs throughout the United States in 2007, it took two months, three companies, several research laboratories, and one federal agency to pin down the toxin (melamine, an industrial chemical) and its origin (China).[12] While this episode involved pet, not human, food, it illustrated the interconnectedness of the world food supplies for people, food animals, and pets. Despite harsh punishment for the perpetrators, melamine turned up in Chinese infant formula and was responsible for causing kidney problems in nearly 300,000 infants. It continued to appear in milk-containing food products around the world throughout the following years.[13]

While international commerce in foodstuffs has become easier and more frequent, establishing political agencies whose authority matches the problems and distances at issue has never been more difficult. Nevertheless, several European countries have attempted to consolidate oversight of food safety into single agencies or institutions. In the late 1990s, Denmark, Ireland, and the United Kingdom (along with Canada) created such agencies, followed more recently by Germany, the Netherlands, and New Zealand. In 2003, primarily as a response to the BSE so-called mad cow outbreak, the European Food Safety Authority (EFSA) was established to provide independent scientific advice on all matters with a direct or indirect impact on food safety. Although the approaches taken by these countries varied, all established a single agency to oversee or to enforce food-safety procedures. Because these benefits have not been fully evaluated and because these countries are all smaller than the United States, officials of U.S. food-safety agencies believe that such approaches have only limited ability in their country.[14]

Overall, economic considerations continue to remain the guiding concern for food producers operating across national borders. As we discuss below, without strong political institutions, the default governing authority for handling international food-safety and production standards is the

World Trade Organization (WTO), whose chief purpose is to end barriers to trade between nation states, not to manage food-safety problems.

FOOD BIOTECHNOLOGY

Some of the most political issues in the food-safety realm, however, are not strictly matters of safety. The catch-all term *food biotechnology* is an imprecise phrase that refers to the use of recombinant DNA technology to adjust or intervene in the genetic processes of plants, animals, and micro-organisms.[15] Applications range from the technology used to *alter* the genetic structure of plants and animals, to the set of reproductive techniques used to clone, or *replicate,* adult animals. These applications are similar in the level of fear and loathing that they generate among the public.

Some characterize the dread and outrage generated by biotechnology as a moral virtue and describe it as "the wisdom of repugnance," while others characterize it as a kind of gastronomic queasiness or, pejoratively, as an expression of scientific ignorance.[16] Whatever its designation, the sense of unease voiced by many consumers about food biotechnology indicates a difficult political problem. Social, economic, and political issues are at stake with biotechnology policies which, in the contemporary policy-making environment, are difficult to discuss, let alone resolve. The result is public anxiety about patenting forms of life, the labeling of biotechnology products, intellectual property rights, long-term social and environmental risks, the implications of the technologies, and the regulatory system itself.[17] Such concerns are often funneled into the one setting in which it is possible and permissible to object to and criticize food biotechnology: the realm of food safety.[18]

Supporters routinely argue that genetically modified seeds provide the solution to hunger, poverty, and the pressures of world population growth.[19] By adjusting plant traits to enable staple crops to weather pests, droughts, and other adversities, proponents argue that agricultural biotechnology can increase harvests and allow farmland to support growing populations. Critics, however, wonder how such benefits are possible when populations most in need of the technology can least afford it, and existing methods of sustainable agriculture are bypassed in favor of technological approaches.[20] Most often, however, these disagreements are discussed not on their own terms, but are instead swept into scientific disputes about risk, safety, and hazards.

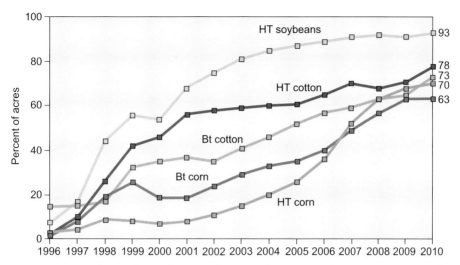

FIGURE 4.1: Rapid growth in adoption of genetically engineered crops continues in the United States. Data for each crop category includes varieties with both HT (herbicide tolerant) and Bt (Bacillus thuringiensis) toxin traits. *Sources*: 1996–1999 data are from Fernandez-Cornejo and McBride (2002). Data for 2000–2010 are available in the ERS data product, Adoption of Genetically Engineered Crops in the United States. Tables 1–3.

Trade disputes between the United States and the European Union, for instance, over the use of biotechnology products in exported agricultural items have ostensibly occurred because of food-safety concerns—despite profoundly different social and political attitudes between these trading partners with respect to biotechnology.[21] In 2003 the European Union enacted a law that required all food products containing genetically modified organisms (GMOs) to be labeled as such and to be traced back to their origins. This traceability, for most Europeans, is seen as a consumer right and thus ensuring a safe and reliable food supply, while for many producers and even consumers in the United States it is regarded as inconvenient at best. The transformation of public mistrust and unease into a discussion of relative safety levels is in part a pragmatic response to a messy dispute, but it is also a successful move on the part of biotechnology companies to control the terms and outcome of the discussion.

Whether in domestic or international political disputes, contemporary regulatory systems that focus on biotechnology as an issue of food safety often pit public concerns and values against corporate interests in a sphere in which corporations have far greater resources. The politics of food biotechnology is consequently about public access and deliberation in a political setting where those with the greatest financial stakes in the debate are also the ones that set its terms. Meanwhile, in other areas of food politics—such as agricultural policies—ordinary citizens have even less of a say in determining long-term plans and principles.

AGRICULTURAL POLICIES

Throughout the twentieth and twenty-first centuries, governments have struggled to ensure that food supplies are not only abundant but also safe, nutritious, and affordable. These attempts can be understood as political interventions into the agricultural economy. Such interventions have taken several paths, ranging from government-run collective farms to government subsidies for private farms. Rarely do these grand schemes begin out of a desire to alter agriculture alone. Guaranteeing an ample food supply can be understood as a political necessity—if not a basic moral duty—of *any* government, but in the twentieth century these obligations were caught up in the concurrent needs of nation-states to transform, maintain, and adjust their economies—needs that continue to the present day.

In the Soviet Union, for instance, the leaders of the 1920s and 1930s embarked on an ambitious plan to industrialize the traditional peasant economy.[22] Doing so required transferring people and resources from small-scale agriculture to large industries—and accomplishing this transition at breakneck pace. In 1917, the peasantry made up 85 percent of the population.[23] Some peasant farmers were compelled to leave the land and work in factories, others were forced or encouraged into state-run collective farms, and many of those who resisted "disappeared."[24] Russian historian Nicholas Riasanovsky estimates that at least five million individuals vanished—many sent to concentration camps in Siberia or Central Asia.[25]

With similar dispatch, the first of several five-year plans to transform the agricultural economy was completed in a mere four years—leading to a series of terrible famines.[26] The worst of these swept the USSR in the early 1930s. Although this famine cannot be blamed entirely on the strict, quick, and unrealistic farming schedules developed by Soviet planners, the adjustment plan almost certainly worsened an already dire problem caused by poor weather, soil, and economic conditions.[27] The result was widespread privation and worse: at the height of the 1932–1933 famine, more than 4.5 million individuals are believed to have perished across the Soviet Union.[28]

The consequences of rapid industrialization in China were even more extreme. Similar to the Soviet Union's programs, Chinese plans for swift industrial development involved bringing agriculture under state control in the form of collective farms.[29] Also similarly, the Chinese policies, launched in 1952, came at great human cost and caused an immediate agricultural crisis. Following widespread upheaval and disarray, grain production fell into precipitous decline by the end of the 1950s. By 1961, the combination of the shortage of food in rural areas, the official disbelief in the shortage, and the inability to redistribute existing supplies is believed to have caused the death of approximately thirty million individuals.[30]

In striking contrast to these stories of hardship, crisis, and collectivization, policymakers in the United States have enjoyed touting the virtues of the independent American farmer and have wrestled with a chronic problem of surplus. However, while American farms have remained private, their very independence and success could be maintained only through vast amounts of government support at levels which continue to this day.

As with agricultural planning in the USSR and China, American farm policies did not originate with a desire to reshape the food system. Rather, they emerged from a perceived need to prop up the entire economic system. In the United States, agricultural assistance to individual farmers was intended to be a short-term tactic to jump-start the economy.

United States' farm assistance was originally enacted into law in the 1930s as a central component of President Franklin Delano Roosevelt's New Deal. The special legislation was intended to bring economic relief to Americans battling the Great Depression. At the time, over one-fifth of the American population was employed in agriculture.[31] Policymakers maintained that providing aid and stability to this crucial 20 percent of the labor force would do much more than help farmers. By enabling farmers to purchase manufactured goods, the direct farm aid would also—planners argued—bring economic stability to the entire economy.[32] The assistance programs consisted of an extensive set of government-backed loans, price supports, and disaster insurance.

The policies were immensely and immediately popular among farmers. Within a few years, more than one-third of gross farm income came from government programs, and farmers quickly came to view these measures as entitlements rather than as historical curiosities.[33] By 1942, the temporary measures of 1933 had been renewed and it was soon evident that the farmers' sense of economic need conjoined with their formidable ability to lobby lawmakers would make the subsidy programs difficult to eliminate.[34]

Because the 1930s legislation creating the programs was provisional, American agricultural subsidies must be continually renewed by Congress—a process which occurs roughly every five to seven years. Lawmakers from farm states soon learned that they could use their votes on *non-farm* issues as bargaining chips, using a vote, say, for a transportation bill, in exchange for a vote for what is now widely known as the Farm Bill. Over time, this process was cemented by tailoring significant chunks of the Farm Bill to suit the politics of urban lawmakers.[35] The 1977 Food and Agriculture Act, for instance, provided the usual agricultural subsidies for farmers, but also included food-stamp programs for city-dwellers, ensuring enthusiastic support from rural and urban lawmakers alike. This long-standing mutual assistance policy of U.S. legislators is an important reason why the (temporary) subsidy programs of the 1930s have not yet been brought to a close. Those with a direct economic stake in the subsidies have successfully captured the political process. The relationships between farmers, their commodity-specific lobbies, and the legislators who bargain on their behalf have proved so impervious to outside influence that they have been enshrined in the study of American politics as the *iron triangle* of influence-peddling: a now-classic example of institutionalized corruption.[36]

Comparable issues bedevil the European Union (EU). European politicians have clung to programs of intensive economic assistance to domestic farmers. The effects of the U.S. and EU systems are similar: both produce too much food. The EU farm-assistance program, however, is certainly more complex than the American system. The Common Agricultural Policy, or CAP, integrates a widely varied collection of national policies into a single, harmonized structure for collecting funds and disbursing subsidies—all while attempting to protect the economic goals and agricultural traditions of very different regions.[37]

A look at Germany's contribution to the CAP illustrates how this works. Immediately following World War II, the West German government gave farmers special economic treatment in order to maintain an adequate

food supply, ensure a stable economy, and lock in the typically conservative votes of farmers and their families.[38] In one stroke, the West German
government remedied a food shortage and made a political commitment
to protect the economic needs of a network of small, traditional family
farms.[39] This promise to uphold the ideal of the small family farm translated into economic policies—namely high levels of price supports and protection from competition—which were, along with the commitment to the
ideal itself, eventually transferred into pan-European policies. Germany's
1955 Agricultural Act, for instance, which decreed a federal commitment
to maintaining a fair standard of living for individual farmers—and did so
through the measures mentioned above—is nearly identical to Article 39
of the 1957 Treaty of Rome—the first declaration of the EU's agriculture
program.[40]

The Treaty of Rome is one of the founding documents of European political and economic unity, and the Common Agricultural Policy laid out in
Article 39 was of particular importance.[41] Much like agricultural subsidies
in the United States, and designs to modernize or support the farm sectors
in other countries, the origins of the CAP are inextricable from the broader
economic goals of the European Union and its member states.

In the decades following World War II, a principal goal of politicians
across Europe was to prevent such a conflict from occurring again. By
forcing historically competitive and hostile nations such as France and
Germany to work together, leaders within Europe hoped to create a single
political and economic community within which war would be unlikely—if
not impossible.[42] To this end, the CAP binds former competitors together
in a system of mutual assistance. The first CAP agreements went into effect
in 1962 with the goal of creating: (1) a single market, in which agricultural
goods can circulate freely; (2) a system of common financing, which col-
lects revenues and distributes benefits as a unit; (3) guaranteed minimum
prices for specified agricultural commodities; and (4) import tariffs to protect CAP member states' agriculture from cheap competition abroad.[43]

Thanks to the importance of agriculture in many European economies,
demands for agricultural protectionism from countries such as Germany, and
the widely varying spectrum of products grown in the European Union, the
CAP remains Europe's single most expensive program—and also one of the
most complex and contested—though reforms have been enacted, including

its decrease in size, decoupling subsidies from production, and the new role of farmers as landscape and environmental stewards.[44] Much like American agricultural policies, the CAP is tremendously efficient in terms of generating an abundance of food. This is an accomplishment not to be overlooked in light of the grave famines that occur frequently in other regions of the world. However, in both the European Union and the United States, these accomplishments can be considered fundamentally inefficient in the sense that they drastically distort the basic relationship between supply and demand.

By supporting what farmers grow—regardless of what they can sell—both the EU and U.S. programs boost the supply of basic commodities well above the level of demand. This can be understood as a benefit in the sense that a reserve supply of food protects national economies from price swings and poor harvests, but this chronic state of excess creates its own set of calamities. Chief among them are nutritional dilemmas, ecological destruction, and international quarrels.[45]

The influence of northern-hemisphere agricultural policies on the economies of southern-hemisphere nations, for instance, is well illustrated by the trajectory of developing-country farm sectors in the later twentieth century. Domestic policies in both developed and developing countries supported a one-way flow of cheap foodstuffs across international borders from the affluent and over-productive north to the developing south. Governments in developing countries watched as cheap imports flooded their markets and drove their own farmers to cities in search of work.[46] In some countries, where the turbulent growth of democratic political systems has coincided with a brisk displacement of agricultural populations, newly unemployed and landless workers have been quick to demand what they describe as their political and economic rights to land.[47] In other places, the rural exodus has been essential to industrialization by creating a burgeoning urban labor pool.[48]

Across the board, the economic interests of the north have shaped the terms, laws, and practices not only of the international trade in food, but also of developing nations' agriculture. Exports from abroad directly affect what developing-nation farmers are able to grow profitably for domestic consumption. In many places, the inability of small domestic producers to compete with the external supply of cheap food has meant that formerly self-sufficient countries became dependent on food imports from the developed world.[49]

Over the course of the twentieth and twentieth-first centuries, while some governments have stepped into the agricultural economy in order to radically transform it, others have thus stepped away from it, subject to the economic policies of more powerful nations. Some governments have intervened in the farm sector in order to preserve hallowed ideals—or to support the economic interests of a narrow sector of producers. In all of these cases, national farm politics have effects that are felt far beyond national borders and impact far more than the lives of farmers themselves. In our widespread nutritional crises of both surfeit and scarcity, in the perplexing political traditions of both right and left, and in the tightly interwoven economic systems of both north and south, the farm politics of the last hundred years have contributed to, and continue to perpetuate some of the fiercest and most deeply felt conflicts of modern life.

DIETARY GUIDELINES

One consequence of the farm-support traditions of the modern developed world is an excess of calories available in the food supply. These complicate the making of dietary guidelines. Although dietary guidelines are supposed to be based on science, they are subject to pressures from food companies concerned about the business implications of advice to restrict certain nutrients or foods.

Advice to consume *more* of a country's agricultural and food products in order to prevent nutrient deficiencies raises few controversial issues. Advice to *restrict* intake of certain foods to prevent obesity and chronic diseases, however, is inevitably controversial. The producers of foods targeted for restriction routinely use the political process to weaken, undermine, or eliminate dietary guidelines that suggest eating less of their products.

The history of dietary guidelines and food guides is rife with examples of controversy over advice to eat *less*. Like any other business in today's global marketplace, food companies must expand sales, meet growth targets, and produce immediate returns for investors. Because all but the poorest countries in the world provide more food than is needed by their populations, the food industry is especially competitive. The U.S. food supply provides an average of nearly 4,000 kilocalories per person each day, nearly twice the amount required by the population. Unlike the situation with shoes, clothing, and electronics, consumption of food is limited even for those with the largest appetites, making competition especially intense. The need to sell more food in an overabundant marketplace explains why the annual growth rate of the American food industry is only a percentage point or two, why food companies compete so strenuously for a sales-friendly regulatory and political climate, and why they so aggressively defend the health benefits of their products and attack critics of their marketing, selling, and lobbying practices.[50]

More often than not, food-industry pressures have succeeded in inducing government agencies to eliminate, weaken, or thoroughly obfuscate recommendations to eat less of certain nutrients and their food sources— or to consume less food overall. United States' policymakers learned this lesson in 1977. When Senator George McGovern's Select Committee on Nutrition and Human Needs released a report suggesting that Americans reduce consumption of meat, eggs, full-fat dairy products, sugars, and salt, the affected industries protested and persuaded Congress to intervene. This level of opposition established an apparently unshakable precedent: dietary advice must never suggest eating less of anything. Over the years, dietary guidelines' committees have internalized this approach.

Since 1980, the USDA and the U.S. Department of Health and Human Services (HHS) have jointly issued *Dietary Guidelines for Americans* every five years as a policy statement on nutrition and health. The *Guidelines* provide dietary advice to reduce risks for chronic diseases for everyone over the age of two years and constitute an official statement of government policy regarding all federal nutrition education, training, food assistance, and research programs. Although they are explicitly set forth as "science based," specific recommendations are invariably influenced by the economic interests of food-industry stakeholders.[51]

The 1980 version of the sugar guideline, for example, simply said, "Avoid too much sugar." By 2005, under pressure from sugar-industry groups, the *Guidelines* used twenty-three additional words to make the same point, beginning with "Choose and prepare foods and beverages with little added sugars or caloric sweeteners."[52]

Such politics extend to the international level. In 1992, Geoffrey Cannon, a British writer on food politics, surveyed dietary guidelines produced by thirty countries, mainly European, and found their content—and the politics behind them—to be virtually identical to those above.[53] More recent guidelines produced by the World Health Organization for the thirty member countries of the European Region continue this tradition,[54] as do food-based guidelines and reports collected by the Food and Agriculture Organization from individual countries in its various world regions.[55] These make it clear that the politics of dietary guidelines remains consistent no matter where the guidelines are issued.

In the early 2000s, the World Health Organization (WHO) began work on a global strategy to help member nations reduce the burden of death and disease related to poor diet and inactivity. The process began with an expert consultation involving international scientists who were asked to review research and make recommendations. Their report, commonly referred to as "Technical Report 916," appeared in 2003.[56] The process also involved stakeholder consultations with member states, United Nations (UN) agencies, governmental and non-governmental organizations, the food industry, and other private-sector groups, as well as negotiation of co-sponsorship with the Food and Agriculture Organization (FAO) of the UN. The final Global Strategy, released jointly by the two UN agencies, was ratified by member states in May 2004.[57] In this process, the dietary guidance components proved especially contentious.

In the United States, lobbyists for sugar-trade organizations induced the HHS to submit critiques of the draft based on materials they provided.[58] Although sugar-trade groups ostensibly based their arguments on science, their concerns were decidedly economic. Such a recommendation, they said, would be likely to produce "serious, detrimental and long-lasting effects on the agriculture and the economy of [sugar-producing] countries."[59] Just prior to release of "Technical Report 916," The Sugar Association threatened to ask Congress to withdraw U.S. funding for the WHO. It demanded that the WHO immediately withdraw the report.

At the same time, industry groups were attempting to convince member states that acceptance of the 916 report would adversely affect the economies of sugar-producing countries. The World Sugar Research Organization, for example, distributed a report illustrating the loss to sugar-producing countries that would occur if global sugar consumption dropped to 10 percent of calories. Despite flaws in this analysis, it convinced many member states to lobby against the recommendation.[60]

In May 2004, the fifty-seventh World Health Assembly endorsed the Global Strategy, but with major concessions to the sugar industry. Analysis of drafts produced between April 2003 and May 2004 provided substantial evidence of industry influence. As ratified, the Global Strategy states that foods high in fat, sugar, and salt increase the risk for non-communicable diseases, but the sugar recommended simply stated, "limit the intake of free sugars." The Global Strategy remains the basis of dietary advice set forth by the World Health Organization.

Even more recent examples abound. The dietary guidelines' committee in the United States that prepared the seventh edition in 2010 was asked to prepare "science-based" recommendations. Once again, lobbyists for every food product or group likely to be affected by the guidelines prepared materials for the committee, testified at committee meetings, and worked behind the scenes to make sure that the guidelines did not suggest eating less of their products.[61] Indeed, the 2010 Dietary Guidelines suggest eating less of "solid fats and added sugars" but say little about reducing intake of the food sources of those nutrients.[62]

HEALTH CLAIMS ON FOOD LABELS

Marketing food to the general population involves another set of political issues. As the food system has grown more complicated, so has the sort of information necessary to understand what is in a particular food and what it does. While food-labeling laws *require* producers to display certain pieces of information on food packaging, regulations about health claims *limit* what food producers may say about their products. The history of health claims on food labels reflects the tension between the interests of food producers in using health messages in marketing, and those of regulators concerned that labels display information that is truthful and not misleading.

Food packages did not always display health messages. Although they might have done so in the nineteenth century, the U.S. Food and Drug Act of 1906 specified that food labels could not bear statements that might be "false or misleading in any particular way"—an interdiction interpreted to preclude health claims.[63] Following legal challenges by food manufacturers, Congress passed the Sherley Amendment in 1912, which prohibited food packages from displaying statements that were both false *and* fraudulent.

For almost a century, the FDA interpreted any statement of health benefit on a food product as meeting both criteria.

The FDA made an exception for statements of nutrient content. Manufacturers began to add vitamins to food products almost as soon as these nutrients were discovered—vitamin D to breakfast cereals as early as the 1920s, and vitamin C, iron, and B-vitamins during the war years of the 1940s. The FDA allowed these additions as part of a general effort to improve the health of men fighting the battles of World War II. In 1955, Kellogg introduced Special K cereal fortified with seven vitamins and iron. But the FDA limited the amounts of nutrients that could be added to levels that replaced nutrients lost in processing.

These limitations weakened after 1969. That year, President Nixon held a White House Conference on Food, Nutrition, and Health for the purpose of recommending ways to end hunger and malnutrition in America.[64] Food companies, well aware of the marketing potential of added vitamins, seized the opportunity to recommend more widespread nutrient fortification. A food industry committee suggested fortifying not only wheat, corn, and rice, but also snack foods and chocolate. But some consumer groups at the conference urged caution, explicitly stating that the addition of vitamins to such foods would promote marketing, not health.

Nevertheless, in response to the conference recommendations, the FDA relaxed some of its restrictions on fortification. It allowed nutrient fortification of certain categories of foods but continued to restrict their amounts. In the 1970s, cereal manufacturers demanded wider fortification. The FDA eventually conceded and permitted labels to say such things as "contains 7 essential nutrients." But the agency continued to refuse to allow statements that the foods could prevent, treat, or mitigate disease. Such statements, the FDA argued, constituted drug claims that required scientific substantiation.

In 1984, unbeknownst to the FDA, the Kellogg Company arranged with the National Cancer Institute to endorse a health claim for All-Bran cereals. Within six months, All-Bran's market share increased by 47 percent, thereby demonstrating that health claims sell food products.[65] Kellogg, although conceding that the purpose of its campaign had been to promote sales of All-Bran, asserted that its actions were a public service in informing the public about the benefits of fiber, and it filed a lengthy citizens' petition with the FDA to allow health claims.[66] In what can hardly be a coincidence,

Congress incorporated the petition's suggestions about health claims virtually intact when it passed the Nutrition Labeling and Education Act of 1990. This act required the FDA to consider ten specific health claims and to permit those that were scientifically substantiated to be displayed on food labels.

Additional acts further weakened the FDA's ability to prevent use of unsubstantiated health claims. In 1994, Congress passed the Dietary Supplement Health and Education Act, which effectively deregulated supplements and permitted them to bear a new kind of claim that a supplement can support some *structure* or *function* of the body. Although this act did not apply to foods, and still does not, manufacturers sued the FDA any time the agency denied a claim. In 1997, Congress passed the FDA Modernization Act, which further weakened the FDA's ability to control health claims on food labels. During the Bush administration, the FDA lost most of the health claims lawsuits and stopped fighting them. The requirements for scientific substantiation weakened and nutrient-content, health, and structure–function claims proliferated on food products.[67]

A fourth category of claims, front-of-package (FOP) endorsements of nutritional quality, began to appear in 1995, with the American Heart Association's symbol indicating that a product is low in saturated fat and cholesterol (but not necessarily sugar). PepsiCo introduced its Smart Spot in 2004, soon followed by Kraft's Sensible Solutions. In 2007, General Mills' cereals displayed tokens indicating the content of specific nutrients, based on European models. Other companies followed suit. FOP symbols proliferated to such an extent that *Consumer Reports* developed a website to track and evaluate them.[68]

Never before in American history have food products displayed so many symbols and statements proclaiming nutrition and health benefits. FOP claims, although often used in violation of FDA labeling regulations, are ubiquitous in food marketing. Recently, the FDA embarked on an initiative to review FOP labeling and asked the Institute of Medicine (IOM) to consider the eventual recommendation of a single, standardized guidance system.[69]

The bewildering array of claims for increasingly remote health benefits has recently elicited political action. The Smart Choices Program, a voluntary initiative involving several food companies and health organizations, became the focus of an embarrassing exposé by the *New York Times* and threatened legal action by the Connecticut Attorney General when its logo of approval appeared on a children's sugar-sweetened cereal. The companies withdrew from the program. The FDA now intends to examine the entire issue of nutrition labeling, but whether the agency will be able to retake control of health claims in the face of food-marketing imperatives remains to be seen. In this arena, as in food safety, the FDA remains handicapped by a lack of political and financial support, and faces powerful industries determined to act in their own self-interest.

A similar situation is occurring in Europe. In Great Britain, for example, the Food Standards' Agency (FSA), concerned about rising rates of obesity, began in 2006 to encourage food companies to use FOP labels to identify levels of fat, saturated fat, salt, and sugars in their products. In particular, the FSA recommended a *traffic-light approach* that marked high levels of fat, saturated fat, sugar, and salt as red, medium levels as yellow, and low levels as green.

The British food industry strongly objected to this approach and proposed an alternative, nutrient-based guidance daily amount (GDA) approach that identifies the percentages of various nutrients in a product. In response to consumer confusion generated by the competing schemes, the FSA conducted a study and concluded in 2009 that the best-understood approach would combine the words high, medium, and low with traffic-light colors *and* percentage GDAs. The food industry continues to object to *any* traffic-light labels, not least because consumers understand them so well and tend to avoid products marked in red. It wants the European Union, which seems much more amenable to food-industry lobbying, to make the final decision. Indeed, the European Parliament narrowly defeated the traffic-light proposal early in 2010, and instead suggested one that allows companies to decide voluntarily how to combine traffic-light colors, text, or percentage GDAs.[70] For food companies, much is at stake in their ability to market products to consumers.

INTERNATIONAL TRADE

The self-interested actions that constitute the politics of food at the domestic level are compounded when food-policy disputes involve other countries, especially when the disputes concern international trade. Political leaders of any country may aspire to keep grocery prices low enough to avoid civic unrest, political instability, and food insecurity, but are often beholden to their own agriculture sectors. Agricultural interests demand government support to keep prices high as well as government assistance to sell their excess goods abroad at competitive prices—goals that sometimes conflict with the needs of nations to develop their own agricultural systems. Aid for such systems can be perceived as helping the competition and hurting the long-term interests of farmers in wealthier nations.[71] Similarly, governments can and do maintain higher-than-normal prices by restricting free trade—either by limiting imports or assisting exports.

In recent years, most countries in the world (150 out of nearly 200) have joined the World Trade Organization (WTO), whose stated purpose is to *reduce* barriers to free trade.[72] It is no surprise that these three goals—supporting domestic growers, placating consumers concerned about food prices, and eliminating trade barriers—often clash. Resolving the contradictions among these goals requires coordinated international action that in turn conflicts with the interests of individual countries.

For the latter half of the twentieth century, international agreements have established rules for navigating these waters. Immediately after World War II, most countries of the world agreed to set up several international political and economic organizations—such as the United Nations and International Monetary Fund—intended to bring a measure of order, stability, and cooperation to world affairs. One of these institutions was a treaty known as the General Agreement on Tariffs and Trade (or GATT). Signed in 1947 by twenty-three countries, GATT was created in order to eliminate trade barriers and end discrimination in international trade.[73] With respect to trade in agriculture, however, trade barriers and unfair discrimination in such areas as domestic farm subsidies proved to be such touchy issues that even talking about these subjects was postponed for three decades.[74]

In 1995, the WTO replaced the GATT framework. In the discussions preceding the creation of the WTO, member states agreed to discuss and even change their agriculture trade policies, but the WTO tools for liberalizing farm subsidies and trade policies have done little to change the national and international organization of world trade in agriculture. The old system of political bargaining—in which nation-states haggle and barter to settle who can produce and trade in what goods—remains firmly in place.[75]

Shoring up the incomes of domestic producers, whether of hogs or sugar beets, often means keeping prices for these commodities high enough at *home* for the growers to make a profit, but low enough *abroad* for growers to be able to sell the excess in world markets. As a legacy of the ongoing farm-subsidy policies, wealthy countries typically have had and continue to have excess food. But their governments, while providing subsidies, must also keep international competition at bay. To do so, they tend to block cheap imports from abroad by imposing boycotts, tariffs, or quotas. Countries that export commodities such as sugar beets or cane are left with few markets in which to sell their products.

This problem becomes worse when wealthy countries that support domestic prices also provide *export subsidies* for commodities. These allow producers from nations with strong political systems and agricultural support networks to flood world markets with artificially cheap goods. By paying growers more for their products than they would receive on the world market, developed countries create outlets for their own surpluses—while undercutting the farm sectors of less developed countries whose governments cannot afford subsidies.

All of these tactics are political maneuvers intended to satisfy commodity groups that double as key political constituencies. The result is that politicians face a *two-level game* when negotiating with other nations—they must represent national interests on the world stage but without jeopardizing their political position in domestic politics.[76] Often, these levels conflict. Supporting domestic industries without alienating trading partners, international allies, or one's own citizens, while at the same time looking out for the interests of developing countries, is usually impossible.

The EU's difficulties with the politics of sugar trade illustrate the problem. Indeed, EU representatives to the WTO must engage with three layers of political and economic conflicts: those of individual nation-states, those within the European Union, and those which the European Union enters into as a WTO member.

Sugar beets, for example, are subsidized heavily by national governments and are among the most profitable and widely-grown crops in the European Union. European Union countries produce so much beet sugar that the region experiences a chronic excess. The European Union has long attempted to keep its sugar producers in business by blocking cheap imports. It further supports growers by helping them sell excess sugar on the world market.[77] Nevertheless, the European Union is obligated under WTO rules to remove trade barriers and cease dumping its excess sugar in world markets.[78] The result is that the European Union produces more sugar than it needs and can export. Yet at the same time, it is a major *importer* of sugar—mainly from African, Caribbean, and Central American countries—in order to meet its commitments to assist these states.[79] The economic absurdity of this position is surpassed only by the political incongruity of EU-wide policies that aim to help the very countries that are harmed by the farm policies of individual EU nations.

As a result of such incongruities, food disputes fuel some of the most controversial trade disagreements in the modern world.[80] However, not all of them concern agriculture. Some have roots in—or make appeals to—food safety. Food-safety standards are governed by a particular WTO accord known as the "Agreement on Sanitary and Phytosanitary Measures," or SPS, for short.[81] The SPS framework relies on the standards for food safety set by an international organization created in 1963 by the FAO and the WHO: the Codex Alimentarius Commission.

The standards agreed upon by the Commission are known informally as the Codex. The WTO uses the Codex, in conjunction with its authority under the SPS agreement, to determine what food-safety measures are appropriate in the context of international trade.[82] The SPS structure seems simple enough: it standardizes requirements for food safety, labeling, and inspections to protect plants, animals, and consumers from potentially harmful contaminants. However, accusations that trading partners have violated food-safety standards are often made in situations where it is uncertain whether food safety, political demands, or economic grievances are the most immediate sources of discontent.

One of the most long-running SPS clashes—over hormones used in American beef—demonstrates why this is the case. In 1987 the European Community blocked imports of American beef by banning six natural and artificial growth hormones used in its production. The United States responded by imposing tariffs on European imports equivalent to the value of the blocked beef exports—worth approximately $100 million.[83]

When the WTO went into effect in 1995, the beef feud was still raging, and the United States sued the European Community, arguing that it had violated the recently adopted SPS measures by failing to conduct a risk analysis on the disputed growth hormones. Under the rules agreed to in the SPS treaty, WTO members must rely on international standards for food safety in the Codex—unless they have commissioned risk analyses that prove the inadequacy of the international standards.

The European Union eventually did conduct risk analyses, but WTO legal panels issued mixed verdicts on the case. These allowed the European Union to continue its ban *and* the United States to continue its punitive measures—which were now extended to retaliatory tariffs on goods such as Bordeaux wine.[84] Since no international organization has the power to force either side to back down, the dispute simmers on—with the United States continuing to argue that the EU's goal is to keep American beef out of its markets. Which side is right? What are the *real* issues at stake? In the context of international trade, the politics and economics of modern food production and distribution are so tightly linked as to be indistinguishable.

CONCLUSION

The steady industrialization of food production has generated new political conflicts about how food should be produced, processed, marketed, consumed, and even understood. The scale and complexity of the modern global food system has increased opportunities for lapses in food safety—deliberate as well as inadvertent. Similarly, in the realm of food marketing, labeling, and nutrition, the need to turn a profit—and an ever larger profit at that—creates stunning clashes of values and interests. In the otherwise volatile politics of the twentieth and twenty-first centuries, the entrenched farm-support programs of the United States and Europe, instituted in times of scarcity, have become irreversible in times of plenty. The vast agricultural output of the global food system has resulted in food excesses that create their own sets of longstanding political conflicts. Yet at the same time, unequal distribution of food and economic resources leave more than a billion people on the verge of starvation.

As the principal stakeholders in these food debates hold economic interests in their outcomes, these case studies illustrate a fundamental point: when food controversies become fodder for major national and international political quarrels, their root cause can often, if not always, be traced to the underlying financial or economic interests of the most influential participants. It is over the distribution and organization of resources that governments, corporations, and other organizations are most likely to engage in bitter and prolonged conflicts. In the cases that we have examined, these conflicts have been gradually incorporated into political institutions, practices, and traditions. As such, they continue to shape the most distant structures and the most ordinary routines of the modern food system.

CHAPTER FIVE

Eating Out: Going Out, Staying In

PRISCILLA PARKHURST FERGUSON

Eat in: 1 Tall Latte

The Tall Latte is the dead giveaway for Starbucks. But in what sense do we EAT IN at Starbucks as the receipt proclaims? Classification becomes more problematic still in this particular instance, since the Starbucks in question is located on the New York State Thru-Way. To be sure, there are tables where one could sit to imbibe the coffee and ingest a muffin but none is connected to Starbucks. Maybe, as a colleague suggested, EAT IN points us back to the car where so much food is consumed. Truly, then, eating turns the automobile into a mobile home.

At Home versus Home Cooked?

A couple of years ago, when a broken wrist hampered my culinary ventures, an exceptionally thoughtful friend had a number of dinners catered for me and my husband. Certainly, we didn't think of the meal as *eating out,* but neither was it *eating in* as usual. It was not a home-cooked meal (though in some culinarily challenged quarters heating the meal does count as cooking). We ate at home, at our table with our cutlery and dishes. Yet, were we eating in? Or, rather, in what senses were we eating in and to what extent were we eating out?

So what *is* eating out? Any number of indicators point to the increasing importance of eating outside the home in contemporary post-industrial societies. According to a 2002 survey of the U.S. Department of Agriculture, eating out has steadily increased since 1972 and now accounts for fully half of all food expenditures in the United States. Some three-quarters of Americans eat out at least once a week.[1] Modernization in its many guises supports this trend toward eating out. A self-consciously modern world vigorously pulls people out of their homes to satisfy not simply their hunger for food, but their desire for pleasure.

The pleasures of eating out are not unalloyed. Nutritionists are troubled about the calorie density and nutritional poverty of meals eaten out. Fast-food outlets and fancy restaurants alike worry about shifts in public preferences, especially in the current state of economic fragility for the post-industrial world. Then there are the differences across class and across culture. What is the analyst to make of the national differences in eating out? The Japanese eat 196 meals out every year, Americans 119, the Germans, the British, the Italians, and the French between 80 and 85; the Dutch and the Belgians come in last with 66–75 meals eaten out per year.[2]

Differences notwithstanding, overall, the past half century has witnessed a remarkable increase in both numbers and the frequency of people eating out in food outlets of one sort or another (as opposed to more informal venues). From 1951 to 1981 in the Netherlands, for example, where there are comparatively fewer meals eaten out than in other European countries, the number of restaurants increased over 150 percent—that of café-restaurants more than doubled while small food outlets increased almost twenty-fold.[3] In Norway, only very recently did the highly traditional food culture adopt the practice of eating out based on (post)modern models that favor professionalized food preparation and make claims to gastronomic excellence.[4]

Undeniably useful in circumscribing the social phenomena attendant upon the consumption of food outside the home, statistics fall short when it comes to the experience of eating out. What meanings does this culinary adventure carry in the daily lives of all those who choose more or less freely to eat out? What drives the many decisions that such a choice entails? What, in sum, *is* eating out?

Every reader can duplicate a hundred times over the permutations noted in the epigraphs of crossover dining. Understandings of *in* and *out* shift over time and place, and, in the end, eating out and eating in are a function of each other: *out* takes us away from a place that we consider *in*. How far does *out* count as eating out? What do we mean by *out*? Public dining? Formal meals? How formal? In what company? With friends? With strangers? In what settings? If home supplies the paradigmatic setting for eating in and the restaurant constitutes the model for eating out, these are only the most marked of innumerable sites and occasions for eating out and eating in. Each instance, each venue, each occasion, each meal, mixes private and public, ceremony and informality, the individual and the collective, the familiar and the new—all of which will likely be construed differently by each of those at the same meal.

Beginning mostly in the nineteenth century in the West and greatly accelerating in the twentieth and twenty-first centuries, each term—*in* and *out*—became manifestly variable and, for that reason, perceptibly unstable. Surely, one of the most striking developments over the past century is the blurring of the distinctions between the two—between what is considered eating in and what is deemed to be eating out. Social and geographic mobility undermined the apparently secure definition of home, which, more and more, changes over time and place, even for the same person.

However, it is the explosion of public or semi-public settings for food consumption that turned eating out into an especially vexed and problematic terrain. Before urbanization and globalization multiplied consumption venues so dramatically, most people in most places most likely took the distinction between public and private consumption occasions as self-evident. The more self-sufficient or autarchic a community, and, therefore, the more isolated it is, the fewer its choices, and, therefore, the sharper the dividing line between the communal and the individual, the private and the public. Today these would be identified as traditional food cultures. In modern, globalizing society where social and economic mobility so decidedly shape the social order, where virtually no community is self-sustaining, those boundaries have become exceptionally permeable. As a consequence,

FIGURE 5.1: McDonald's on Wheels in Washington, D.C. Photo by David Fernandez. Reproduced with permission.

the contemporary dining landscape is not simply broader but of a very different order of complexity than a century ago.

CULINARY MODERNITY

This complexity of dining out is a function of a more general condition of culinary modernity. One of our most intimate activities—eating—is also one of our most social activities. It at once ties individuals to, and makes them dependent upon the social order. For that order supplies and prepares the food and defines the occasion. Small wonder that eating is so fraught with anxieties. Consumers worry about noxious substances, fearing for the integrity of their bodies and their sense of self. They also worry about the integrity of the social body of which they are a part. The socialized consumption of the meal obliges participants to come to terms with others, however temporarily. Where food is consumed cannot be indifferent. This choice too fills us with apprehension, whether we know it or not, though usually we are well aware of the consequences of our choices: in or out, we ask ourselves with trepidation, is this place safe, is it good, is it right for *me?*

What counts as eating out? We assume a consumer who moves away from a fixed base. Yet *how* far, physically, culturally, socially, must one travel to eat out in the fullest sense of the term? To what sort of setting? Eating in hospital is not eating at home for either patients or staff, but, given the constraints on choice, does it count as eating out? The same absence of choice characterizes fare as different as offerings in a school cafeteria, grub in prison, industrial canteens, or the dwindling number of airline meals (do we purchase food when it is not offered? Is that a *real* choice?). What about the hotdog from the street vendor that we eat on the run, or at least at a walk? Food brought in to office, class, or home from the local deli? Frozen food? Does the food define the meal or the setting? Or the company? Guests in a private home are eating out, but what about the hosts who receive these outsiders?

Today, more than ever, the culinary landscape offers an astounding array of consumption choices. How do prospective diners weigh the desirability of the food proposed against the site of consumption? The increasing unpredictability of response, which is compounded by the ever-greater number of possible sites for consumption, reveals much about the different ways in which women and men today manage their lives and define their selves. For, whether in or out, meals not only allow but, more significantly, demand negotiation of relationships with the world and with the self.

WHAT IS A MEAL?

To say anything useful about either eating out or eating in, we have to ask when? Where? What? Why? With whom? In other words, what is a meal?

By the thirteenth century, the meal had acquired its now indelible association with food, thus coinciding with the Latin inflected *repast*. In Old English, however, as the Oxford English Dictionary informs us, a meal referred to a unit of measure and a unit of time. This original sense, suitably updated, points us to the meal as a specific social enterprise situated in time and bounded in space. The three elements of time, space, and social setting give the meal rules and endow it with form. Rules and forms vary according to the purpose of the meal and the conceptions that any culture has of the proper structure for a meal, the sequence of dishes, the content of courses, and the times and places reserved for given repasts. Following dinner as it moved from mid-day to the end of the evening and then somewhere in between, should disabuse anyone who might assume that our current meal times are fixed once and for all.[5]

Granting the fundamental unevenness of the schedule of meals over the day, week, month, and year, today's culinary mores also blur the boundaries of any given meal.[6] The question is not so much what counts as eating out and eating in as what counts as a meal—a *real* meal. With so many choices competing for attention, confusion reigns. The sheer number of possibilities eradicates the boundaries that situate a meal in time and space. If the repast commonly called *breakfast* still mostly comes at the beginning of the day and is associated with certain foods, what do we make of this same meal when restaurants boast of serving breakfast all day long? With scrambled eggs and bacon at 6 P.M. in an American setting, what becomes of dinner? More and more, the answer is left to the individual. Generally characteristic of post-industrial countries from the mid twentieth century to the present, such a spectrum of choices for eating out encourages a radical individualization of food choice. Think of the food courts in malls across America today that turn eating out into a shopping expedition (and vice versa). The distance could scarcely be further from the forms or sequence associated with almost any meal a century ago.

The late eighteenth century opened up this path of culinary individualism, and it did so with that new, exemplary urban institution—the restaurant. The originality of the restaurant lay precisely in giving unprecedented scope to individual selection of foods and services. This new site for consuming food in public not only allowed individuals to order (in all senses) their own meals, but it required that they did so.[7] In a great innovation that trumpeted the possibility and the necessity of choice, the printed menu displayed the selections (and their prices). Choice distinguished the restaurant from previous modes of public dining such as the boarding house, the inn, the banquet where the diner ate what was offered. To be sure, no matter how laissez-manger the contemporary culinary scene, restaurant menus generally correspond to a sequence of courses. But no one need follow that sequence, and more and more often, twenty-first-century diners range across the menu as their fancy dictates—two hors d'oeuvres and no main course, no cheese but two desserts, and so on, with perhaps an appetizer taken for the dessert course. From individual choice on a menu in a single establishment to a great selection in many different establishments represents a shift of degree, not in kind.

Meals do not loom large in the social landscape simply because humans need to eat. Meals reach beyond appetite to orchestrate the distinctive rhythms of our lives because they connect us to our fellow human beings. Once we move beyond sheer instrumentality—food as fuel—the meal appears as a cultural space and time for the performance, the making, keeping, and at times, the breaking of social relations. Eating together is a fact; the pleasures of commensality are the goal. For a dramatically, memorably good meal is rare. As the gastronomic commentator J.A. Brillat-Savarin recounts in *The Physiology of Taste* (1826), and as every one of us knows from our own food encounters, a stellar meal leaves us satisfied in body and in spirit. A good meal leaves the consumer/guest/diner not simply replete but profoundly content with self and with the world. Such a meal depends on the confluence of several factors, of which the food consumed is but one. As Brillat-Savarin impresses upon his readers, the most important elements of a meal have to do with the promotion of sociability—good wine, good guests in a good mood, and time to savor both.[8]

Other critics who focus on the meal as a collective gathering emphasize the fragility of the social equilibrium. The sociologist Georg Simmel addressed the central paradox of the meal, namely, that an activity common to absolutely every human being—eating—engenders a form—the meal—that produces such blatant inequality.[9] All humans eat, but they differ quite spectacularly in how they do so. Hierarchy and difference dominate. Almost as if to obliterate the commonality that insistently ties humans to their animal nature.

Socially weighted distinctions are made manifest in the refinement of the food and the setting, in the selection of company, in the inclusion of some individuals, and the exclusion of others. By admitting insiders and keeping outsiders from disrupting the cohesion, the meal presents a splendid opportunity to define the social group.

INSIDERS AND OUTSIDERS

As Norbert Elias noted in his study of court society under Louis XIV, the increasing refinement of table manners from the Renaissance on, as with the proliferation of specialized table utensils, serves to bar the collectivity to "foreigners"; that is, those who have not been trained in the usages that mark members in good standing.[10] As consumption settings diversify and as mobility puts more and more people in new places, the customs at table exert ever-greater influence as mechanisms of social control, determining access to the group.

Innumerable instances come to mind, fictive or actual, where a newcomer feels and is meant to feel an outsider, one who does not know which spoon, which fork, which knife to use for which task, how to read the menu, or what not to talk about. A paradigmatic scene occurs in the film *Titanic* (1997) when the hero, travelling in steerage, finds himself invited to dine in First Class. He encounters strange food (caviar) and unfamiliar utensils (caviar spoon), insider talk, and formal dress (tuxedos, evening gowns); all of a very different order from what he is used to. Everything about the meal, all the accoutrements, conspires to impress upon the young man that he does not belong. In a different mode, using ethnographic and survey data on contemporary culture, Pierre Bourdieu's work argues on a broad scale that taste, both literal and figurative, operates to identify and demarcate a given social group.[11]

Demonstrating that one belongs at table is so important because commensality—eating together—connotes equality. Exalted individuals such as monarchs or popes, who can have no equal, invariably ate in a separate space and often at different times than others. For less exalted gatherings, the equality is temporary, to be sure, but the very fact of commensality implies connection. For Brillat-Savarin, coming together at meals offers a modicum of compensation for being apart the rest of the time: love of good food promotes "the spirit of conviviality that brings different social classes together every day, gives them a single goal, stimulates conversation, and softens the angles of ordinary inequality."[12] Dining, then, in this mode, occupies a temporary space that brings individuals together. The ideal meal proposes a space of equality against the hierarchies that intrude from the world beyond the dining room.

Clearly, Brillat-Savarin had private dining in mind as the paradigmatic meal. Its restricted physical and social space allows for, as it assumes, control, over the food and over the company, certainly in comparison to restaurant dining (about which the critic says very little). Accordingly, the host is enjoined to take especial care in producing the occasion. Moreover, the heightened sociability hoped for in commensality has to contend with material constraints. The typical oblong dining-room table reproduced as it reinforced the family hierarchy: the father at the head of the table, the mother at the bottom, children in between. At official or formal meals, precedence is a vital concern in seating—perhaps one reason that restaurants make round tables available. Nevertheless, hierarchy is never eliminated entirely. In the absence of great care, division and distinction resurface to disrupt the conviviality of the meal.

The semi-public dining in an eating establishment is rife with ambiguities. What is our relationship to other diners whose space we share? Does equality prevail as it does when we eat in or is every table a world unto itself? Does the thrill of eating out not lie precisely in this ambiguity and the attendant excitement, in the possibility of connecting with people perhaps very different from ourselves? Celebrity sighting brings the most obvious thrill. Does the presence of Chef Mario Batali as a guest at a nearby table not tie me to his culinary celebrity and validate my choice of restaurant? The current trend toward informalization of dining confuses the hierarchy without in the least eliminating differences.

PLAIN AND FANCY

What, then, determines eating occasions as *in* or *out*? Although cooking alters all food, the high degree and visibility of those alterations are sure signs to eating out. The greater both the material and the social transformation of the foods concerned, the more the occasion is likely to be defined as *out*. That is, the greater the difference between the raw and the cooked, and between the food consumed and the foods of everyday life, the more *out* the meal will be. Not abundance, but complexity and refinement identify eating out. The more complex the dish and the more intricate the sequence of dishes, the fancier the meal. Take the hierarchy for the lowly celery. This humble vegetable wants work to become worthy of an extravaganza meal out. If raw celery sticks will do at home, guests require a dip. A particularly festive occasion might stuff the stalks with blue and cream cheese. The celery root in mustard-mayonnaise sauce that is standard in French cafés already suggests greater transformation, and, finally, cream of celery soup with crème fraîche and a dab of truffle oil translate the verifiably plain into the authentically fancy.

Until relatively recently, the formality of the meal has gauged the distance from the everyday. At least until the late twentieth century in Western cultures, one sign of distinction from everyday dining is specialized cutlery and dinnerware, the confusing number of forks, spoons, knives (fish, salad, meat, dessert), and plates, proliferating as hosts and restaurateurs competed for elegance.[13] A special-use celery dish transforms and in so doing promotes the plainest of celery sticks (especially if it is in cut glass). A demitasse does not just serve less coffee than a regular cup (and still less than the more informal mug); it serves a socially superior coffee. The specialized function of the demitasse depends on the moment and occasion in which it is served. The size of the cup comprises a necessary but not sufficient criterion of distinction, which can only be situation specific. The diminutive capacity notwithstanding, the small espresso cups served in cafés or similar eating establishments do not carry anything like the prestige of the demitasse.

There is an intimate connection between the complexity of the food—which should be of a sort that will not normally be served at home—and the formality of the meal—an elaborate sequence of courses quite the opposite of informal family-style meals. *Fancy* food, or so it was long assumed, accompanied, because it deserved, *fancy* settings. Food and setting acted in concert to define eating out in terms of difference from the usual state of culinary affairs, which was in turn coded as *home*. The putative connection lies at the heart of the debates over the validity of the judgments rendered by *Michelin Guides* to restaurants: just what is the correlation between the knives and forks that Michelin awards to restaurants for elegance of setting and the stars awarded for the quality of the food?[14] Empirically, most notably in the rarefied circle of the restaurants that boast three stars bestowed for culinary excellence, the correlation is extremely high. Should it be? Can one not find superior cuisine in a simple setting? But where three stars are concerned—which propose that the restaurant is worth the trip—surely the whole experience should be taken into account?

INFORMALIZATION

The most striking shift in late-twentieth-century dining that has brought this question to the fore is the increasingly notable informalization of

eating out. The formal complexity of the food served is no longer invariably tied to a formal setting. Expectations of the experience of dining out
have changed considerably. The elaborate and complex food preparations
that are the sign of avant-garde *creative* cuisine are no longer necessarily
consumed in an elaborate décor marked by extensive specialization of setting (silverware, dinner ware). Finally, undoubtedly the most noticeable
sign of change is the more or less informal dress of customers. In short,
fancy food no longer entails dressing up as it once did in many milieus.
Whereas eating out once demanded dressing up to meet the difference of
the restaurant experience, formality now looms as an obstacle to enjoy-
ment, most noticeably among younger generations and those who, for one
reason or another, have not mastered the codes that allow the production
of an egalitarian dining space. For all of these reasons it is now the restaurant that *dresses down* to attract customers by meeting them on their
chosen level.

The flip side of Brillat-Savarin's egalitarian dining utopia exposes the
meal as a battleground of insiders against intruders. As public establishments dependent upon an ever-renewable clientele, restaurants cannot, for
the most part in the twenty-first century, exercise blatant discrimination
of the sort depicted in *Titanic*. Yet every restaurant reaches toward new
customers whom it hopes to attract and discourages others. The posting
of menus, once outside the restaurant and now online, puts customers on
notice about the financial resources required. There are many other indicators of exclusivity, some obvious, some subtle: menus listing dishes in
another language, the waiter visibly impatient with questions that betray
the neophyte, a confusing assortment of knives, forks, glasses. The same
principle applies to every dining establishment, no matter how plain. When
eating out merely extends eating in, there is diminishing profit in going out.
If the experience does not stand apart from the everyday, eating out comes
to look an awful lot like eating in.

The informalization of the past quarter-century or so has skewed
the stratification system of eating out. It was once relatively clear that
informality–formality covered both food and venue. No one expected either soufflés or tuxedos in a bistro, and one would not be surprised to see
both at a formal dining occasion. Such is no longer the case. Strict dress
codes are no longer applied as they once were. How many establishments
today require that men wear a tie? A few upscale restaurants require a

jacket, though they keep ones on hand for unadorned customers. Women no longer think about wearing trousers, whereas not so long ago the better spots turned away any woman not in a skirt, however elegant the pant suit and whoever its designer.

Informality is not without its disadvantages. On the one hand, the diminishing distance between the everyday and exceptional dining experience would seem to make eating out more welcoming to a broader range of individuals. On the other hand, that same informality reduces the incentive to eat out in the first place. Why go out if it is not much different from home, especially given the many possibilities for lessening the burdens of the home cook (take out, frozen foods)? Why, in the current economic crisis, spend more money for less? What value does the restaurant add?

Responses to this dilemma vary greatly from one end of the eating-out spectrum to the other. Some businesses emphasize the connection with the good side of home cooking by serving comfort food, with a price point that makes the meal affordable and a convivial atmosphere. This is the standard for diners (whose task is made easier by restricting service to breakfast and lunch), bistros, coffee shops, and neighborhood establishments generally. Such eating establishments choose the familiar, defined by the more or less local clientele.

TRADITION AND INNOVATION

Reproduction of tradition relies on codes, whether the dish is a pot-au-feu or a BLT (bacon, lettuce, and tomato sandwich). These are comfort foods in the broadest acceptance; that is, foods that make the consumer comfortable. As with all food preferences, comfort food is defined by people and by places, with a strong bias toward childhood favorites. Food comforts us because we can expect to relive a valued experience—say, one's grandmother's chocolate pudding or, in a more modern household, the chocolate pudding that came out of a mix. Or the vegetable dish in the film *Ratatouille* (2007) that conjures up his mother's love and sends the severe food critic into bliss.

In contrast to the reference to tradition and its familiarity, self-consciously avant-garde cuisines draw attention to the novelty of the culinary experience proposed, and to the invention and innovation that a given dish expresses. In short, the avant-garde looks to the culinary unknown. Newness character-izes eating out—we expect the unexpected, whether preparations are from an acknowledged authority (preferably charismatic) or unusual ingredients.

However, the unknown cannot pass unaided. Bridges are needed to the known—whence the often lengthy descriptions of dishes that translate the innovative into familiar terms. Menus now customarily list ingredients in detail. The codes that once designated dishes—boeuf à la mode, coq au vin, or, in another culinary world, the BLT—reproduced tradition. Today, given the emphases on the creativity of the chef, and on local or exotic ingredi-ents, menus need clarification. It is not a question of mastering a code, for the chef makes his mark by breaking or, at the very least, tweaking those codes. The succinct code name of a dish yields to a description to explain the dish and make the customer aware of what this particular chef brings to the plate.

STYLIZATION, MEDIA, AND MENUS

Whereas explanation of the dishes reaches out to the customer by translat-ing the new into familiar terms, stylization celebrates the difference of eat-ing out. A contemporary décor conveys the novelty of the cuisine, which is why elite restaurants regularly update (or "refresh" as one New York City restaurant proclaims on its website) the dining room. Good dining value requires a dramatic break from everyday routines.

Flowers, for one example, have taken on enormous significance as markers of difference, whether in a large single bouquet on the bar (long a hallmark of the classic French bistro) or extraordinarily artful blossoms in spectacular, and very costly, arrangements. Flowers, it would seem, impress without intimidating. They mark difference, but they do so without raising barriers to inclusion. No one need master a code or fear missteps to take pleasure in floral displays. The greater the competition—in large urban centers for example—the greater the need to be up-to-date in every domain including the floral display.

More important still, as the setting and the customers become more informal, thus bringing the meal into familiar if not home territory, in an unsurprising development, the food preparations themselves become more elaborate. Stylization extends to the foods themselves. As every restaurateur knows, the appearance of a dish is a crucial to drawing diners. *Plating* has become a subset of design. The humble vegetable dish in the film *Ratatouille* that overwhelms the severe food critic benefits not only from an unexpected, non-traditional preparation but also from a new, highly stylized plating. Both signal its promotion to high-end cuisine. Some luxury restaurants in China, I have been told, put tantalizing photographs on their menus to bring the customer-reader into the heart of the culinary experience. Most others entice customers with visually arresting websites.[15]

What drives these developments? What accounts for the simultaneous blurring of, and emphasis on the distinct nature of eating out? What are we supposed to make of informalization accompanied by stylization? Some explanations are familiar: travel after World War II, itself a function of increasingly widespread economic prosperity; immigration, especially from countries outside of Europe, which brings vastly different culinary repertoires into the everyday lives of an ever-broader public; transportation technologies that turn once-exotic foodstuffs into staples on the other side of the world; and globalization, which sends singular foods around the world. All of these changes combine to produce a marked sophistication in culinary matters of greater and greater numbers of people.

Channeling and shaping all of these factors are the media. They have been crucial in breaking down the barriers between home cooking and restaurant cuisine. First, television and, latterly, the Internet, bring the most extravagant, most aggressively creative chefs and their dramatically different cuisine into the home. Need inspiration? Just Google the ingredient. You will be overwhelmed with the number of recipes that turn up on the many websites devoted to spreading culinary news and knowledge.

At the most elemental level, the media facilitate and also encourage the sharing of information. However, television does much more because it brings professional cooking into the home. It goes beyond explaining the ingredients of intimidating culinary productions to showing, step by step in real time, how they are made. Julia Child was by no means the first television personality on American television to make this translation, but she was the most charismatic at a time before celebrity chefs did not fill every slot on the as yet non-existent Food Network. Beginning with the paradigmatic *French Chef* in the 1960s, Child's programs dramatized what her cookbooks taught. Although Child's cookbooks and shows stressed food preparation in, and for everyday life, many of the dishes that she presented were not the versions that would be served in the French households that she took as her standard. Often, she invited viewers and readers to try their hands at a more elaborate version of the basic dish—what one would serve to guests. To be sure, the dishes were traditional French dishes, known as *cuisine bourgeoisie* rather than haute cuisine, but Child's preparations were often more appropriate for a restaurant with an extensive set of kitchen equipment and an extra set of hands. The recipe for, say, Veal Orloff, took the home cook a few steps on the road to the restaurant kitchen and therefore to understanding what *fancy* entails.

Perhaps as important, recipes such as this one that engaged the viewer made that restaurant cuisine familiar to thousands of people who would not have had a clue what a given preparation should look like. The film *Julie and Julia* (2009) presents the French stew, boeuf bourguignon, for example, as a true labor of love, requiring more steps, more ingredients, and more time than a servant-less cook ordinarily has at her disposal.[16] But today, in the early twenty-first century, if there are fewer and fewer servants, catalogues, stores, and websites sell a raft of often highly specialized kitchen equipment. With the food processor at the head of the line, the home cook can undertake the most arduous tasks that once could be achieved only in a restaurant kitchen. Beyond machines and devices, the home-kitchen adventurer can call on labor-saving ingredients, from frozen puff pastry and fresh pasta, to dried mushrooms and fish sauce. And if your local emporium does not stock the item that you need, a click or two opens up the vast storehouse of the Internet.

NEXT?

What, then, can we conclude about eating out today? In the twenty-first century, more than ever, dining out will be about producing difference. Even so, if that difference requires distance from the ordinary and the everyday, no dining establishment can afford to cut itself off from the everyday altogether. Diners need to recognize and gauge the distance that separates eating in from eating out. The greater the difference from everyday life, the higher the meal scores on the prestige scale. In this sense of distinction (which may or may not correlate with quality), breakfast at a diner is superior to and better than breakfast at home, hot dogs on the street beat out hot dogs at home, and hot dogs at a French restaurant served with high-end culinary inflection top both—as they must if the restaurant is to survive.[17] The production of difference is so crucial in an increasingly competitive culinary world because eating out implies and requires choice. The variety of eating out is also a function of the variability of the everyday. The ordinary fare of one group turns out to be exotic for another.

The tensions that shape individual decisions will continue to characterize the culinary field as a whole. The charisma of the chef and the spectacularity of the cuisine make eating out extra-ordinary. But that charisma works against the team model of coordination necessary for any eating establishment to function. By deflecting the focus of the meal away from consumption to production, the salience of the chef also undermines the sociability of dining together. Conviviality among equals cedes to admiration of the outsider in the kitchen.[18]

From the ferocious television cook-offs to the turnover of restaurants, the competition rampant in this world counters the communitarian commitment to promoting food across the board. The democratization manifest in the informalization of eating out comes up against the economic stratification that remains in force. And finally, the globalization that makes so much available to so many over such distances must contend with a localism that is increasingly important in orienting both individuals and restaurants. Stratification and differentiation are old culinary stories, to be sure, but today, more than ever, they work separately and in concert to make eating out a complete social experience—a space where individuals negotiate their relationships to the society that feeds them and which they, in turn, feed.

CHAPTER SIX

Kitchen Work: 1920–Present

AMY B. TRUBEK

Cooking and eating are fundamental to all human societies, necessary and constant, every day and everywhere. Such ubiquity means that both human practices are difficult to contain, practically and analytically. Can cooking be similarly defined from place to place and era to era? Can the people responsible for transforming food from the raw to the cooked be neatly categorized? And what about where humans cook and eat—can consistency be located? If historian Fernand Braudel's perspective of the *longue durée* is adopted, moving between long historical trends and more transient activities, layers of continuity appear, although constantly intersected with fascinating variations. Oftentimes food scholars have assumed that underlying all this variation was a singular continuity: kitchen work as an individual or family dominated domestic task, with only elites capable of commanding the resources to have other people cook. New research over the past decade reveals much greater fluidity between domestic and public cooking, especially over the past two centuries.[1] And as Jacobs and Scholliers point out, the many forms of cooking and eating that emerge often "confront and interfere with each other."[2] In the modern period people have become increasingly able to make *multiple* choices about what to cook and eat: from day to day (lunch at home or lunch at a tavern); from place to place (on a country farmstead or at an urban boardinghouse); and from country to country (food cooked by slaves on a plantation or by wage laborers in a commissary kitchen).

This shift away from individual or family subsistence as the primary mode of obtaining food to increased reliance on others to perform such labor can be examined using Braudel's classic division of history into events, cycles, and structures.[3] Such a shift has been a long-term structural change revealed in varied patterns (small-scale domestic cookery versus commercial kitchen work) and events (purchasing a meal or components of a meal). Manifestations of this shift, seen in broad trends and localized actions, included new forms of kitchen work and types of kitchen workers in both domestic and public domains of social life. By the mid-twentieth century this long-term shift in fact creates startling new realities for the location, practice, and status of kitchen work. And these new structures in turn create new forms of identity, meaning, and value for all aspects of making and consuming food.

Identifying the possible forms of labor and the primary locations for transforming food from the raw to the cooked now involves multiple sites including bakeries, slaughterhouses, creameries, factories, restaurants, and finally, homes. This can be understood as part and parcel of a long-term integration of economic and political systems with the increase in scope and scale of imperialism, nationalism, and capitalism. This means that by the late nineteenth century, the organization of the modern food system and associated values both reflect and shape persistent structural shifts in the organization of everyday life such as the increased movement of people from rural to urban areas, the changing organization of work and leisure time, industrialization of food production from farm to table, and increased use of technology in all forms of kitchen work. In this context, the everyday decisions about what to cook, how to cook, who to cook for, or whether to cook at all are powerfully influenced by how individuals intersect with larger social, political, and economic institutions. Most notably, when looking at cooking from 1920 to the present, this necessary practice becomes increasingly less *contained* in the domestic sphere—defined as a physical space where families are cooked for and fed each day. This essay looks closely at cooking that might involve, but extends beyond, familial relations, exploring continuities and changes in this ubiquitous practice. Three themes are highlighted: the role of gender in the division of culinary labor; the methods, meanings, and motives involved in organizing cooking practice; and the changing form and content of disseminating culinary knowledge, or the discourse around cooking.

The complexity of considering cooking, thus, lies in its very fluidity. Understanding cooking as a form of paid labor needs to account for cooking as a form of domestic duty, and vice versa, for the myriad everyday individual choices ultimately making the modern culinary system constantly move between domestic and public domains. Clearly from 1920 onward, though, paid cooking labor shifts increasingly *out* of the home kitchen (a general decline in domestic servants) and into commercial kitchens (a concomitant increase in service workers). At the same time, food cooked outside the home becomes a more constant everyday option for all manner of people, from poor to rich, from west to east.

GENDER AND KITCHEN WORK

Anthropologists have documented the near-universal cultural connection between women and cooking; a 1973 survey of 185 cultures by George Murdock and Catarina Provost reported that "[w]omen were predominantly or almost exclusively responsible for cooking in 97.8% of societies."[4] Richard Wrangham argues that the sexual division of labor understood as crucial to the evolution of modern humans long relied on women being in charge of cooking food for entire families.[5] From small tribes of hunter–gatherers to apartment dwellers in vast urban areas, women have been primarily responsible for feeding families, however culturally defined. This labor thus is widely understood to be women's work, as linked to biology as it is to culture. Among the Inuit of the Arctic, women were solely responsible for transforming raw seal, caribou, and other animal meat hunted by Inuit men into palatable meals. In rural Mexico, women have long been responsible for making tortillas, the caloric and symbolic center of Mexican cuisine. The daily responsibility for food production has remained strongly associated with gender in all manner of modern societies: urban and industrial, west and east, north and south, rural and agrarian,

hunter–gatherer. And yet, this universal assumption has not been universally *practiced;* close examination reveals regular confrontations and interference, especially over the past century. To borrow a nutritional term,
women now predominate as food *gatekeepers* in the domestic sphere, but
not all women are food *producers.* Shifting the definition as such opens up
the wide array of food work being done by other people in many different
kitchens around the globe.

A nineteenth-century Parisian cabinetmaker chose to purchase all his
workday meals at the local tavern, and his wife "often fetched her own
meals from a local restaurant."[6] In Philadelphia, Joseph V. Horn and Frank
Hardart transformed their lunchroom into a series of twentieth-century
automated waiterless restaurants where the food was brought in from a
central commissary kitchen and transported to various sites, meeting the
needs of office workers and laborers with only thirty minutes to eat lunch.[7]
Some of the middle-class women writing fan letters to Irma Rombauer, (author of *The Joy of Cooking*) in the 1940s and 1950s wrote about their new
need to learn how to cook since they no longer were in households with
domestic servants. In all these cases the task was to feed one's self and one's
family, but in every case the solution was different.

Such a shift is long-term, best seen as a continuous *process,* with many
implications for cooking practices. The global demographic shift of people
from rural to urban areas accelerated the movement of some domestic culinary tasks out of the household or village milieu; in the twentieth century
bread-baking is generally seen as the work of laborers outside the home,
unless an individual *chooses* to do so. There has been an interesting shift
along the same lines in the making of flatbreads such as chapatti, roti,
and tortillas; these are now widely made in either small artisan or larger
industrial settings and sold at markets. Today in Oaxaca City, Mexico,
fewer and fewer women make tortillas by hand inside the home each day.
Rather they purchase them from other women selling them on the street, go
to a local *tortilleria* where tortillas are made by machine, or buy packages
stacked on shelves in the chain supermarket.

This shift in cooking practices has transformed women's roles as the primary cooks and bakers, creating culinary practices and culinary discourses
with links to the past, but also new iterations. The increased differentiation
between paid labor and domestic duty that has emerged has generated new

ideas about required forms of culinary knowledge and expertise. From a historical perspective, as the *daily* burden was no longer exclusively the responsibility of individual women, new associations between cooking and identity were generated. Commercial kitchen work has long involved both women and men, and thus other ideals beyond domesticity emerge to inform cooking practices, such as quality, aesthetics, efficiency, health, and mastery. This has created contemporary confusion about the link between gender, kitchen work, and mastery. Are those who cook for pay or those who cook out of obligation best able to teach about kitchen work to others? And where do cooks derive legitimacy from the point of view of skill and knowledge?

COOKS, KITCHENS, AND DINING ROOMS AS CATEGORIES

United States Census Bureau statistics on labor occupations reveal the changing location of kitchen work in the industrialized West over the course of the twentieth century. In the census data a clear demarcation is made between private-household workers and service workers. Within the private-household-worker category there are a number of intriguing sub-classifications, particularly a distinction between workers living in and living out, and a distinction between housekeepers and laundresses. By 1950, baby-sitter becomes a demarcated sub-classification under domestic-service worker, and this category gets larger and larger between 1950 and 1970, while the category that captures domestic work beyond childcare consistently declines.

A review of major occupational groups in the Historical Statistics of the United States shows that in 1940 there were 2,111,314 domestic-service workers (of which 93.3% were female) with the household labor tasks not clearly differentiated. This year appears to reveal the peak of this occupation, with a subsequent steady decline, with a total of only 521,839 in 1990. During the same period of time, people reported in the occupation of cooks, except private household, increases in number from 300,088 to 2,106,500.[8]

Who were the domestic servants working for remuneration over the twentieth century? The specifics vary from country to country and era to era, although the American census data confirms the general trend that they were primarily women. Other studies indicate that migrants, from country to city, from region to region, from continent to continent, were primarily employed in domestic service. Census data reveals that although by 1970 the occupational categories had shifted again, the general trend remains the same: more and more employed kitchen labor occurs outside of the home. However, another trend is equally as important to consider: employing someone else, in some manner, to do the cooking has always been vital to moving food from the raw to the cooked in the modern period. What changes are the *locations* for paid kitchen work.

If transforming food from the raw to the cooked moves increasingly outside of the home over the course of the twentieth century, where does it happen? Priscilla Parkhurst Ferguson has pointed out that the restaurant has been a "privileged location" for the study of public cooking and eating, and although, as she points out, the restaurant is a "central site of the service economy," in order to do justice to the vast array of sites of public production and consumption available to modern consumers, the restaurant needs to be considered one among many possible locations.[9] By 1920, an increasing number of people were living in urban areas, often residing in small, cramped quarters with little kitchen space. Thus numerous methods of procuring and preparing food were required. By this time as well, the necessity and availability of transportation allowing people to travel long distances, whether it be for leisure, work, war, or other reasons, also created another set of reasons for procuring food from people and places outside of their known world. Commercial kitchen work expands by every means possible, sometimes with a genealogy harkening back to the elite beginnings of the invention of the restaurant in late-eighteenth-century Paris, but as often committing allegiance to the older traditions of so-called street food; for example, the itinerant peddlers of the medieval Crusades or the Chinese noodle vendors in urban areas. Chaucer, in his *Cook's Prologue and Tale* talks of the suspect merits of food purchased on the road, "Many a pilgrim's cursed you more than sparsely/When suffering the effects of your stale parsley," revealing a *necessary evil* analysis of purchasing prepared food that remains through today.[10]

First there were bakeries, restaurants, street carts, taverns, boarding houses, summer camps, hotels, resorts, hospitals, trains and train stations, religious centers, and outdoor markets; then there were drive-ins, drive-throughs, airports, airplanes, cruise ships, sports arenas, concerts, and supermarkets; and, finally, the emergence of restaurant take-out, market take-in, and all manner of call up, dial up, and order up. All these public locations for purchasing and (most often) also consuming food now required cooks: cooks with some level of training and some level of paid compensation for their labor. As the American census categories reveal, paid labor for kitchen work in homes tends to be bundled with other domestic tasks. A black maid working in a Southern white household, or a South Asian maid working in a Saudi Arabian household would be expected to clean, cook, do laundry, and oftentimes help take care of the children. Over the course of the twentieth century, with the rise of non-domestic service workers, a more precise differentiation of these domestic duties emerges. Categories for kitchen work in the 2008 Labor Statistics include the following descriptions: "Fast Food Cook: prepare and cook food in a fast food restaurant with a limited menu; Institutional and Cafeteria Cooks: Prepare and cook large quantities of food for institutions such as schools, hospitals and cafeterias; Restaurant Cooks: Prepare, serve and cook soups, meats, vegetables, desserts, or other foodstuffs in restaurants. May order supplies, keep records and accounts, price items on menu, or plan menu."[11]

As such precision develops, the act of cooking becomes a job, a craft, a profession. This type of kitchen work now involves millions—men and women—in all corners of the globe. Where were these new jobs? Commercial kitchen work has long been firmly entrenched as part of commercial enterprises in urban areas. Paris, which in 1900 had a population of almost two million had "1,500 restaurants, 2,900 hotels, 2,000 cafés and brasseries and 12,000 wine merchants (of which 75 percent offered food)."[12] In the late nineteenth century, historical accounts of travelers to Mexico City commented on the foods: "women wandered the streets with baskets of corn confections such as tamales and quesadillas, while men carried improvised ovens with pastries and *barbacoa.*"[13] The density of urban areas, the often-cramped living quarters, and the lack of ready access to arable land conspired to make cities around the world natural sites for public cooking and eating.

The other natural location for hotels, inns, taverns, and ultimately restaurants were travel and tourist destinations—increasingly an intrinsic part of modern life. The rise of industrial manufacturing and the concomitant rise of population in towns and cities where manufacturing jobs were located created an interest in rural tourism. This leads to new temporary migrations, "[w]hen late nineteenth-century consumers grew uneasy with

FIGURE 6.1: 802 Hull Street. *Source*: Adolph B. Rice Studio, 1955. Library of Virginia.

the world they had helped to make, tourism offered an escape from that world."[14] These establishments catered to all different types of clientele, from rich to poor. In the generally poor, rural state of Vermont inns serving food for travelers and tourists could be found all over the state, including Woodstock, Rutland, and Manchester, even during the Depression. Earlier taverns primarily served business travelers, but by 1920 urban tourists became the primary guests at the bed and breakfasts, inns and resorts that increasingly defined village centers, towns, and vacation destinations.

The increasing popularity of the automobile in Europe created regional tourism opportunities; for example, Parisians streaming out of the city on holiday and thus spurring the creation of many small *auberges* and cafés in the towns and villages found throughout the country. Ultimately, eating out became instrumental in the decision to explore the countryside, as seen in the popularity of the Michelin travel guides, which created sophisticated analyses and rankings of food and lodging establishments throughout the French countryside as well as other European countries. Another site that emerges after the rise in the automobile as a primary mode of transportation is the quick-stop roadside restaurant, and fast-food restaurants are the increasingly global answer to the dilemma of what to eat while on the road. In 2007 the Kentucky Fried Chicken franchise included 11,000 restaurants in over eighty countries.[15]

In industrialized nations, the overall trend during the twentieth century has been towards a greater percentage of an individual's food budget spent on food prepared outside the home, in all the iterations discussed above. The U.S. Department of Agriculture Economic Research Service reports an increase in the proportion of total food sales that come from food and beverage operations from 20 percent in 1940 to 50 percent in 2007. The increase in sales are derived from eating and drinking places; hotels and motels; retail stores and direct selling; recreational places; schools and colleges; and others. The increase in the scale and scope of public cooking and eating is clear.

LABOR OF COOKING

Just as in domestic settings, not all cooking in the public sphere has been organized in equal manner. Kitchen work varies greatly depending on the number of people to be served, the type of food to be made, and the social messages to be communicated. As well, the natural and physical location of where the food will be made and consumed profoundly shapes the organization of labor involved in moving food from the raw to the cooked. When examined closely, preparing food to be sold in the parking lot of an alternative rock concert may have little overlap with preparing food to be sold in a multi-course banquet at a mega-hotel in Taipei, save for the fact that all the cooks should expect to go home with money in their pocket. There are other common threads, however, in particular a certain organization of production that considers all the parts involved in making the final whole: a finished hot meal ready to be eaten by a prospective diner.

Since the nineteenth century the ways of knowing and doing involved in preparing food in an individual, free-standing restaurant, the larger space of a grand hotel and other similar public settings have been dominated by the French standard of professional kitchen organization. This has been particularly strong in public milieus with a strong investment in communicating messages about elite social status, although the French standard can be seen in some variant in kitchens serving food of all categories. In this model of kitchen organization, adequate professional performance is associated with the mastery of a set of cooking techniques and methods. These techniques and methods emerged in France first in the large kitchens of the royalty and became a standard of practice that then moved to urban public restaurants first in Paris and then in urban areas around the globe. As Jeffrey Pilcher notes for Mexico City, "By the end of the [19th] century talented [French] chefs such as Paul Laville and V. Barattes could sell their talents to the highest bidders in a number of exclusive restaurants and social clubs."[16] By 1920 the famous New York City restaurant Delmonico's had been in continuous operation for almost a century, serving dishes such as *macaroni à l'Italienne* and turtle consommé. The food served at these sites clearly needed to fulfill certain social expectations: Delmonico's regularly served the Four Hundred during the Gilded Age and was a frequent stop for Broadway actors and actresses, and even early Hollywood movie stars. Aesthetic expectations, both sensory and visual, were at the foundation of the ingredients, techniques, and methods disseminated through the overall organization of kitchen work in these settings.

Until the mid-twentieth century such mastery was primarily disseminated through a system of apprenticeship, where young men (generally between fourteen and sixteen years old) worked to learn by doing and by gaining low-level employment in elite restaurants and hotels, and gradually working their way up the kitchen hierarchy. Apprentices would start their sojourn in the professional kitchen by doing scullery work: this included washing and peeling fruits and vegetables, stoking coal fires, and doing dishes. If deemed worthy of taking on more tasks, an apprentice could move to *garde manger* or cold prep work, eventually moving up to work at the stove, preparing the final dishes for the customer. The organization of the modern public kitchen was heavily influenced by the work of Auguste Escoffier, credited for developing the *brigade* system, which broke down cooking tasks in a fairly linear fashion—something akin to the modern assembly line. He developed his ideas working with Cesar Ritz, first at London's Savoy Hotel and then, by the late nineteenth century as the Ritz-Carlton hotel chain expanded, throughout Europe, North America, and Asia. By 1920 Escoffier's system became standard operating procedure in restaurants, hotels, clubs, and even cruise ships. Although the apprenticeship system remains an inviolable aspect of kitchen training for elite settings, vocational culinary schools are now increasingly important and viable methods of obtaining culinary mastery.

In the United States the Culinary Institute of America was founded in 1945, the first dedicated vocational culinary school, and the school's curriculum has been dominated by a European culinary approach. Before that time, restaurant kitchens were dominated by European-trained chefs overseeing large numbers of poorly educated workers, as not only were there no culinary schools, there was also no state-supported apprenticeship system. The American Culinary Federation, founded in 1929, did work to promote an apprenticeship system, but the Great Depression and World War II intervened, and vocational schools ultimately emerged as the dominant method for gaining credentials.

Alain Drouard argues that even in France, ground zero for the modern apprenticeship system, many changes occurred after World War II. A new government charter was elaborated in 1928 specifying the conditions of cooks' training, and which guaranteed their (social) rights. After World War II even more changes occurred, with the French state being increasingly involved in the oversight of professional cooking, including domestic cooks. Chefs also increasingly became restaurant owners, thus less dependent on separate owners.[17]

Other forms of kitchen work evolved, which rely on forms of mastery, but are not necessarily as strongly linked to certain sites in the rapidly expanding service economy of the twentieth century. One obvious example is the emergence of fast-food restaurants, initially in the West, but now found across the globe. Although there is a long global history of street food—the pushcart vendors selling sausages in New York City, the women selling tamales in Mexican markets—fast food is characterized by meals prepared quickly that can be eaten in a restaurant setting. Although McDonald's often gets credit as the first fast-food establishment, some food historians identify White Castle as the original. This kitchen work relies even more on an assembly model than Escoffier's brigade system, or perhaps more accurately, an organization of labor even more embedded in an industrial mode of production. Fast-food restaurants are now found around the globe and increasingly define people's public eating and dining experiences, leading to a global labor market for these venues.

Another form of kitchen work that becomes increasingly important is cooking in, and for, large institutions such as schools and hospitals. Part of the long-term shift away from cooking in the domestic sphere and into the public sphere lay in new ideas about how to feed children, the ill, and the elderly. As these groups no longer resided exclusively in the home, or spent more time in larger public institutions (for example, schools and hospitals), their feeding became less and less the sole responsibility of families. For example, to differing degrees, depending on cultural practices, feeding children and young adults has become either the sole or partial responsibility of educational institutions. Higher education that involves students boarding in hostels or dormitories with cafeterias is now the norm in most Western nations and is also the case in other locations, including India and China. Feeding groups in such settings is now big business and also a major mode of employment. The concepts of culinary mastery in this setting overlap somewhat with the model of restaurant and hotel cooking (many of the methods of procurement and preparation are the same) but a major difference lies in the organization involved in the transformation of food from the raw to the cooked, and how food is served to the diner. In institutional settings much of the work is done in advance, or with batch cooking, rather than cooking to each individual order. This approach is in fact closer to fast-food preparation, although the greater variety of choices for every meal period and also the array of dishes prepared over a menu cycle require a larger set of culinary skills.

Large-scale catering also has similarities to institutional kitchen work, although the more episodic nature of cooking for large functions such as banquets and weddings can create kitchen work that is a hybrid of *à la carte* and *batch* cooking. The larger culinary expectations can have a tremendous influence on how such kitchen work is carried out as well. For example, Indian weddings are famous for involving large and elaborate meals; however, if the meal is prepared in a traditional hall people will sit at long tables where various vegetable and meat curries, dals, condiments, rice, flatbreads, and more are served directly on a banana leaf from a large, stainless-steel serving bowl. If the wedding is in one of an increasing number of large luxury hotels (such as the Taj chain found throughout South Asia), the food may be served in the European style, either from large steam tables or on individual plates. These two styles of wedding banquet have an impact on every stage of the organization of work, from preparation through service.

A commonality among all forms of kitchen work, whether in a three-star Michelin restaurant or a small roadside stand, is that most commercial cooking still requires strenuous and often tedious forms of manual labor. George Orwell's description of a large Parisian hotel kitchen in the 1920s is echoed by more recent descriptions by chef and writer Anthony Bourdain and journalist Bill Buford. Orwell writes: "The kitchen was like nothing I have ever seen or imagined—a stifling, low-ceilinged inferno of a cellar, red-clanging of pots and pans."[18]

In the United States and elsewhere the rising number of available jobs as well as an improved social perception as to the status of kitchen work has led to a dramatic increase in vocational culinary schools, especially over the past thirty years. By 2003 there were approximately five hundred degree-granting programs for the hospitality industry, with a large number involving culinary training. These programs are found in private schools (Culinary Institute of America, Institute of Culinary Education, Cordon Bleu Cookery School), community colleges (Kingsborough, Brooklyn), and universities (Boston University, Cornell University). Educating rather than just training people to work in food service has now become big educational business.

Over the same period a slow shift in the definition of culinary mastery for those engaged in contemporary kitchen work has emerged. This shift involves a general expectation that attaining high status in the culinary profession requires formal education as much as, or more than an apprenticeship. The declining importance of mastering French culinary skills to attain the status of a *chef* is another element of the changing definition. Other forms of mastery are now becoming as relevant to success: molecular gastronomy, nose-to-tail, farm-to-fork, Asian fusion, and more. The end of French culinary hegemony in fine dining restaurants is seen everywhere, witnessed in the food prepared, the style of service, and the kitchen hierarchy. Ferran Adrià is a contemporary chef often credited with helping create this paradigm shift. His Michelin three-starred restaurant, El Bulli in Catalonia, Spain, both embraced and defied many elements of the French model. His restaurant kitchen was compared to scientific laboratories, and

his food considered an early manifestation of so-called molecular gastronomy, where scientific principles and technologies were used in creating the
complex dishes served to diners, who often waited for months to get a
reservation and were willing to pay the exorbitant prices. Adria continues
to promote his new vision of the form and content of haute cuisine; he
now uses his restaurant as a teaching laboratory for his new culinary academy. At the same time, in culinary schools and in restaurant kitchens the
French influence remains strong; for example, most kitchens continue to
use the brigade system for organizing the moving of food from the raw to
the cooked. Many culinary techniques considered fundamental for mastery
(knife skills, sauce making) remain marked by the French tradition.

THE DISCOURSE OF COOKING AND KITCHEN WORK

The long-term shift in the definition and practice of kitchen work to the
present spectrum of possibilities, inside and outside the home, has led to
new forms of meaning. The deep and broad connection of cooking to gender has been primarily associated with social ideals of duty and obligation rather than monetary remuneration and professional reward. This
has meant that the discourse around kitchen work has been informed by
a marked divide between private and public spheres. And as many food
scholars have pointed out, traditionally most kitchen knowledge was orally
transmitted, told by mother to daughter, or by chef to apprentice.[19] The
twentieth century, however, was a period of fluorescence of documentation
of kitchen work in many forms of media. Newspaper sections, magazines,
pamphlets, recipe cards, cookbooks, cooking shows, websites, and now
blogs are all devoted to kitchen work. In all of these genres, a notable trend
is the increasing importance of the trained and paid cook or chef as the
expert over the knowledgeable home cook. In this discourse the definition
of expertise in kitchen work is *owned* by those whose primary training has
been outside of the home, even if the primary audience is the home cook.

The first edition of the iconic American cookbook *The Joy of Cooking*
by Irma Rombauer, published by Bobbs Merrill in 1936 and continuously
in print for almost eighty years, has for a subtitle, "A Compilation of
Reliable Recipes with a Casual Culinary Chat." Rombauer continues the
informal tone in the preface, where she says, "I have attempted to make

palatable dishes with simple means and lift everyday cooking out of the commonplace."[20] In the 1946 edition, by which point the book had become hugely popular, Rombauer understands the broad sweep of culinary skills possessed by her fans with full acknowledgement of their gender: "Written in a method so clear that a child can follow it, its instructions cannot fail to help and inspire the novice. The experienced cook will find in it innumerable practical and novel suggestions to spur her on to new efforts."[21] At the same time, she understands the landscape of kitchen work in that era: "Encouragement came from many sources—especially from the eloping bride who telegraphed her family: 'Am married—order announcements—send me a Rombauer cookbook at once';…and from an unknown Cincinnati maid who stole her mistress' copy of *The Joy of Cooking*." Rombauer's ability to acknowledge her readers' skills and varied backgrounds but also provide inspiration to move beyond the everyday is clear in every chapter. The sauce chapter includes recipes for hollandaise sauce, easy hollandaise sauce, cheese sauce one (with mild cheese), cheese sauce two (with processed cheese), chestnut sauce, and barbecue sauce. Rombauer understood that American home cooks increasingly had greater *aspirations* than *skills*. As a young, female college student explains in her fan letter, dated September 29, 1954: "The most unique thing about your book is the fact that it assumes the reader knows *nothing* [sic]—which in my case wasn't far from wrong!"[22]

By the 1975 edition, with the advent of the women's movement, the decline of domestic servants, and the increased involvement of Marion Rombauer Becker, Irma Rombauer's daughter, the tone has shifted somewhat. The possible means of using *The Joy of Cooking* has been cast wider, "Choose from our offerings what suits your person, your lifestyle, your pleasure; and join us in the joy of cooking," but also the necessary knowledge for being able to cook. Marion Rombauer Becker continues the emphasis on cooking technique when she describes how to use the index: "There is a back-door key, too—the Index. This will open up for you and lead you to such action terms as simmer, casserole, braise and sauté; such descriptive ones as printanière, bonne femme, rémoulade, allemande and meunière."[23] She adds, however, that cooks now need to also understand nutrition and provides a new section that aids the home cook in trying to navigate such knowledge.

Although *The Joy of Cooking* remains a popular and best-selling cook-book in the United States, a new trend in the cookbook genre not embraced by this now-classic tome is a necessary connection with other media forms, especially television. For example, Jamie Oliver, a restaurateur and chef from London, England, demonstrates the ability of chefs to now become media celebrities through cookbooks, television shows, blogs, and even social-networking sites. However, Oliver demonstrates another quality of the contemporary culinary discourse. It is now possible for a celebrity chef to wield influence on all domains of contemporary kitchen work. Oliver first attained international prominence with his cooking show, *The Naked Chef,* which focused on simple preparations and attention to the quality and provenance of ingredients. This led to a series of books designed for the home cook, including *The Naked Chef* and *Jamie Oliver's Dinners.* Oliver, who also owns the restaurant Fifteen in London, then started to turn his attention to the food served at schools all over the United Kingdom. In his documentary series, *Jamie Oliver School Dinners* (2005), Oliver chronicles his attempts to change the food preparation and consumption at a large public school in Greenwich, outside of London. Over the course of his year working at the school, Oliver realizes the deep divide between the kitchen work in his fine dining establishment in London and the kitchen work in an institutional setting such as a school. The four-part documentary ended up emphasizing the importance of dinner ladies, or the hourly workers who make the food each day, to any understanding of British school din-ners. Nora Sands, the head cook at the Kidbrooke School in Greenwich, ultimately went on to write a cookbook and consult with other dinner ladies. Sands, originally from Ireland, was first hired as a kitchen assis-tant and ended up working her way up to manager, though she says on her website she prefers to be called a dinner lady. There was widespread public engagement with his efforts, which resulted in the Feed Me Better campaign, attempting to get more government support for "ban[ning] the junk served in school canteens and get the kids to eat fresh, tasty, nutri-tious food instead," as Oliver puts it in his "Manifesto for School Dinners" found posted on his website. His campaigns include creating Jamie Oliver's *Ministry of Food,* an initiative that includes a cookbook, cooking shows, and now cooking centers, one in Rotherham and one in Bradford. These shops have been funded by regional government grants; for example, in

FIGURE 6.2: Chef Jamie Oliver personally carries out food for the G20 delegates and guests at dinner at Downing Street, London, on 1 April 2009. *Source*: Courtesy Getty Images.

Bradford the local city council and National Health Service office provided resources. The general public can come and take cooking classes where the techniques and recipes are created by Oliver. Partially as a result of the public outcry after the showing of *School Dinners*, the United Kingdom's Department of Education and Skills started a School Food Trust in 2005 to work on improving school dinners.

Now Oliver has turned his attention to the United States. In 2009–2010 he helped create a reality TV show that was shown on network television to great fanfare, in the city of Huntington, West Virginia, because the city was awarded the *most obese population* status by the Centers for Disease Control. The latest in his "challenges," was to get "a whole community cooking again." In Oliver's words, according to his website, he wants to "get everyone back in the kitchen and making tasty meals with fresh ingredients—no packets, no cheating. He's starting a new revolution: to get people all over America to reconnect with their food and change the way they eat."[24] Oliver now effectively has irons in the fire in almost every category of contemporary kitchen work: home, restaurant, and schools. His powerful multi-media presence and his ability to garner an audience and resources to extend his message across classes and nations reflects the porous borders between domestic and professional kitchen work in the contemporary period.

Of particular note is Oliver's quest to "get people back in the kitchen." Echoing beloved American culinary icon Julia Child's efforts both in cookbooks and on television, part of Oliver's appeal is his commitment to democratizing cooking and his casual and approachable demeanor. In the over forty years since Child published *Mastering the Art of French Cooking* and began her cooking show on public television, however, the culinary system has markedly changed. In Child's case she assumed someone was in the kitchen, cooking. She wanted to *expand* people's culinary repertoires. The domestic sphere was Child's primary bailiwick. Oliver wants to *change* culinary repertoires. Accomplishing such a task requires both an engagement with multiple culinary sites as well as a critique of present practices. Helping people cook at home increasingly seems to require convincing people to not engage with other people's kitchen work.

CONCLUSION

If the events, cycles, and structures involved in kitchen work over the past century tells us anything about long-term trends, Oliver may be swimming upstream in his calls for people to start cooking at home again. Kitchen work remains fluid, but the currents all seem to be moving toward those who cook as a form of paid labor, rather than out of duty or obligation, or possibly, love.

CHAPTER SEVEN

Family and Domesticity

ALICE JULIER

DEFINING FAMILY AS AN EXPERIENCE AND INSTITUTION

There is no more iconic or culturally significant image than one of people eating together in a domestic setting. The home, while no longer centering on the hearth, is still the site where people believe sustenance and meals should take place. Most significantly, food preparation and food sharing are intimately associated with family life. The twentieth century has seen a reconfiguration of domesticity, meals, and family where the cultural assertion of that trinity is more powerful than the actual material realization of commensality.

Food is often the centerpiece of domestic organization, determining the configuration of members, status relations, and the longevity of the household. Producing and eating food together is one basis for human society. Anthropologist Audrey Richards elucidated the cross-cultural observation that nutrition was more important than sex in determining social arrangements.[1] The household unit that generally organizes daily life is called *family*. But what constitutes family? Its purpose, membership, rights, and responsibilities are as much ideological as social, seemingly natural but shaped and mobilized by states and political economies to justify a larger framework for production and reproduction of people and goods. In surveying types and interpretations of households, Gubrium and Holstein conclude that no single unit is sufficient to determine the concept of family.[2] While family is created both discursively and interactionally, for most people it is a specific local enactment, grounded in the material organization of care and sustenance.

Sustenance, in the form of meals, is tied to relations of kinship, work, and exchange. The idea of family exists in most societies, with the understanding that members contribute to the group in multiple ways. With varying degrees of flexibility, families often center on a division of labor based on gender and age, with women bearing the major responsibilities for childcare and feeding work. The experience and evaluation of that work—how it is viewed—is linked to the overall social organization of labor and the political and social values that shape the culture. Thus, family and domestic life are frequently the rationale for the policies and processes of states, institutions, and commercial markets. Citizenship is linked to fulfilling rights and obligations related to households: for example, government-supported food-assistance programs are often based on a need to care for mothers with dependent children.

Sociologist Marjorie DeVault summarizes the basic contours of family:

The groups we call families are built on patterns of shared activity, and that the shape of such a pattern—who does what work in each society—produces a characteristic pattern of opportunities and relative power for typical men and women…when we speak about contemporary families, then, we refer to two kinds of realities, to both experience and institution.[3] As experience, *family* refers to the activities of daily lives: to small groups of men, women, and children who usually share material resources, who may work or play together, who sometimes love each other and sometimes fight. Experientially, households are sites of material interdependence, of care (both material and emotional), and often, of affection and respect. They are also arenas for social conflict…where power relations are reproduced. They are also dangerous for some members…but the word *family* refers to an idea (or social institution) as well. It is a term whose meaning has emerged historically, a construct rooted in discourse as much as in immediate experience.[4]

Meals are both social and material. While the modern experience of family is deeply associated with close social relations, in historical terms the types of families prevalent as well as the domestic expectations in the household are predicated on the dominant economic means of production.[5] In the twentieth century, the Global North rapidly moved into an industrial, technological market economy, while the Global South continues to contend with the legacies of colonialism and imperialism. While this chapter uses the Western experience as a primary lens, it is with the understanding that such a story reproduces some inequities in historical experience. With those limits, the dominance of this story helps explain the contradictions between contemporary cultural ideals about family life and food, where the relationship between a desire for global economic prosperity and a nostalgia for a mythic agrarian past compete in determining the shape of today's domestic commensal settings.

Families in contemporary global society are often at the fault lines of economic and social forces over which they lack control. Positively, globalization offers increased communication, knowledge, and cultural transmission, but negatively, people in household units are often at the mercy of market logics that determine how their work and time are configured, where their meals are made, who is expected to make them, and at what costs.

FOOD IN HOUSEHOLD AND WAGE ECONOMIES

Worldwide the most common configuration of families is organized around a household economy. Because the spread of industrialization and technology has been more rapid in some regions and countries than in others, the contemporary trajectory of family life has been mixed between longstanding maintenance of agrarian-based households and rapid transitions in wage-based consumer households. These trends do not represent straightforward progress into market economies, but the dominance of such approaches is a hallmark of the current global economy.

Until the twentieth century, the majority of the world's households were shaped by a need to produce food and goods within small to midsize communities. Trade and commerce were part of everyday life, but the productive nature of family was integral to its continued existence. Eating together, both in routine daily meals and special communal occasions, was a hallmark of group membership. While most families did not eat together at every possible instance, the majority organized their labors in a way that allowed them to consume the main meal of the day communally. What constitutes a meal varies greatly from society to society, but the centrality of a particular starch, often indigenous to the region in question, and some form of protein constitute the heart of a successful eating event.[6] For example, rice and beans are staples in many cultures, although the type of rice and kind of beans, as well as the spices and vegetables vary greatly. Cultures created the guidelines for family life, meals, and social norms, but the material labor of producing family meals occurred in individual households through dinners and holiday celebrations.

With the shift to industrialization, the household was no longer viewed as a site of production but of reproduction and consumption. The household economy often had a division of labor that may have been based on gender and patriarchy but required interdependence among everyone, whether it be a middle-class home with boarders and servants, a slave plantation, a small village of extended and fictive kinship, or a colonial hacienda.[7] While some items may have been acquired through purchase or trade, or even collectively produced (such as in village bread ovens) most food production was generated by the labor of household members. Work was coordinated and shared among men, women, and children. Cooking that occurred outside the household was often for groups who had to labor away from domestic settings or for men, who were granted more public opportunities to eat at taverns, coffeehouses, and pubs.

Food, labor, and ideals of family shifted with the social and economic transformations of industrial capitalism and the consolidation of agricultural production. As capitalism spreads globally, so do family forms based on conjugal relations and emotional ties rather than economic needs. The shift to a market economy, where goods were produced outside the home and work moved to a wage system in a centralized setting such as the factory, meant a dramatic change in the nature and meaning of work. Some household members (often young farm women) left home in order to work in better paying jobs. The demand for factory labor meant that immigrants and freed slaves migrated to urban centers, competing for the same jobs at lower wages, rather than less desirable work in households as boarders or servants. As a result of the wage economy, the nature of men's and women's work changed, such that labor within the household was now viewed as less significant than work outside the household, particularly as families became dependent on the income that generated money necessary for buying goods.[8] While food was still produced and consumed in households, the work shifted in meaning and value.

The development of wage labor, first in Europe and North America, reinforced existing hierarchies of labor based on race, gender, and class. Marriage and childrearing were asserted as the most significant bonds within a household. Goods and then services were produced outside the household, effectively privatizing that space. The function of the domestic household was more centered on consumption, negotiation for services, social reproduction (child care), and emotional support for both dependent children and wage earners. Caregiving, which included feeding the family, became a naturalized extension of women's activities.

Reliance on the marketplace for goods also created a gendered dependence whereby women did not receive wages for their labors within the home, and men were excused from them by the nature of their work outside the home. While food labors and cooking were still highly valued as part of family life, the shift reinforced a gendered division of labor which suggested that unpaid work done in the household was less critical than work done for wages.[9] This also helped change attitudes about domestic cooking. While advertising and processed commercial foods played an important role in re-shaping both cooking and the ideals around it, the devaluation of domestic food labor was intertwined with its association with unpaid but expected caring labor. At the same time, the celebration of domestic cooking and the individuation of culture within households increased as such work became deeply associated with acts of caring and love rather than straightforward sustenance or the assertion of communal ties.

Reinforcing this problem, across the globe ideals of domesticity subordinated women economically. In Europe and North America, women's work in the household was shifted to emotional support, even as their actual labors remained significant. In Asia and Latin America, patriarchal values created additional support for male dominance: in households, men expected to be fed.

Although the commercial marketplace took over many of the functions that men did within the household, the development of new technologies and commercial products did not significantly change the number of hours women spent on household labor. An increase in standards and expectations as well as new caring labors kept women tied to domestic work.[10] Children were increasingly viewed as precious dependents in need of nurturance rather than *little adults* who could contribute materially to the household. Along with other domestic tasks, feeding children became a science learned through home economics and nutrition, as well as a calling exclusively for women. New fields of marketing, psychology, and medicine each exerted new influences on family food choices. Science took a front-row seat in teaching parents how to feed children, helping them discover the importance of cow's milk, fruit, and vegetables. Meals were a site for socialization as citizens, consumers, and class members.[11] While dietary social reforms were often done in the name of the larger social good, they were also often centered on creating good citizens, compliant workers, and a populace that was less dependent on assistance from the state. For example, although vitamins were a general scientific discovery, reformers and government agents promoted them after World War I because they worried about the supply of healthy potential soldiers.[12]

Making households independent units of consumption was central to the global rise of industrial capitalism. One means of doing so was by giving workers incentives to care for dependent family members. The breadwinner wage was a means by which employers (with the support of government policies) coerced working-class men into respectability and compliance, forced women out of waged labor and into the home, but also kept some workers—working-class women, immigrant men and women, indigenous peoples, and racial minorities—available as a cheaper backup workforce.[13] Gender ideologies about women as workers and homemakers, and men as economic support were used to justify shifts in the workplace that benefited industry rather than families. Women workers could be paid less because they were presumed not to have dependents and *they ate less*. In reality, the breadwinner wage was more of an ideal, often unattainable for even the middle class. Not accidentally, the emphasis was on the power to purchase comestibles even as expectations remained for women in households to procure and produce meals. Providing meals—whether by growing and making the food or by purchasing it—became more and more centrally defined as a domestic responsibility for women. This change is more profound when we recognize that prior to this time, even barely middle-class families had servants, and working-class families relied on extended kinship networks. While the pattern of non-kin participation, servants, and household economic production remained in colonial and non-Western countries well into the middle of the twentieth century, the general trend has been, and continues to be a shift in reliance on paid services outside the home.

In many countries, migrants worked in industries that mirrored domestic labors in the household economy. Chinese men made up 90 percent of domestic and laundry workers in California well into the twentieth century. Mexican Americans were concentrated in service work and food processing. African Americans were concentrated in heavy labor, domestic service, and agriculture. Global migrations in Asia meant that women from poorer regions and countries often found domestic employment in wealthier households. For any racial–ethnic migrant group that was able to find regular employment, the wages were lower and it was easier to fire people whose citizenship was usually legally restricted. The types of labor limited opportunities for family life. Most obviously, the federal restrictions often meant that men migrated to wealthier countries and women stayed behind. Across the globe, groups that migrated experienced difficulties that undercut their ability to marry and have children. For example, work–family life for Asian immigrants to Europe, Australia, and North America often meant that family entrepreneurship collapsed the workspace and household. Immigrant entrepreneurs were often highly successful, but children were conjoined to work in the family business at the expense of education and wives were employed in ways that belied wage earnings. This is particularly true in businesses that mirrored domestic production, such as restaurants and food service.

Today, the global economy continues to depend on women's food labors, although many of the tasks they performed in the household are now being done for very low wages in factories, farms, supermarkets, and fast-food restaurants. These women are often unable to provide meals for family members because their wages and work hours do not give them ample opportunities. While wealthier families can outsource their domestic needs with great flexibility, families with less resources and time are often dependent on poor-quality commercial foods.

IDEOLOGIES OF DOMESTICITY

Hierarchy within households and labor markets was frequently established and maintained by many stereotypes of men's and women's nature. The current understanding of domesticity is a modern construct with ideological roots in earlier eras. For example, the continued growth of the middle class in the United States was fueled by the prevalence of servants in the north and slaves in the south. While men's work allowed their wives to focus fully on the home, other women did much of the production work, including food preparation and cooking. With industrialization, native and immigrant women who previously worked in domestic service flocked to the better paying factory jobs. African American women were often blocked from factory employment and although a substantial proportion managed to find paid employment elsewhere, the vast majority of domestic-service jobs were held by black women well past the Civil Rights era. With the decline in paid in-house service, women in all families except the very wealthy took on the household jobs that they had previously shared or supervised.

At the same time, in most countries so-called separate spheres was not a reality for many families. Regardless of the steady increase in women who participated in the paid economy, in general, the ideology of the breadwinner wage meant that women's work was seen as secondary and supplemental, even if she provided the main income in a household. In particular, the notion of separate spheres is problematic when examining the experiences of ethnic- or racial-minority families. In these households, men were often denied access to better paying jobs and women worked for wages. Immigrant households were also often organized around family businesses. This complicated the divide between so-called public and private realms and made the ideal of domestic life more difficult to achieve. According to Overacker in the United States,

> Black women and men have never experienced the luxury of developing separate spheres with concomitant roles which stemmed from the man engaging in the public realm and insuring the economic viability of the household while the woman stayed home and made that household a serene and wholesome place for both husband and children…Recognition by family and friends as a good mother, cook, and housekeeper gave many black women a sense of accomplishment and satisfaction not possible in their paid work lives.[14]

Narratives of racial–ethnic women's lives from the early twentieth century suggest that even while working for pay, cooking for their families was a means of asserting some control over their lives and insuring the well-being of the household.[15] In some cases, women exercised collective power through kin-based cooking, by sharing foods across generations, and by deciding who was worthy of participating in cooking.[16] Using migrant women's tamale-making, Williams suggests that food distribution among kin and non-kin was a means of demonstrating one's standing. A man who beat his wife would not receive tamales while working in the fields. Similarly, Counihan illustrates how Italian mothers offered favored children more delectable foods as a means of coercing others to behave well. At the same time, McIntosh and Zey caution against confusing examples of women's responsibility for food labors with control over them, as they do not always coincide.[17]

While women were often seen as the keepers of culture, passing on cooking traditions and family practices, in racial–ethnic and immigrant families the men often participated in the food production, particularly for holidays and special events. In some cases, the demands of the marketplace meant that everyone in the household still contributed. Both African and Gullah-Geechee traditions along the coast of the Southern United States dictated that knowledge of rice cooking was commonplace knowledge, so that everyone knew how to "throw down" in the kitchen.[18]

The new field of psychology reinforced the rise of the companionate family. Marriage partners and children became a source of friendship and love, with an emphasis on relationships and togetherness. Affect was now at the heart of family life. At the same time, as home-cooking became less essential materially, it became reinforced as a domestic task most closely associated with women. Without servants, feeding the family became a moral and emotional imperative. Frances Cancian asserts that love became *feminized,* making it difficult to interpret men's household labor contributions as anything but instrumental.[19] The family built on affection could also become an oppressive place for family members who no longer had the ability to rely on extended kin and community when relations within the household became problematic. At the same time, poor families were unable to match this ideal at all—or resisted it as a response to colonialist versions of patriarchy.

CONSUMING MODERNITY AT HOME

The years between 1920 and the 1960s saw a profound shift in where and how people purchased food. The largest change was in the development of energy and new technology: manufactured goods, utilities, and appliances were all developed and sold with greater regularity in more affluent countries. Greater availability of energy changed the domestic environment and the work within it: people began to purchase appliances for individual homes such as electric ranges, dishwashers, and refrigerators. In more affluent countries, rapid urban electrification meant new customers for these items. Promoted in world fairs and expos, ideal-home expositions, and domestic-science classes, the combination of science and technology along with efficiency was an easy sell even among people affected by war and economic difficulties. By 1929, the most common electric servants for food production included refrigerators, toasters, percolators, and corn poppers. Public access to household power was often a project of modernization. In the United States, until the New Deal rural-electrification project began in 1935, large portions of the country were still reliant on older forms of food labor. Hot and cold running water as well as central heating were not commonplace outside of affluent areas until well into the 1940s. Comparatively, large segments of the non-Western world have only begun to have similar stable municipal services. As the marketplace was unreliable, canning, preserving, and growing food in garden plots were still commonplace practices, reinvigorated by national propaganda campaigns in World War II, and supported by cooperative extension services in rural areas. Home food preparation and preservation remained more common in countries that had uneven industrialization and trade.

In the war years, the number of meals eaten in a day or eaten together varied greatly, although it is clear that industrialization took the midday meal out of many households and encouraged the development of cafeterias, street vendors, and restaurants. Restrictions on women's public eating changed as restaurants and eateries recognized their power as a consumer market. In the era before World War II, there was a push to develop new commercial foods, which in the United States included mayonnaise, cookies, Crisco, cereals, pancake mix, hot dogs, and rice, and in Italy included canned tomatoes. New foods and brands such as Ritz crackers, Wonder Bread, and Spam were all developed and marketed in the 1930s. Fresh, dried, canned, and prepared foods, from sardines to pasta and vegetables, were promoted and sold in chain groceries and large supermarkets in European countries before and after the war. Companies such as Nestle and Armour began greater international distribution. Cookbooks and magazines promoted one-pot meals such as macaroni and cheese, chili, and casseroles served with inexpensive vegetables. The American government tried to promote soybeans as a meat-replacement with little success. Bread and soup lines were commonplace, as war created scarcity. Regional food-ways still dominated the daily food choices people made, which suggests that locally available or familiar products were a significant part of family meals. Ethnic crossover in culinary traditions was rare.

NOT YET THE NUCLEAR FAMILY

The Depression and World War II pushed families in many countries back into cooperative, extended-kin living situations, delaying marriage, and postponing childbearing. At the same time, global social disruptions of war and migration created the groundwork for new household forms. World War II engendered a major shift in women's paid employment: middle-class women were pulled in to work by wartime. In most countries directly affected, working-class women and ethnic–racial women who had worked prior to the war were able to get better jobs in factories, away from domestic service—albeit often at different pay rates.[20]

With mostly men at war, food was diverted to the effort of feeding soldiers. This meant that women's food labors on the home front became even more complicated. What people ate and how they came by it became more obviously entrenched in political and social significance. American Victory Gardens were a prime example: many people maintained small vegetable plots prior to the war, but during the war gardens in North America and Europe took on an added significance. Although urban and suburban populations had already become reliant on newly available processed commercial foods, governments promoted less commercial consumption and more local and homemade products. In contrast, contemporary government promotions in wartime equate good citizenship with good consumer behavior. In many wars, good citizenship became associated with good eating and the home became a metaphoric *front* for defeating the enemy with intelligent household practices.[21] Women were enlisted as the generals in a fight to save the economy at home by running efficient and frugal homes. In this case, family preferences were subordinate to making ends meet.

In the same era, advertising became a full-fledged cultural power, reaching more people with the rise in leisure and entertainment such as radios, cinema, paperback books, and print magazines. The links between science and marketing were established early on in the food industry. Manufacturers developed some of the first foods and goods to be mass marketed, such as cereals and ready-made clothing. Many early food producers had to overcome existing fears of contaminated food. Standardization—combined with ideas about scientific advances in disease prevention—was sold as a way of countering food-safety concerns. For example, milk was increasingly advertised as a scientifically manufactured, safe product, with images of men in lab coats gazing assuredly at test tubes, replacing older images of mothers and children set in nature.[22] American industry in particular focused on domestic life, creating needs through the new avenues of radio and print ads. Bakery bread, factory canning, and refrigeration were new developments. A famous change came with Clarence Birdseye patenting an approach to frozen foods in 1929 and marketing it heavily in the 1930s. Appliances were standardized and promoted in a variety of ways. By 1944, almost three-quarters of American households had refrigerators. "Selling Mrs. Consumer" became an important profession that defined women's household roles as the mediator of the commercial marketplace. For example, processed foods, especially canned fruits and vegetables which were welcomed as bringing variety to one's diet and as year-round sources of vitamins, were incorporated into cookbooks without guilt or celebration.

Although the Depression and Great War caused dramatic shifts in industry, the idea of the home as a locus of consumption was beginning to take hold. Suzanne Morton's study of a working-class suburb in Halifax in the 1920s and 1930s demonstrates that home community and family were important as deindustrialization was already occurring, but mass culture made commercially prepared goods more relevant and important despite the economic fears.[23] People were able and willing to purchase foods they could store and goods they felt would last. Imports and so-called foreign products, often part of the colonialist past, met with both resistance and incorporation.

THE RISE OF SUBURBIA

The end of World War II meant major disruptions and migrations, as well as global re-construction of industries and countries whose economic mainstays were destroyed. The end of many colonial empires, including British rule over India, resulted in even more complicated and violent migrations. As many countries struggled, the United States began a period of economic and social dominance. The economic machine that produced wartime goods was turned on domestic production. Foods developed for wartime were marketed to the general public after the war was over. Sold with convenience in mind, they had mixed success until the 1950s and the rise of suburbia. Marketing of commercial convenience foods trod a careful line between making things easier and demonstrating care. Manufacturers of canned soup such as Campbells, played on women's desires to be good homemakers, using anxiety as a tool. The pressure for variety in cooking created more work, since it was no longer enough to simply cook for a family but it had to embody excitement and modernity.[24] Many goods were sold through variety. Betty Friedan lamented the advertising contradictions exhorting women to "buy processed foods, but cook from scratch; be creative but follow directions precisely; accommodate all family members' preferences, but streamline the food purchasing and preparation process; work part time, but be a full-time homemaker and do it all with little or no training."[25]

Postwar infrastructure projects such as highways increased people's mobility, while federal financing allowed white male veterans to go to college and buy homes in newly constructed suburban developments such as Levittown. Women in particular embraced cars and driving, transporting food from new supermarkets and children to activities that were once nearby. Although the 1950s were often seen as the era of the nuclear family, with male breadwinner and women homemakers, labor statistics show a slight but steady increase in the number of women who worked for pay. Working-class women, recent immigrants, and women of color continued to rely on paid employment, but middle-class women also often held jobs that were seen as supplemental and part time.

Stephanie Coontz points to nostalgia for the 1950s nuclear family, a historical boon for many people who experienced stability and economic comfort for the first time in their lives.[26] At the same time, the standardization of culture also posited assimilation as the key to good citizenship and family life, with ethnic difference and gender variation presented as dysfunctional. Second- and third-generation immigrants explained their discomfort often through foodways. Arlene Voski Avakian's memoir explores how her initial rejection of all things Armenian could not hold up when it meant embracing bland foods.[27] As her relatives described it, Americans did not know the taste of their own tongues. The reality was that American women, immigrant or native born, were pushed by a food industry desperate to sell products, into embracing a contradictory ethos of care and convenience embodied by meals in tin-foil trays. At the same time, regional and ethnic foodways remained strong throughout the decade.

SOCIAL CHANGE AND INEQUALITY

From the 1950s and into the 1980s, global social movements emerged. In the United States and Western Europe, growing, but unequally distributed affluence allowed people to claim new identities and challenge existing forms of social life. From the Civil Rights movement to second-wave feminism, environmentalism, and whole foods, people asserted new racial, ethnic, and sexual identities that would not have been possible in different economic and social conditions. John D'Emilio points out that the notion of a gay identity could only have emerged after advanced capitalism had freed people from the necessity of living in family units centered on reproduction.[28] Work and consumption in modernity did not require the standard family form, so people were free to develop affective attachments and lives outside the domestic realm. At the same time, such movements were tied to the existence of a commercial marketplace that could provide goods and services. With the stagnation of real wages in the 1970s, people in affluent societies found the gap between rich and poor growing larger rather than smaller, dividing the population further. Identity-based politics was also easily co-opted by corporations. As Belasco explains, the origins of the whole-foods movement may have been a re-configuration of society and the way we produce and consume food, but the food industry eagerly took advantage of the relationship between healthy planet and healthy individuals, suggesting that the best route to social change was through consumption.[29] The larger effect of wage stagnation was greater difficulties for many families to meet breadwinner ideals, relying on two incomes to accomplish what their parents managed on one. The time bind and the inequities of the division of household labor became more of a collective problem as white middle-class people began experiencing what poor, working-class people and racial–ethnic minorities had experienced throughout the twentieth century.

For poor families, extended kin networks remained the key to survival, although they also required a reciprocity that made upward mobility difficult. Carol Stack's study of low-income black families in an American industrial city demonstrated that "what goes around comes around," including food, diapers, and daily essentials such as milk, that were shared among kind and fictive kin as a means of making ends meet and insuring networks of assistance.[30] Around the world, middle-class families began to experience similar pressures balancing work and family: many men and women defined the family itself as the locus of conflict. Gender inequality generated malaise and confinement, especially for those who had been educated and sequestered in the middle-class and elite suburbs that proliferated after World War II. For working women, poor women, women outside of heterosexual marriage, women without breadwinners, and women of color who experienced a mixture of race, class, and gender oppression, the distinction between public and private troubles was problematic. African American writer and cook, Verta Mae Grosvenor, asserted her own liberation through cooking: rather than seeing it as a gender restriction, she claimed, "my kitchen was the world."[31]

Changes in migration patterns and ease of global travel also meant that the everyday patterns of domestic life were changed. Beloved American culinary icon Julia Child brought French cooking to Western men and women through television; ethnic and regional foodways were celebrated and asserted internationally; and global cuisines were embraced as part of the postwar experience. In the United States, ethnic restaurants began a steady surge of success, albeit with different groups becoming mainstream and hybridized over the latter half of the twentieth century. In the domestic setting, eating together became more complex. The food industry, including new fast-food restaurants, began to assert a wide-ranging dominance over the availability and symbolic meaning attached to various foods. While food movements challenged that dominance, corporate food producers have been able to use global markets to create new needs where none existed prior.

THE DOMESTIC SPACE: HOMES AND KITCHENS

In the twentieth century, kitchens have moved forward from the back of the house, where they were space reserved for servants that also kept cooking smells contained away from living quarters. Haciendas, courtyards, and traditional hearths gave way to distinct rooms for cooking and eating. In the 1930s and 1940s, with the fields of home economics and social work burgeoning, women were hired to reform each other's domestic environs. International development projects, public policy changes, and federally funded home-extension services brought household rules about sanitation, safety, scientific management, and basic home improvement to rural households. These practices were supported by media-based discourses of assimilation and upward mobility: etiquette books sold briskly from the 1920s onward, giving middle-class women the information they needed about serving food and bringing guests in to their home.

As part of this so-called civilizing process, the ideals of modernism were applied to both domestic entertaining and home décor.[32] An increase in standards of living and new living spaces meant that privacy also became a hallmark of modern family life. The shift away from extended kin and non-kin household members coincided with the development of houses and rooms that were more intimate and more isolated: people required individual bedrooms and kitchens became a single-function space.

Twentieth-century expos and world's fairs featured modernist furnishings and kitchen designs, offering an end to Victorian clutter. Magazines promoted eliminating bric-a-brac and demonstrated futurism in appliances. Domestic advice in the 1940s began to use the family as an organizing principle for the American home.[33] The rubric for home design was *togetherness*. The era launched the open-space floor plan, first promoted by American Prairie School architects and then incorporated into suburban housing tracts. Families chose the house layout and opened up the kitchen. Dining rooms were optional for middle-class living, since they defied the relaxed atmosphere of suburban life. Deep freezers became an icon of freedom and plenty, offering the assurance of security and safety. Backyard barbecues gave men the illusion of frontier expansion safely contained. Betty Friedan surmised that the open floor plan was perhaps part of suburban women's oppression, since it constructed a world in which it was never possible to find privacy from children and household responsibilities.[34]

In the 1960s and beyond, the fitted kitchen became a commonplace expectation of modern Western homes, replacing free-standing appliances.

The design, which began as a U.S. trend but has made headway in other countries, became standard for all new construction, and only in recent years have interior architects promoted purchasing separate furnishings and appliances to suit a less modular approach to kitchens.[35]

With a new discourse of domestic cooking as art and entertainment in the 1980s, kitchens were larger and organized to allow for more traffic and social gathering. At the end of the twentieth century, the kitchen became an expensive part of household design and renovation, while some surveys suggest that people are cooking less, relying on value-added prepared foods that now dominate the supermarket. The general story of the kitchen has been its movement from a shared space, to a private space, back to a public space. As cooking has become more visible and less of a private act done prior to social gathering, the possibilities return that people work together rather than in isolation.

THE GLOBALIZATION OF CONSUMPTION: CONTEMPORARY DILEMMAS

Whether real or perceived, social concerns about family meals often focus on a general anxiety about cultural atomization, including the individualization of preferences, divergences of taste, diffused household time schedules, and the de-centering of households, which might disrupt ideals and experiences of family life. Contemporary family life is deeply varied, shaped by geographic location, migration, gender, class, and race. In 2001 two-thirds of all married women with children worked outside the home. Globally, between one-third and one-quarter of all children live with one parent. Rates of single and never-married households without children continued to increase.[36] For most people, global migration has a profound impact on family life, particularly as adults are forced to live great distances away and send monetary remittances as a form of caring rather than engage in daily caretaking and meals. The general decrease in government investment in social services has also meant an increase in caretaking and family-related labor that occurs in the household. The story of the contemporary era is one where increased variety and individualization have become wedges used to create new hierarchies and issues for families who are expected to socialize children over daily meals.

While family forms continue to diversify, the ideological construct of a particular normative kind of family continues to shape people's interactions with social institutions such as schools, workplaces, and governments.[37] Family forms that do not match the ideological code are constantly trying to make up for it or counter the impression that they are inadequate. The political and religious backlash that asserts a single, dominant family form taps into these deep-seated beliefs and anxieties, considering diversity a problem rather than an asset for a culture. Worries about the decline in the family meal become a way of expressing concerns over shifting gender expectations and economic conditions. At the same time, the growing power of giant corporations that produce and sell food illustrates how these fears are grounded in historical experience with institutional incursions into everyday life.

Social reformers, governments, and the food industry have increased the pressure and expectations attached to family meals. Despite international surveys, there is very little information about whether or not people actually eat a regular family meal together and if so, how often.[38] Eating together has such high social value that people are unlikely to admit that they were unable to attain that goal on any given week. Concerns about the family meal surface at various points in history and disappear again, regardless of any real drop in aggregate numbers. Anne Murcott suggests, "The anxiety lest the family meal is waning is also to be understood as if it were a standing item on the agenda of twentieth century public commentary on the nature of family life."[39]

Today, family meals in post-industrial societies are rooted in a contradictory framework of pleasure and struggle. On the one hand, the commercial marketplace and the global diffusion of people and goods have made eating together adventurous and enjoyable. On the other hand, only a segment of society is capable of achieving that kind of experience at the table. Women's labors continue to provide both the food cooked in the household and the vast majority of food produced outside the household. Current affluent discourses of *good* food have shifted to assert local, organic, and non-meat foods as the pinnacle of proper eating.[40] While these may be laudatory assertions for individual health, the global environment, and local economies, many people cannot accomplish meals with these kinds of products or ingredients because they lack access, knowledge, or time to prepare such foods. This is particularly true when supermarkets and other food venues offer inexpensive alternatives that may allow people to feed their families and manage to fulfill 24/7 work obligations. Simultaneously, people in developing economies see meat-eating as a sign of affluence. Across the world, the family meal is newly disrupted by global capitalism.

In contemporary times, the family meal has become the locus of concern for food and for social and political development. For example, childhood obesity is a public health dilemma in contemporary times: the causes remain unclear, but increasing research funds and studies attempt to demonstrate that eating family meals decreases the possibilities of obesity and increases child literacy. However, these studies do not control for the enormous influence exerted by a food industry that has taken over everyday food production and created food products that are ubiquitous and unhealthy by any standard. They ignore the political and economic conditions under which families must try to provide meals. In 1990, DeVault's landmark study of family meals demonstrated that providing meals had different meanings and power for families from different socioeconomic backgrounds. Invisible labors include negotiating the marketplace, making sense of individual preferences, dealing with limited or extensive financial resources, and attending to the expectations of variety and taste. DeVault concludes, "In families with more resources, food becomes an arena for self-expression, providing a chance to experience family as a reward for achievement; in poor families, feeding and eating are themselves the achievement. Since the ability to maintain family members cannot be taken for granted, all family members are recruited into interdependence through necessity."[41] Ultimately, food remains a key resource in domestic life.

CHAPTER EIGHT

Body and Soul

WARREN BELASCO

For most of human history, the soul aspired to far more than the body could achieve. While even the poorest of cultures could conjure soaring fantasies of spirit, bodies could barely keep up. Souls longed for greatness, but bodies, stunted by a limited menu of genes, food, and medicine, wore out early. In perhaps the most tragic of bargains, reproductive sex condemned countless mothers to early deaths in childbirth. And if bearing children did not kill you, then *libertine* behavior might do so through endemic venereal disease. No wonder that dualistic philosophers assumed the body to be inferior to the soul (or, in its secular version, the mind).

Modern times upset this assumption. Beginning with the Columbian Exchange of 1492, and accelerating with the technological breakthroughs of the nineteenth century, food became more abundant, medicine and sanitation improved, and, thanks to global migration, gene pools broadened.[1] Almost overnight bodies became taller, rounder, longer-lasting, and more fun. One's body was no longer a heavy burden or Hamlet's imprisoning "mortal coil" to be "shuttled off" after a brief sojourn on earth, but rather a marvelous gift to be treasured, shaped, and refashioned many times over an extended lifespan. As new birth-control technologies disentangled sex from reproduction, modern mass-production of clothing, cosmetics, and food enabled consumers to emulate the sexually supercharged forms suggested by modern mass media. While height was largely beyond the individual's control, the chest, abdomen, and facial regions were more malleable.[2] Of particular interest here is how modern people attempted to sculpt their bodies through conscious manipulation of food consumption.

While the opportunities to mold and perfect the modern body could seem miraculous, the challenges could be quite unsettling. The old dualistic assumptions may have been dreary (for the body at least), but they were predictable: the body was weak, beauty ephemeral, vanity a sin, sickness and suffering inevitable, and death brought blessed release from material constraints.[3] True, the body needed to be fed, for as the Burmese proverb put it, "a full gut supports moral precepts," but the word *supports* was a crucial reminder of the stomach's subordination to the head, whose needs were far more complex, as the German proverb noted: "It is easier to fill the stomach than the eye."[4] Accepting these certainties, the mind (or soul) was better occupied with the higher goals of service, truth, art, and salvation.

Once the body became more enjoyable, however, minds were more easily distracted from the ethereal agenda. Instead, they found themselves dedicated to savoring, preserving, and improving the bodily sphere. For those of the old school, such collaboration between soul and body could seem idolatrous, immoral. Hence the fierce Victorian condemnation of Walt Whitman's proclamation, in "I sing the body electric," of the body's equivalence, if not superiority. And once modern contraception decoupled sex from reproduction, the potential for licentious behavior expanded exponentially. Not coincidentally, parallel breakthroughs in veterinary sexual technologies improved livestock and expanded the fresh-meat supply— thereby broadening opportunities for *carnal knowledge* of both the sexual and culinary variety.[5] The sensual exploration that had once been reserved for aristocrats and libertines now became a democratic entitlement.[6] Many of the culture wars of the modern era were conflicts between modernists who celebrated the carnal body and conservatives who sought to preserve the hegemony of the soul. In fact it was a long time before the word *body* could even be used in polite company, except perhaps as a synonym of *corpse*—a body whose soul has departed for a better place.

As late as 1930, the notion that a soul might be subordinated to fleshly appetites could still provoke scandal, as when radio stations in the United

States refused to air the hit show tune, "Body and Soul," a song of abject hunger, loss, and desperation. No mind-over-matter mastery here, nor any contemplation of the safely conventional prerogatives of unrequited love—chastity, sacrifice, sublimated service in a convent or classroom. Instead, pure desire and lust prevail, with the jilted lover groveling for another chance—"I'm all for you, body and soul." During this same transitional period jazz and blues composers found innumerable ways to erase the older distinctions between romance (the realm of the soul) and animal lust (body), and their primary metaphorical tool was food, particularly meat, whose carnal associations were already well known, envied, and feared. Thus in Andy Razaf and Eubie Blake's soft-porn classic "Kitchen Man," (1929), the "deluxe" Madame Bucks defies the traditional Victorian lady's disdain for meat and grieves the departure of her personal chef Dan, whose "frankfurters are oh so sweet"—not to mention his "sausage meat." Addiction looms: "I can't do without my kitchen man." When soul is enslaved to appetite all caution is thrown to the wind. "Life's a wreck," the song "Body and Soul" concludes. In the modernist nightmare of many horror films, unleashed bodies, depicted as mindless hunks of meat, run rampant—an apt metaphor for an age of plenty when bodies grew to extraordinary sizes only to fall prey to unprecedented diseases of aging and affluence.

However, modern bodies were not *completely* out of control. Culture—the collective soul of a people—still had its tools of order, particularly the power to classify, prescribe, and proscribe. Through careful categorization, culture attempted to contain or normalize the body—perhaps not to the extent of the old mind-over-matter dualism, but at least within manageable boundaries. Once disciplined, bodies could be clothed, shaped, and the subject here, fed in systematic, even profitable ways. Or, to put it in musical terms, modern culture set up basic motifs that were open to numerous variations—much as the tune "Body and Soul" could be played in a wide variety of styles, from Billie Holliday's torch song to John Coltrane's polyphonic improvisation. This chapter sketches four of these themes: the efficient body, the authentic body, the busy body, and the responsible body. Each type embodied particular ideals, drew on its own sources of authority, and assumed its own infrastructure of food provisioning and consumption. While the different types clashed with each other in some ways, all addressed a key question: how, under conditions of plenty, might the body be nourished, protected, and directed towards loftier, more soulful goals?

THE EFFICIENT BODY

In a textbook case of normalization, the efficient body ideal directed bohemian body ideals into serving the needs of modern industrial capitalism. What was once deviant—the thin, hard, youthful body—became an emblem of maximum utility.

Much of the spadework for this transformation was completed before 1920. Two accomplishments are worth noting here: thinness became both sexy and scientific. First, by 1920 thinness had replaced fatness as the standard of beauty and wealth. Several historians have dated this remarkable change from the nineteenth-century cult of romantic poets, composers, and artists, many of them dying from tuberculosis, or consumption, a wasting disease that depleted body fat and produced a wan, feverish physique that some admirers considered more passionate, even "spiritual."[7] That many of these artists were in fact quite poor and thus ill-fed furthered their ascetic, otherworldly aura. Such notions may have had roots in more distant ideals of *holy anorexia*—ultra-religious people who starved themselves for sacred ends.[8] But what made the so-called tubercular-poet model more distinctly modern was that it was associated with earthbound love *without* reproduction. The dying artist was very seductive but not particularly interested in, or even capable of having children.

In the early twentieth century, the thin ideal did lose some of its more sickly connotations, as newfound interest in sports, exercise, and militarism favored more robust versions—for example, the muscular Christian, the football hero, Teddy Roosevelt's Rough Rider, and the Gibson Girl, the 1920s personification of the idealized curvaceous female form.[9] And through the somewhat perverse dynamics of social distinction, dieting became associated with great wealth. Whereas feudal aristocrats had valued fatness as a sign of their command of food surpluses, by the early twentieth century their descendants were moving beyond conspicuous consumption to conspicuous abstinence, whose axiom, "You can never be too rich or too thin," would soon be attributed to assorted super celebrities. By 1920 advertising and movies were primed to bring such ideals to the masses, or more precisely, the middle-class targets for such media. For the poor and pre-modern, rounder body types remained attractive.[10] Immigrant grand-mothers still pinched young cheeks fattened by overdoses of pure heavy cream, but their more assimilated bourgeois children increasingly equated fatness with laziness.

The association of thinness with a middle-class work ethic was aided by the rise of scientific nutrition at the end of the nineteenth century.[11] According to the emerging dietetics, food was largely energy or fuel—measured in kilocalories—and sedentary office workers needed less of it than their agrarian ancestors. Moreover, even those doing physical labor were shown to be eating far more extravagantly than nutritionists deemed adequate. As chemical nutrients such as protein, vitamins, and minerals became identified, dietary needs were calculated and specified. Following one's own sensory desires was not so much sinful (the old religious moral-ism) as inefficient (the new scientific moralism), especially for the poor, who were urged to substitute cheaper beans and whole grains for more prestigious, but nutritionally superfluous meat and white bread.

According to this emerging ideology of quantified nutrition, food was an amalgam of elements that could be rearranged and synthesized by chem-ical engineers. Much of this had been anticipated by far-sighted Victorians: Justus von Liebig's infant-milk formulas and beef extract, John Harvey Kellogg's granola, Gail Borden's condensed milk and survivalist beef bis-cuits. With analogues such as saccharin and oleomargarine already on the market by 1890, synthetic meat seemed just around the corner. Why would sensible, modern people waste resources on raising cows for chops, French chemist Marcellin Berthelot asked in 1894, when "a tablet of factory-made beefsteak" could be produced so much more cheaply from an array of "compounds," and with far less damage to landscape, animals, or diges-tion? Noting the link between female and animal enslavement, feminist veg-etarian Mary K. Lease dreamed of a "small phial" that would free women from kitchens and turn slaughterhouses into "conservatories and beds of bloom."[12] While meal pills took the reductionism a bit too far for most tastes, wartime food-conservation efforts did educate many consumers to look for cheaper substitutes for scarce luxuries. Thus, during World War I Americans tried to go meatless on Tuesdays and Europeans learned to eat canned foods.[13] And the constant discovery of new vitamins encouraged people to seek their vitality not from recognizable dishes, but from hidden chemical elements.

With modern science's focus on what historian Joseph Amato calls "the small and the invisible," power came through "the control of miniature things."[14] The early twentieth century witnessed the rise of a powerful infrastructure of laboratories, research universities, government bureaucracies, social workers, public-health agencies, and affiliated professional organizations dedicated to counting and regulating the unseen elements that form the essence of life—in food, mainly calories, bacteria, and chemical compounds. The light and imperceptible trumped the heavy and obvious. Tradition—the dead weight of the past—was yet another mortal coil to be shuttled off, as elements were rearranged in the most economical manner, thereby reducing waste and freeing up time and money for higher pursuits, whether women's liberation, the contemplation of unspoiled nature, or national defense.

In effect, mind controlled body once again, and the lean, well-managed body stood as proof of that mastery. The key difference from traditional dualism was that whereas the old arrangement disdained animalistic sex, the modern, disciplined body relished it. Indeed, feral sex was an expected perquisite of slimness. The efficient body thus reconciled the seemingly incompatible—wild lust and sober rationality. No wonder it possessed such seductive appeal and wreaked such psychological havoc.

Building on these foundations, post-1920 culture extended the calculus of efficiency to farm, factory, and kitchen. The food industry trimmed waste by consolidating and rationalizing every aspect of food production, whether assembly (canning) or disassembly (meat). Applying the same techniques and mindset, home economists conducted time–motion studies to reduce surplus steps in the store, kitchen, and dining room. Institutional feeders—schools, hospitals, prisons, hospitals—all merged Fordist production with scientific nutrition to generate cheap, standardized, balanced meals. Physically embodying the ethic of leanness, tractors, barns, locomotives, trucks, corporate offices, grocery store flow patterns, even toasters and refrigerators were all *streamlined*—a newly coined word suggesting aerodynamic sleekness, swiftness, and youthful slenderness.[15] Paradoxically, as scientific management improved productivity while reducing labor, energy-dense food became both more available and less necessary. The result was an oversupply of calories that would bankrupt farmers and soon threaten to make people fatter—the opposite of the efficient-body ideal.

Depression and another war delayed the full impact of this metabolic imbalance; if anything, the widespread deprivations of the 1930s and early 1940s restored some plumpness to beauty norms that had become almost prepubescently skinny in the 1920s. In the 1950s, newly prosperous Americans paused to relish the profligate *inefficiency* of a culture symbolized by extra-large cars, fatty steaks, and double milkshakes. Citing major breakthroughs in agricultural efficiency, a *Life* magazine editorial boasted in 1955 that "nearly all Americans not only enjoy a national diet but a luxury diet. Their land is so increasingly productive that they can afford the luxury of using up 10 calories of corn and forage to produce one calorie of beef."[16] Whereas progressive-era reformers would have decried such wastefulness, Cold War propagandists flaunted it as a sign of capitalist superiority. Widespread famine abroad, including in the European homeland, encouraged Americans not to cut back, but rather to clean their plates on behalf of the starving. The unprecedented fertility of the postwar Baby Boom was reflected in the maternal curves and forgiving A-lines of high fashion.

In the 1960s, however, body culture resumed its march towards lightness, recapitulating the early twentieth-century merger of bohemian and quantitative paradigms. Like the dying-artist cult of the nineteenth century, countercultural sexuality valued pre-marital skinniness over parental plumpness. For shorter-haired rebels the space program served a similar, dying-poet function; displaying the *right stuff* through ritualistic suffering, early astronauts all lost a lot of weight on NASA's tubed food diet—itself the ultimate outcome of generations of research in scientific nutrition.[17] The statistical case for thinness came from a combination of epidemiology and economics, as public-health officials warned that the cost of treating the newly recognized cardiovascular "diseases of affluence" might bankrupt governments and businesses alike.[18] Moreover, in a highly competitive world, how could a slothful people keep up with the lean and hungry communists, hard-charging Japanese and Chinese, or, in the post-Cold War era, the sleeker Europeans?[19] Worse, as oil supply crises, costly wars, looming environmental disasters, corporate outsourcing, and assorted neo-liberal economic policies shelved postwar expectations of the benign, corporate welfare state, how could people keep up with their neighbors? Postwar dreams of abundant energy too cheap to meter, *populuxe* automation, thirty-hour work weeks, lifelong job security, and cushy retirement at fifty seemed remote indeed. It was time to toughen up.

Dieting was an ideal ritualistic response to a world seemingly out of control. First it suited the modern faith that nature—here, the body—could be managed and rebuilt, especially after the depredations of the holiday season. Moreover, dieting assumed a mechanistic view of the body: its ca-loric inputs and outputs could be closely measured, and its parts could be tuned up with ultra-specialized, shiny exercise equipment. It also reflected the democratic belief in individual willpower: you could lose weight if you *wanted* to. At the same time it served the needs of consumer capitalism; since almost all diets failed, there was considerable repeat business. The diet industry exemplified capitalistic enterprise built around perpetual ob-solescence—the constant flow of new and improved goods and services. And the diet business also offered excellent synergy with the mass-mediated entertainment and sports industries, which served up impossibly thin and hard body images and severely stigmatized those who failed to keep up.

In all, the diet industry was a well-oiled, elegantly designed apparatus that *should* have worked as effectively as the efficient body it idealized. Yet it failed spectacularly. Despite the well-synchronized efforts of public-health experts, diet entrepreneurs, and media celebrities, people actually got fatter. Apparently, mind had less control over matter than the efficiency experts had hoped.[20] Explanations for the spread of fatness throughout the modern world range widely, from the psychological and genetic, to the environmen-tal and economic.[21] Here it might be useful to focus on an important cultural conflict: the efficient-body model failed to satisfy the longings expressed in other body types, particularly the desire for authentic social experiences.

THE AUTHENTIC BODY

When efficiency triumphs in modern science fiction, the results are gener-ally quite horrifying—ranging from the quiet sterility of *Brave New World,* where people are programmed to mistake security for happiness, to the screaming nightmare of *Soylent Green,* where, to conserve scarce resources, pragmatic engineers recycle cadavers into food. (Why waste perfectly good protein?)[22] Rational utilitarianism is scary in these dystopian stories because people crave more than security and sensibility; real bodies want real sensations, real *experiences*. "All history is the history of longing," Jackson Lears writes.[23] One problem with modern consumer culture, however, is that it offers so many potential experiences to long after. Given the oversupply of options, what's real now can seem rather superficial later. As Czech novelist Milan Kundera suggests, the very "lightness of being" in the modern world can seem "unbearable."[24] The longing for a heavier reality translates into a desire for what *other* people do, have, and are. And of other people, the pre-modern seem more rooted, fixed, *authentic*. Paradoxically, people with fewer options appear more real than people who have many. Hence the modern fascination with the primitive.

Authenticity-seekers sample other people's worlds. Before the twentieth century, most people did this sampling vicariously, through stories. While such armchair tourism employed the two higher senses, sight and hearing, few people could actually put their whole *bodies*—including the lower senses of taste, smell, and touch—in another place.[25] The limits of technology, economics, geography, and tradition kept most people at or near home; even those who migrated across continents and oceans did their best to take home along with them in the form of familiar icons, clothes, melodies, and foods. But thanks to modern transportation, mass production, longer education, and globalized warfare, more bodies could now experience the authentic other *physically,* primarily through travel, dance, costumes, food, and occasionally, sex. Such encounters may not have been subjected to the calculus of efficiency, but they were powerful nevertheless—and often quite profitable for smart retailers of other-body experiences.

Through the twentieth century we see a steady growth in such entrepreneurial opportunities. In the food business, tastes of the Other were served up by foreign-trained chefs, immigrant restaurateurs, ethnic street-festival stand operators, culinary tour guides, world-fair exhibitors, food-court franchisees, food memoirists, and cookbook authors. An early example was the appearance of roadside restaurants in the 1920s. Catering to the needs and fantasies of newly (auto)mobilized bodies, these eateries offered exotic food experiences in neo-colonial tea rooms, half-timbered inns, castled burger stands, carnivalesque fried-clam shacks, and building-size root-beer barrels. Such vernacular architecture also lined county, state, and world-fair midways, as well as the neo-Victorian main streets of the postwar Disney parks. Capturing space-age aspirations in the 1950s, some restaurant designers affected futuristic arches, parabolas, pylons, and boomerangs—for example, early McDonald's, Burger King, Dairy Queen, and California's famous *googie*-style coffee shops.[26] Whether set in the pre-industrial past or intergalactic future, the authentic was most definitely *not* in the here-and-now. No *today-land* existed at the Disney parks; similarly, tourists to the Old World tended to avoid the more contemporary neighborhoods where real people actually lived, worked, and ate.

The longing to be anywhere-but-here also resulted in a strong neo-agrarian pull near the end of the twentieth century. As farmers lost economic clout—for instance, in 2005 they accounted for just 2.5 percent of the U.S. workforce and received less than a fifth of the retail food dollar[27]—they accrued moral stature as embodiments of pre-modern craftsmanship, diligence, sacrifice, and loyalty to place.[28] To be sure such virtues tended to be projected more on white farm owners than on the brown migrants who actually produced much of the modern food supply on factory farms. But urban consumers were fascinated by subsistence farmers who resisted the temptations of the urban market and stayed home. No one published the ad hoc recipes of illegals who crowded in small apartments while laboring in Kansas or Hong Kong slaughterhouses, but chain bookstores stocked walls of cookbooks full of the grainy dishes of peasants living in huts fashioned from mud, stone, thatch, and sticks. Sophisticated retailers found scarce shelf space for gnarly artisanal cheeses, sausages, and breads. Natural, organic, ethnic, and slow foods all gained appeal precisely because ordinary daily life seemed artificial, fragmented, bland, and rushed.[29] Indeed, even seasonal and local foods could seem exotic to consumers accustomed to accessing the world's produce year round at the neighborhood hypermarket.[30] The fascination with truck farms, small corner groceries, Victorian-era public markets, farm stands, backyard vegetable plots, home brewing, and micro-butchering—all displaced by mid-twentieth-century modernization—was matched by intense nostalgia for another mainstay of localized production, the bread-baking, peach-canning, stay-at-home mother. Like the small farmer, the domesticated mom gained mythic standing as she lost daily economic relevance. As the subject of a host of bestselling food memoirs, however, she endured profitably.[31]

Of course the more ubiquitous and accessible the experience, the less real it seemed. It was remarkable how similar local fare could begin to taste, especially when served at micro-breweries that all appeared to be run by the same person, usually a blue-jeaned early retiree from the financial world who decided to give back by opening a community pub serving freshly baked focaccia piled with a neighboring farmer's pulled pork and mesclun. Readers of one too many ode-to-mom memoirs could experience a similar sense of déjà vu. So food adventurers were constantly seeking out new experiences, exposing their finds to the world, and then tiring of the latest discoveries once they became popular. Even modernist icons such as Jell-O, Kool-Aid, TV dinners, Space Sticks, Tang, and the canned, precooked pork product SPAM could be reborn as nostalgic relics of a lost faith in the industrialized future.[32] The authenticity market was thus one of the more volatile segments of the consumer economy.

No doubt there were less faddish, ephemeral, or voyeuristic ways to experience Others, especially through the relatively quiet encounter of the shared meal. Dining with kin and friends has long been a way to escape loneliness, expand horizons, and restore a sense of perspective. And preparing food for others can be a powerful way to air one's voice and reward allies. There is considerable evidence that people continued to cook and eat socially throughout the modern period, even as they complained steadily about not having time to do so.[33] Like the efficient body of the progressives, the commensal body of communitarians had to compete with yet another major body type of the modern era—the busy body.

THE BUSY BODY

Much of the hunger for anywhere-but-here stemmed from a basic failing of the here-and-now: in a cruel joke, consumer capitalism provided more options than ever, but not nearly enough time to enjoy them. Modernity tantalized the five conventional senses with an array of possibilities, and then added a sixth sense that frustrated the whole deal, the feeling of being rushed. Indeed, the very wealth of options added to the sense of being overwhelmed. It is not entirely clear, however, whether modern people in fact had less time than their agrarian ancestor-idols, as farmers and artisans had certainly worked long, hard days. Employed mothers working a second shift at home had good reasons to feel hurried, but so too had nineteenth-century female factory workers, as well as the moms who did most of the food work and childrearing in hunter–gatherer societies. It is possible that raised expectations for domestic chores, combined with a decline in the employment of domestic servants, contributed to the feeling of "more work for mother," whose tasks seemed "never done."[34] No doubt modern bodies did spend more service time idling in traffic, but such time was not necessarily wasted, as car radios kept minds informed, or at least occupied. Moreover, even as they complained of a time deficit, they still devoted many hours to surfing television channels and websites; as they did so, many multitasked—an activity at which working mothers were particularly adept. Thus people may have been busy, but it was not necessarily at paid jobs. Expressions of feeling too busy may have offered some compensatory satisfaction in a culture that still valued the work ethic and had not quite elevated the leisure ethic to equal status. And it also served to bolster the self-esteem of the professional-managerial classes, who did the most complaining yet worked fewer hours than their blue-collar fellow citizens.

Still, when it comes to the senses, perception is all. Modern bodies may have lived longer, but they still felt worn out. The consequences for food production, distribution, and consumption were enormous. Too busy to shop, cook, or even eat a formal meal, modern people relied heavily on the food industry to do the work. Selling convenience was in fact the food industry's primary service, forming the basis of a multi-trillion-dollar business. Fed by commercial-food services, the busy body morphed into the incorporated body—the corporeal result of numerous corporations competing to *do it all for you*. This was not quite the sleek, modern body that the efficiency experts had in mind, as it ingested too many calories, especially from energy-dense snacks, soft drinks, and convenience foods. Here was the body in service not of higher ideals (whether mind or soul) but of the bottom line.

Getting to this state took some time and effort. Consumers initially resisted many of the main technologies of the convenience-food system, particularly refrigeration, canning, chemical preservatives, and plastic-wrapping. Inherited notions of freshness, romance, health, tradition, and morality tended to get in modern marketers' way. Mindful of the historic struggle to put food on the table, many consumers rightfully doubted anything that came too quickly or too cheaply. Toughened by generations of being cheated by canny peddlers, early modern food shoppers were well acquainted with the hallowed Latin concept of *caveat emptor*—let the buyer beware. Gadgets that preserved food beyond what seemed its natural lifespan were initially viewed as attempts by hucksters to corner a market or to foist spoiled supplies on an unwary public.[35] Furthermore, because many housewives were socialized to believe that domestic service was their sacred calling, they hesitated to forego the hard kitchen work that earned them respect, martyr points, and even power.[36] Otherwise-marginalized women may have seen complex scratch cooking as a form of networking. For example, anthropologist Brett Williams has shown how even the most rushed, impoverished Tejano (Texan of Mexican descent) farm workers in the United States will find the many hours required to make tamales, which serve to bind husband and neighbors in the tight migrant community of the road.[37] Reliant on loyal kin for survival, many immigrants refused to feed families from a can. Bodies fed by quick-and-easy foods were less likely to be faithful and grateful.

To overcome consumer resistance, marketers often clothed convenience products in the more attractive garb of authenticity. Thus, canned fruit drinks were sold as vitamin-rich repositories of Mediterranean sunshine (otherness). As if to anchor its steel-milled corn flakes in an agrarian past, Kellogg's ads and boxes still feature an iconic rooster. Since 1921 the focal point of a package of Land O Lakes butter or margarine has been a stereotypical Native American woman whose people were displaced long ago by industrial dairy and corn farmers. In the United States, brown skins sold white goods, as when the R. T. Davis Milling Co. created the mammy, Aunt Jemima, to hawk its convenient pancake mixes and syrups (1893), North Dakota millers invented chef Rastus to sell Cream of Wheat (1893), and Converted Rice, Inc. concocted Uncle Ben to represent its quick rice (1943).[38] Less racially tinged but still fabricated was Betty Crocker (1921), who reassured that a real mother was somehow, somewhere involved in the mass production of General Mills' cookies and biscuits.

This was the recombinant or post-modern strategy outlined in 1902 by futurist H. G. Wells, who anticipated that modernization would leave consumers longing for "the second-hand archaic" and "old-fashioned corners"—for example, nostalgic touches such as sham chimneys with artificial smoke, automatic windows with medieval mullions, and court-style, mass-produced clothing. Most food would come from corporate laboratories, Wells predicted, but consumers still might want to grow something in a quaint garden behind their electrically powered cottages and then heat it up on a "neat little range." Universities might even employ a few "ramshackle Bohemians" to give romantic color and character to an otherwise bland modern civilization.[39] Quick to recognize and capitalize on such ambivalence was Henry Ford. Behind the scenes, Ford employed a full array of Taylorist techniques and technologies to cut costs, but to the public Ford presented himself as an illiterate tinkerer who just wanted to supply the masses with a simple, unadorned horseless carriage—"any color as long as it's black." Also in the United States in the 1930s, a similarly clever backstage–frontstage approach popularized Howard Johnson's so-called family restaurants, which dressed factory-style food production in the garb of a colonial, New England town hall, complete with white steeple and fake dormers with green shutters. Johnson, the efficiency engineer, also added orange roofs to the mix—a calculating acknowledgement that speeding tourists needed considerable advance notice to slow down before turning off into the parking lot.[40] Simultaneously in Berlin, the Aschinger brothers staffed their quick-lunch buffets with bartenders in lederhosen and waitresses in dirndls, although the tempered rusticity of these pseudo-Bavarian touches had little practical utility in an enterprise organized around thoroughly modern self-service.[41] After World War II the same recombinant formula—scientific management + escapist whimsy—would be copied and perfected by countless fast-food chains; for example, Taco Bell, Pizza Hut, Arby's, McDonald's, as well as by the world's most powerful authenticity merchant, the Disney Company, whose *imagineers* catered to a wide variety of fantasies. But perhaps the most remarkable recombinant strategy was practiced by mega-retailer Wal-Mart, whose corporate trademark reduced a universal repertoire of folksy gestures, emotions, and relationships to a single smiley face—itself a relic of the 1960s counterculture.[42]

THE RESPONSIBLE BODY

The counterculture was not entirely co-optable, however. Its compelling ethical claims challenged the prevailing consumerist drift, chastening people to think about the wider political, economic, ecological, and so-cial consequences of their eating behavior. Inviting you to "have a nice day," the smiley face also nudged you to *be* nice. The same voyeuristic fascination *with* Others that powered the search for authenticity could also induce people to *care about* Others. In food terms, caring meant being willing to pay the full cost of a meal. No deadbeat, the responsible consumer examined how each meal affected the welfare of people and creatures around the globe and across generations. The responsible body personified conscience, altruism, foresight, and empathy—the more sober attributes of soul.

The search for an ethically clean bill was by no means a modern phe-nomenon. All cuisines are shaped by notions of purity and equity. We are as much defined by what we will not eat as by what we do eat. Disgust is as much an identity-shaping social tool as a self-protective biological one. What distinguished the modern era was a widening sense of moral entanglement. The same technologies, media, and institutions that length-ened lifespans and widened experiences also broadened people's awareness of connections and consequences. In the globalized food chain, consumers depended upon ever-more distant suppliers. Understandably, marketers did their best to hide the uglier side of such connections, particularly those involving slavery and imperialism. Thus a 1701 report on one of the first modern multinational food corporations, the East India Company, noted, "We taste the spices of Arabia yet never feel the scorching sun which brings them forth."[43] This distancing from the *scorching sun* of spice procurement was no mean accomplishment, as it took quite a lot of bloodshed to stock middle-class kitchens with highly valued aromatics; as historian Andrew Dalby notes, "spices are truly a dangerous taste."[44]

By the mid-nineteenth century spices were by no means the only dan-gerous taste, as consumers became more accustomed to enjoying foreign grains, meat, and fruits. Thanks to global trade and conquest, British econ-omist William Jevons boasted in 1865, "the plains of North America and Russia are our cornfields; Chicago and Odessa our granaries; Canada and the Baltic our timber forests; Australia contains our sheep farms, and in South America are our herds of oxen; the Chinese grow tea for us, and our coffee, sugar, and spice plantations are all in the Indies."[45] Anticipating this global consciousness, the same romantic rebels who starved themselves

fashionably voiced moral concerns about the cosmic impact of eating decisions. As Lord Byron put it with considerable understatement in "Don
Juan" (1823):

> All human history attests
> That happiness for man
> The hungry sinner—
> Since Eve ate apples
> Much depends on dinner!

For abolitionists in the United States, the *much depends* included the price
that slaves paid to grow sugar, tobacco, cotton, tea, and other agricultural staples for metropolitan markets. Setting an example later copied
by anti-imperialists, British abolitionists pushed the substitution of East
Indian sugar, supposedly harvested by free labor, for that grown by West
Indian slaves.[46] As modern urban life widened the circle of complicity, fol-
lowers of American health reformer Sylvester Graham extended their abstinence strategies to include not just sugar but all industrially produced,
impure stimulants, including alcohol, caffeine, white flour, and red meat.[47]
Opposed to slavery as well as the Mexican War, Henry David Thoreau
probably had such principled avoidance in mind when he refused to pay his
poll taxes—the subject of *Civil Disobedience* (1849), a primary source for
ensuing non-violent resistance movements. In *Walden* (1854), he penned
what has become an axiom of conscientious consumption: "The cost of
a thing is the amount of what I will call life which is required to be ex-
changed for it, immediately or in the long run."[48] While labor reformers
were tallying the full costs in human lives, vegetarians added the costs to
animals and to future human needs. In an early calculation of the ecological bill of animal husbandry, Byron's friend—and prototypical dying
poet—Percy Bysshe Shelley goaded the meat eater who would "destroy his
constitution by devouring an acre [of grain] at a meal. The quantity of nutritious vegetable matter, consumed in fattening the carcass of an ox, would
afford ten times the sustenance if gathered immediately from the bosom
of the earth."[49] At the end of the nineteenth century, scientific nutritionists
used such computations when urging the substitution of beans and grains
for wasteful animal products. However, these arguments held less sway

with working-class eaters facing economic scarcity than with middle-class consumers seeking moral purity.[50]

The case for disciplined refusal gained a wider following in the twentieth century, when muckraking writers such as Upton Sinclair, Carey McWilliams, and John Steinbeck in the United States exposed the hidden costs of the global food chain.[51] Abolitionist-style boycotts were adopted by civil rights' activists throughout the American South as well as in the colonial world. For example, a 1933 boycott of the Hamburger Grill in Washington D.C.'s U Street ghetto forced the owner to rehire fired black workers—at higher pay. The action led to the formation of the New Negro Alliance, which, under the banner "Don't Buy Where You Can't Work," picketed segregated lunch counters, ice-cream stores, and groceries. Ultimately, such protests led to the 1953 Thompson Restaurant decision in which the U.S. Supreme Court voted 8–0 to require all D.C. restaurants to serve "well-behaved and respectable" customers regardless of race.[52] Boycotts became a worldwide tactic, employed most successfully by Gandhi against British goods in India, by black protesters in Alabama, by striking farmworkers in California, and by opponents of South African apartheid. Hunger strikers took principled abstinence one step further by refusing to eat anything until their demands—whether for suffrage, political independence, or release from jail—were met. Black students staging sit-ins at segregated cafes in the United States added yet another twist to the strategy of bodily protest: instead of refusing to eat, they *demanded* to be fed, thereby linking digestion and integration. Along the same lines, white sympathizers deliberately sought strength by eating the dark foods of the Black Power and anti-colonialist movements. Eating the Other thus took on a dual dimension: by eating the foods of the enemy you disarmed him, and by eating the foods of your allies, you absorbed their souls. Either way, bodies were right on the front lines of political action.

The counterculture also revived Shelley's old case for ecological vegetarianism. For example, in *Diet for a Small Planet* (1971), Frances Moore Lappé dusted off USDA statistics that demonstrated the inherent wastefulness of converting feedgrains into animal products. Such numbers had particular resonance at a time when Malthusian worries about future food supplies had resurfaced in a variety of media, from biologist Paul Ehrlich's stark predictions in *The Population Bomb* (1968) to the cannibalistic application of scientific nutrition in *Soylent Green* (1973). Lappé's presentation was especially effective because her ethnic-style vegetarian recipes—"sweet and sour couscous for Arabian nights," "feijoada with tangy black beans," "Greek Gala moussaka"—married scientific calculations of dietary adequacy and environmental impact with a strong bow to the authenticity hunger of postmodern culture. In a countercultural twist on the recombinant formula, the responsibly fed body was both efficient *and* exotic. Almost forty years after Lappé's first edition, the 100-mile diet proposed the same mélange of quantitative science and culinary tourism: precisely calculated doses of ecological footprint and carrying capacity, spiced with wistful invented traditions, and tangy *terroir*.[53] It was a tempting promise—yet another attempt to reconcile the material demands of the body with the noble longings of the soul.

CHAPTER NINE

Food Representations

SIGNE ROUSSEAU

Representations are essentially stories. They can be visual, oral, written, or numerical. Sometimes they are life-like in their accuracy, but like a photograph, even the most objective representation has a framework that not only directs our focus, but more importantly excludes what lies beyond it. Representations are also our basic means of communication, and so the stories that we tell—and hear—can have profound implications for how we live our lives. When it comes to food, this can extend from the mundane, such as buying *Mastering the Art of French Cooking* in order to bring a version of Julia Child into your kitchen (or simply because the movie *Julie & Julia* [2009] convinced you that it was a hip thing to have on your bookshelf),[1] to the much more serious, such as relying on one set of statistics to persuade you that your life, or perhaps your child's life, is in danger because you live in an obesity epidemic.

This chapter focuses on cultural and discursive reflections about food in the twentieth century and beyond. While we cannot with certainty distinguish the modern age as one in which people were (and are) more obsessed with food than ever before, the twentieth century is historically unsurpassed in terms of the *quantity* of food representations. This is thanks largely to development of new media such as television and the Internet (including the refinement of technology such as radio and *talkies,* or films with spoken dialogue), which have at once supplemented and perpetuated demand for more traditional forms of narrativizing food, such as in cookbooks, literature, and the arts (painting, sculpture, photography). Many of these are now also reproduced in digital form. All of these channels combine to create multiple—and often interacting—layers of representations, not unlike Michel de Certeau's description of (Western) society as one that "ceaselessly reproduces and accumulates 'copies' of stories. Our society has become a recited society, in three senses: it is defined by *stories* (*récits*, the fables constituted by our advertising and informational media), by *citations* of stories, and by the interminable *recitation* of stories."[2]

Nowhere is this more striking than in the steady increase of food-related media in the twentieth century, because although representational channels have multiplied exponentially, there remains a notable continuity in the *content* of reflections about food over the century. Cookbooks may have developed in style, design, and tone (not to mention price!), and they have also played an important role in normalizing new food products over the decades, but they continue to reproduce scores of the same recipes, albeit updated or, more reflective of a celebrity culture, personalized (deciding to cook *boeuf bourguignon* may involve deciding between a Julia Child or Rachael Ray recipe, or opting for Gordon Ramsay's speedy version).

Similarly continuous are some of the anxieties that underlie many modern representations of food, such as a concern with counting calories, already in evidence on some U.S. restaurant menus in the 1920s[3] as part of a burgeoning trend in *new nutrition,*[4] or so-called scientific eating, that reduced food to its chemical components. This was made possible by the nineteenth-century scientific advances which also helped to reconfigure cooking as a domestic science,[5] and for government agencies to begin publishing guidelines for healthy eating.[6] This reductionist approach to food, known later in the century as nutritionism, continues into the twenty-first century, particularly with artificially fortified foods that are marketed as functional, or what Marion Nestle calls techno-foods, which often obscure the conceptual boundaries between food, dietary supplements, and medicine.[7] One result of this is a persistent trend of polarizing foods as good or bad, based not on taste or appetite, but rather on composition ratios (fats to proteins to carbohydrates), on a particular constituent (ketchup, for example, is *good* for you because tomatoes contain lycopene, while butter, full of unsaturated fat, is *bad*), or on how *little* nutrition it contains (Barry Glassner dubs this *the gospel of naught*—"the view that the worth of a meal lies principally in what it lacks. The less sugar, salt, fat, calories, carbs, preservatives, additives, or other suspect stuff, the better the meal").[8]

But one man's meat, so the saying goes, is another man's poison, and lay perceptions about food are not formed in a vacuum, nor dictated exclusively by government directives. They are equally informed by advertising, by journalism, or by anecdotes—more stories, each with variously vested interests. These competing representations contribute to what has been described as the "dietary cacophony"[9] of media-saturated environments, where it has become entirely normal to be confronted with a continuous stream of (sometimes conflicting) information about what, or what not, to eat. Media portrayals of obesity as an epidemic sweeping the planet[10] also belong to this cacophony, as do increasingly regular muckraking works about the industries that produce some of the food on our plates (here, another continuum from Upton Sinclair's 1906 *The Jungle,* to Eric Schlosser's 2001 *Fast Food Nation,* to the 2008 documentary film *Food, Inc.*). One ironic result of this age of information, then, is a perceptible lack of certainty about food—one perhaps best summarized by the title of a 1975 book entitled *Eating May Be Hazardous to Your Health.*[11]

Unsafe food creating a "toxic environment"[12] is one representation of food that has taken strong hold in the collective imagination of the late twentieth century. So has the (largely negative) representation of a globalized world with reference to food products, such as McDonaldization and Coca-Colonization[13] (perceived homogenizing forces which, in academia, are countered by a focus on foodways, or on how individuals negotiate and perform their identities through food). However, these stories face equally strong counter-narratives that have celebrated food throughout the century, from pen, to keyboard, to canvas, to screens (small and big), as well, of course, as on the plate.

FOOD IN BOOKS

Counting among them the *Larousse Gastronomique* (first published in 1938) and recipe pamphlets supposedly authored by the fictional Betty Crocker, the twentieth century has produced a range of iconic cookbooks that reflect both the interests and preoccupations of their time, many of which continue to be reprinted today. Published in the United States in the wake of the Depression, the first edition of Irma Rombauer's classic *The Joy of Cooking* (1931) contained recipes for unusual and cheap meats such as squirrel. Subtitled "A Compilation of Reliable Recipes with a Casual Culinary Chat," its informal tone and emphasis on home cooking set it apart from the detached approach of domestic scientists who championed industrially prepared foods.[14] A ninth-revision seventy-fifth-anniversary edition was published in 2006. Thanks to Rombauer's grandson, Ethan Becker, it includes recipes familiar to the modern reader, such as for sushi and corn dogs.

Faced with scarcity and rationing, World War II cookbooks naturally focused on thrift, and their immediate successors on celebrating a newly emerging abundance.[15] But when Elizabeth David's *Mediterranean Cooking* was published in Britain in 1950 after she had been abroad for most of the war, her inclusion of ingredients that were not *yet* available to the British consumer was met with consternation rather than celebration: "Hardly knowing what I was doing," David later reflected, "I sat down and started to work out an agonized craving for the sun and furious revolt against that terrible cheerless, heartless food by writing down descriptions of Mediterranean and Middle Eastern cooking. Even to write words like apricot, olives and butter, rice and lemons, oil and almonds, produced assuagement. Later I came to realize that in the England of 1947 those were dirty words I was putting down."[16] The book nevertheless proved a great success (to be followed by several other publications, and "The Elizabeth David Kitchen Shop" which operated in London from 1965 to 1973), and David was ushered in as a pivotal figure in British food consciousness. *Mediterranean Food* unveiled a hunger for that breed of food fantasy now often described as culinary tourism,[17] and which television chef Keith Floyd would later take to its logical conclusion by pioneering television cooking shows staged outside the studio.

Across the Atlantic, the success of exotic cookbooks after World War II is exemplified by the approximately one hundred French cookbooks published between 1959 and 1969,[18] though more specifically by Julia Child's *Mastering the Art of French Cooking* (1961, co-authored by Simone Beck and Louisette Bertholle), and M.F.K. Fisher's *The Cooking of Provincial*

France (1968)—the latter the first volume in the *Time-Life* series of "Foods of the World."[19] The Francophone interest extended to (and likely also from) Jacqueline Kennedy, who famously employed a French chef in the White House. The different styles of these books reflect two competing interests of those decades: increased travel, on the one hand, which gestured to the demographic movements of an emergent global village, and television, on the other hand, which helped to make this village accessible without having to leave the home. Child's book—and more obviously its offspring TV show *The French Chef* (1963–1973)—appealed to this second demographic as she demystified French food by giving it an American outfit ("the book could well be titled 'French Cooking From the American Supermarket,'" wrote Child[20]—though she did inspire a demand for French cooking equipment such as charlotte molds and copper bowls).[21] Fisher's volume also contained recipes that could be reproduced in the home, but with clearer limitations. The short section on bread, for example, contains a color plate identifying the different kinds of bread, but no recipes. "Traditionally and almost universally," Fisher explained in the accompanying text, "the French do not bake their own bread…and to bake it successfully without having French flour and other French ingredients on hand is most difficult." In contrast to Child's translation of French food to an American kitchen, *The Cooking of Provincial France* is more suggestive of a readership who were likely to travel to try new foods for themselves, or if not, to limit their experience of foreign foods to an authentic vicarious experience. The *Time-Life* series prefigures others such as *Culinaria* (Könemann) and *The Beautiful Cookbooks* (Harper Collins), which reflect the cross-cultural interaction—both actual and imaginary—that characterizes one version of globalization.

Penned by another seminal figure who already had several publications behind him (and, having appeared on the U.S. television network NBC in 1946, is also considered the first American television cook), the 1959 eponymous *James Beard Cookbook* typifies another trend of demystifying food, but here the food was more familiar, and the intended reader a complete novice in the kitchen.[22] The book, in his words, was for "those who are just beginning to cook and say they don't even know how to boil water." Beard's legacy continues today in the prestigious James Beard Foundation (dedicated to "celebrating, preserving, and nurturing America's culinary heritage and diversity"), as does the market for an ever-simplified approach to food, with titles such as *Cooking for Dummies* (co-authored by superchef Wolfgang Puck),[23] *The Absolute Beginner's Cookbook: Or, How Long Do I Cook a 3-Minute Egg?*, and more to the point, *How to Boil Water: Life Beyond Takeout*.[24]

In keeping with the spirit of Betty Friedan's influential *The Feminine Mystique* (1963), Peg Bracken's *I Hate to Cook Cookbook* (1960), *I Hate to Housekeep Book* (1962), and *I Still Hate to Cook Book* (1967) reflected the growing women's liberation movement by challenging the patriarchal stereotype of woman as cook and homemaker. This theme of manipulating food to give the *appearance* of being an accomplished cook was typified in the United Kingdom with books such as Delia Smith's *How to Cheat at Cooking* (first published in 1971, and re-issued in 2008). In the following decade, Erin Pizzey's *Slut's Cookbook* (1981) abandons pretence and embraces the convenience of fast food, particularly for children. "Don't force your children to eat your carefully prepared home-made stews when what they really want is fish fingers and beans," advised Pizzey, "Remember that kids get addicted to hamburgers for years of their lives. They don't like them home-made; they like them from the take-away, so don't whine—get them a take-away when you can afford it."

Exemplary of giving in to the toxic food environment that would become associated with obesity in years to come, this representation of food contradicted the counter-cultural movements of the sixties and seventies, for which food was one channel to protest mainstream corporate agendas: wholegrain brown loaves instead of Wonderbread and home-made granola instead of mass-produced cereals (little wonder Warren Belasco recalls them as the "crunchy old days").[25] Here came books such as Molly Katzen's (hand-written, vegetarian) *Moosewood Cookbook* in 1977, featuring recipes from the collective-owned Moosewood Restaurant (London's equivalent was the wholefood, vegetarian restaurant-chain Cranks, the first of which opened in 1961, though *The Cranks Recipe Book* was not published until 1982). Together with figures such as Alice Waters, who opened her California restaurant Chez Panisse in 1971, the Moosewood collective epitomized the values of the cooperative garden, described as an "edible dynamic"—a "living medium through which people can relate to each other and their nourishment."[26]

The creed of favoring whole, natural, organic, and more recently local and sustainable foods continues to be in evidence in modern cookbooks, though critiquing the industrial mass-production of food has shifted more visibly to book-length exposés, and to the rapidly growing academic field of food studies. Dominant on the twenty-first-century cookbook market are titles by celebrity chefs: in 2009, Jamie Oliver was declared Britain's best-selling author (outselling J. K. Rowling's *Harry Potter* books in that year), while in India, celebrity chef Sanjeev Kapoor has sold an estimated ten million copies of his cookbooks.[27]

While writing about food is practically as old as writing itself, the term *food writer* did not appear in print until 1950.[28] This moment not only in-augurated a new literary genre, but also the retrospective representation of almost any literature which includes food as potentially belonging to that genre. In his 2002 anthology of "Food Writing from Around the World and Throughout History," for example, Mark Kurlansky includes writings by authors as diverse as Herodotus, Christopher Columbus, Anton Checkov, and John Steinbeck. Among the generation who were writing about food when the genre was christened, M.F.K. Fisher famously stated that "I do not consider myself a food writer,"[29] yet she continues to be cited as one of America's finest of the kind. So lucrative would the profession be that by the turn of the century, (food writer) Regina Schrambling reported that "Fisher, Elizabeth David and A. J. Liebling are no longer seen as the only real writers in food town," having been joined by a new generation whose books "sell like Big Macs." More telling than using the analogy of the most standardized product in the world to describe books about food is Schrambling's description of what makes them sell: a "voracious appetite" for all things food.[30]

This metaphorical appetite (or the *Hungry Mind*, as Schrambling's piece is entitled) underpins the great success of what has become an explosive industry of food representations in the latter half of the twentieth century, across all media platforms. This boon is equally expressed in the popu-larization of such terms as *foodie* (coined by Paul Levy and Ann Barr in their 1984 *The Official Foodie Handbook*), and *food porn* or *gastro-porn*, which first appeared in a 1977 cookbook review to describe that which "heightens the excitement and also the sense of the unattainable by proffer-ing colored photographs of various completed recipes."[31] Notwithstanding that many people do reproduce recipes in their kitchens, and do eat food prepared by others in restaurants, *unattainable* in this review stresses the vicariousness of much of our engagement with stories about food, whether reading a (recipe) book, or watching a dish being prepared on television.[32]

That these representations can stimulate actual hunger is little surprise, given our biological proclivities for thinking about our next meal. Yet there is equal sense in the argument that the sheer amount of food-related media contributes to creating and sustaining the hungry mind, also usefully described as *hedonic hunger*: "thoughts, feelings and urges about food in the absence of energy deficits."[33] M.F.K. Fisher's response to this reported effect of her writing is a noteworthy reminder of the power that food representations can have, regardless of its author's intentions:

> Very nice people have told me, for a long time now, that some things they have read of mine, in books or magazines, have made them drool...They are grateful to me, perhaps, for being reminded that they are still functioning, still aware of some of their hungers. I too should be grateful, and even humble, that I have reminded people of what fun it is, vicariously or not, to eat/live. Instead I am revolted. I see a slavering slobbering maw. It dribbles helplessly, in a Pavlovian response. It drools...I feel grateful but repelled. They are nice people, and I like them and I like dogs, but dogs must drool when they are excited by the prospect of the satisfaction of alerted tastebuds, and two-legged people do not need to.[34]

FOOD AS SPECTACLE: EXTREME EATING, FOODSCAPES, AND MOLECULAR GASTRONOMY

Cinema is one of the great developments of the modern era, and has also provided another platform for dramatizing food, with such classics from around the world as *La Grande Bouffe* (France 1973), *Tampopo* (Japan 1985), *Babette's Feast* (Denmark 1987), *Eat Drink Man Woman* (Taiwan 1994), and *Big Night* (The United States 1996). Food on the big screen is extra-ordinary because it is spectacular, yet it is also ordinary in that it (usually) appeals to our natural hungers, both literal and metaphorical.

If, by contrast, there is one food circumstance which patently has no rela-
tion to biological hunger—nor, conceivably, to stimulating hunger—it is
the spectacle of competitive eating. While public gluttony is nothing new,
it was not until the twentieth century that it was officialized as a specta-
tor sport, particularly with the establishment of events such as the annual
Nathan's Famous Hot Dog Eating Contest in 1916, now overseen (along
with approximately eighty other yearly events) by Major League Eating
(MLE) and the International Federation for Competitive Eaters (IFOCE).

Here food (and drink, as the story of a woman who died from water in-
toxication in 2007 while taking part in a "Hold Your Wee for a [Nintendo]
Wii" contest reminds us) is a vehicle for pushing the body beyond its natural limits. The pay-off for the winner—barring a *reversal of fortune,* as a
disqualifying regurgitation is dubbed—is a cash prize and the opportunity
to become a hero, as Joey Chestnut did when he famously took back the
Nathan's Mustard Belt from Japanese rival Takeru Kobayashi in 2007 by
eating sixty-six hotdogs in twelve minutes. "Unbelievable valor from that
man, right there, Joey Chestnut," the ESPN commentator reflected, "he may
indeed have changed the course of the nation…of our nation…Chestnut
is a true American hero. On this Independence Day, we're actually not far
from where George Washington began to fight the British."

Competitive eating has become so institutionalized that Kobayashi and
Sonya *The Black Widow* Thomas appeared in a Mastercard Paypass advertisement in 2007, where they used their Mastercards for an impromptu hotdog chow-down. Celebrating everything but the food itself, extreme eating
is a "barrel of laughs, it's a death cult, it's a protean myth, it's deeply mysterious," writes one chronicler.[35] However, in a competitive market economy
that encourages individualism, it is perhaps nothing but a logical reflection
of the tendencies to overindulgence that have flourished alongside—and
sometimes because of—messages advocating moderation throughout the
century, from the sanctioned (deep-fried) gluttony at state fairs, to thumb-
ing your nose at the proverbial food police by eating at Arizona's Heart-
Attack Grill, or anywhere else that prides itself on offering excess.

Though his was a very different agenda, Filippo Tommaso Marinetti
(1876–1944) also used food contentiously in his 1930 "Manifesto of Futurist
Cooking." Claiming that eating pasta was "an absurd gastronomic religion" that made Italians lethargic, he called for its complete abolition to

inspire bodies that would be "agile, ready for the featherweight aluminium trains which will replace the present heavy ones of wood iron steel." The creed of futurism was *antipassatista,* or against the past (for futurists, technological innovation would always trump history and tradition), so the *anti-pasta* stance served a useful linguistic polemic. However, Marinetti's program more obviously aligned itself with Mussolini's wish for an autocratic Italy, which included severing its dependence on wheat imports that were crucial to the pasta industry.[36]

While Marinetti's pasta-abolition scheme never came to fruition—nor, thankfully, his ultimate vision of replacing everyday meals with pills, rendering actual food purely aesthetic—some of his ideas are manifest in a number of later culinary representations that challenge the boundaries between food, art, and science. Two Marinetti-inspired art installations from 2009 are most directly representative. The first, as part of SFMOMA's "Metal + Machine + Manifesto = Futurism's First 100 Years" (the original "Futurist Manifesto" was published in 1909), featured a group of women chefs carving an entire (cooked) beef carcass in the midst of a crowd of onlookers—this presumably a response to Marinetti's call for more meat and the "invention of appetizing food sculptures" to replace traditional pasta-laden meals. Second was a pasta sauna at Performa 09 by so-called eating designer Marije Vogelzang, who paid ironic homage to Marinetti by creating a sauna using water from boiling pasta, "giving audience members the chance to be as lazy and un-energetic as they want." (Visitors who had also attended Performa's inaugural installation, a feast called "Creation" by Jennifer Rubell featuring two-thousand pounds of ribs, were no doubt delighted by the invitation to be lazy.)

Leaving aside for the moment food that is artfully presented on the plate, there are by now numerous examples of food-related art as social and political comment, including video-artist Martha Rosler's 1974 *The Art of Cooking,* featuring a mock-dialogue between Julia Child and restaurant critic Craig Claiborne discussing the status of food as art, complete with references to Kant's *The Critique of Judgment.*[37]

More recently, the art world has seen a proliferation of foodscapes: photographs of landscapes comprised partially or entirely of food. Wisconsin-based Nicolas Lampert's meatscapes substitute natural formations such as mountains with various forms of meat as a comment on the amount

FIGURE 9.1: The Ride to Sausage Mountain. Photo by Nicolas Lampert. Reproduced with permission.

of landscape (for grazing, food production, water sourcing) he believes is wasted in the production of meat for human consumption (see figure 9.1). British artist's Carl Warner's foodscapes, inspired by healthy-eating campaigns in the late twentieth century, are constructed entirely of foods, while Gayle Chong Kwan creates "mythical mise-en-scene landscapes, installations, and environments out of disturbing arrangements of waste, food and found materials." Playing on the saying "You are what you eat," Lauren Garfinkel's "Feast for Bush" creates a memorial menu for George W. Bush, including dishes such as terror-alert jello, potatoes Abu Ghraib, and Baba Rumsfeld. Mark Menjivar's "You are what you eat" series, by contrast, photographically documents the insides of refrigerators across the United States in the hope that people will be inspired to think deeply about how they care for themselves, for others, and for the land.

The question of food as art is a centuries-old debate, and examples of chefs specializing in artful food that arrests the eye, and presumably the tongue, include Vatel's seventeenth-century extravaganzas, and later Carême's elaborate early nineteenth-century confectionary. The 1973 "Manifesto for Nouvelle Cuisine" followed Escoffier's early twentieth-century lightening of haute cuisine by stressing simplicity and individuality, but this movement ultimately failed, according the manifesto's author Henri Gault, in part because "fashions, mannerisms and trickery attached themselves to this new culinary philosophy: miniscule portions; systematic under-cooking;...excessive homage paid to the decoration of dishes and 'painting on the plate'; and ridiculous or dishonest names of dishes."[38] Yet it was not until the rise of what is popularly, though erroneously, known as *molecular gastronomy*[39] (pioneered by chefs such as Heston Blumenthal and Ferran Adrià, whose cooking befits Marinetti's avant-garde visions of using a "battery of scientific instruments in the kitchen," and that the perfect meal should display "absolute originality in the food") at the turn of the twenty-first century that institutional reflections of food and chefs re-invigorated debates around the relationship between food, art, and science.

In 2000, for example, Adrià was ranked as an innovator in *Time*'s annual list of the 100 most influential people in the word. In 2004, he was listed under artists/entertainers. For the first time the Raymond Loewy Foundation's Lucky Strike Award in 2006 went to a chef: Adrià (previous recipients include Karl Lagerfeld and Donna Karan). He was also invited to participate in the 2007 *Documenta,* a five-yearly exhibition in Germany reputed as "one of the biggest events in the contemporary art calendar." These public recognitions clearly fuel representations of food as art–science and of the chef as artist–scientist. However, during a public conversation between Adrià, food and science writer Harold McGee, and journalist Corby Kummer held at the New York Public Library in October 2008, Adrià took the opportunity once again to debunk the notion of his cooking as molecular gastronomy, or indeed as scientific by stressing that while science is fundamental to what chefs are able to do in the kitchen, conflating the two risks trivializing the scientific endeavor: "Chefs have to cook," he explained, "and scientists have to help us to make a better world through our cooking, but not to turn...something as serious as science, into a show."[40]

These discursive deliberations tell us more about a cultural need for categorizing than they do about the food itself. From Escoffier's modernist cooking to the nouvelle cuisine of the 1970s, to the fusion food of later decades, to molecular gastronomy (re-christened *techno-emotional cuisine* by Spanish journalist Pau Arenós in 2008), what all these movements share is a culinary dynamism that reaches beyond the ordinary—which makes them all, in their time, avant-garde, or ahead of their time. Until, that is, we settle on a name for them, and they pass into history, making way for the next wave of modern.

FOOD ON NEWS STANDS, ON TELEVISION, AND IN THE NEWS

In keeping with postwar economic booms, the second half of the twentieth century has seen a massive rise in the number of foodie media (magazines, newspapers, radio, television, Internet, blogs), where food often functions as a pleasant diversion from real life, even as much food television has taken on Reality formats. On the other hand, food has been making increasingly regular appearances in the news proper, particularly in the more real context of health and safety.

Gourmet ("the magazine of good living") was launched in the United States in 1941. Unlike the reproaches of *Good Housekeeping* during

World War I that food extravagances were "little short of treasonable,"[41] *Gourmet*'s inaugural issue saw fit to publish a recipe for *pheasant à la bohémienne* ("Pluck and clean a young pheasant [unmortified], rub it with lemon juice inside and out, then salt and pepper to taste. Sew. Truss. Melt 3 tablespoons of butter or, still better, use the butter in which a fresh goose liver, larded through and through with small sticks of raw black truffle, has been poached and then cooled"). As Laura Shapiro summarizes, "there's never been a time that wasn't fitting for *Gourmet*, even when real life seemed to race in the opposite direction."[42] *Gourmet* published its last issue in 2009, but it set an enduring prototype for a market soon populated by the likes of *Bon Appétit, Saveur, Food & Wine, Cooking Light, Every Day with Rachael Ray*, and in the United Kingdom, *Delicious, Good Food, Olive, Easy Cook*, not forgetting its most recent addition, the *Jamie* [Oliver] *Magazine*. (These global trends are naturally reflected in domestic publications in other parts of the developed world, and in other languages.)

Newspapers and non-specific lifestyle (fashion, design, home, garden) magazines have also become standard channels for representing food, both digitally and in print. Major broadsheets and tabloid-style papers alike now publish regular food features, if not dedicated dining sections incorporating restaurant reviews, recipes, and answers to readers' queries. In a 1957 essay, French cultural critic Roland Barthes characterized the recipes in *Elle* magazine as "ornamental" or "idea" cookery, by which the photographic representation of food—typically glazed or coated as per the vogue then—created "objects at once near and inaccessible, whose consumption can perfectly well be accomplished simply by looking."[43] While many contemporary food media do address pragmatic issues, particularly with the increasingly interactive nature of digital media such as blogs and websites, Barthes' stress on visual, or vicarious, consumption remains fundamental to the modern food-media industry, if for no other reason than that the copious amount of available information about food and what to do with it far outweighs the possibility of putting all that information to practical use.

Instead, new media allow us to spend more time watching what other people do with food (and for some of us, to publish our own stories on blogs), and if we like what we see, we can join the narrative by commenting online, sharing (tweeting, digging), or as de Certeau would have it, interminably citing and re-citing the representations available to us. The story of

Julie & Julia, which began its life as a blog telling stories about a cookbook, before becoming a blook (a book based on a blog) and finally a motion picture, is instructive of a popular appetite for consuming other people's food stories, as is the trend of photographing meals and publishing the pictures online (even if they are meant to scare people, as at the self-explanatory "This Is Why You're Fat" website—also now available as a book).

However, for most of the twentieth century, television was the great innovation when it came to representing food, and in some respects it still is as new styles of programming reflect cultural shifts in how we see food. Although channels dedicated entirely to food are relatively recent, food television as a genre grew concurrently with the medium itself: in the United Kingdom, viewers could watch cooking demonstrations as early as 1936, the year of the first British television broadcast.[44] Television did begin to rival radio as a primary source of information and entertainment in those early years, but it was not until after World War II that the industry took flight. Like so many new products on the market, television provided convenience—not having to leave the home—while new food products such as TV dinners provided the convenience of not having to spend more than a few minutes away from the screen (thanks to that other new convenience, the microwave).

So what is food television? In the twenty-first century food television, like food literature, appears to be anything that involves food, including travelogues (*Planet Food*), professional competitions (*Iron Chef, Hell's Kitchen*), amateur competitions (*Come Dine With Me*), nutritional interventions (*You Are What You Eat, Supersize vs. Superskinny*), and social campaigning (*Jamie's Food Revolution USA*). Unlike the instructional premise of many early food shows (entertaining as Julia Child or Keith Floyd may have been, they were there to teach their viewers), a significant portion of today's food television has dispensed with the cook-and-stir approach. Instead of being directly addressed through the screen, modern viewers are more frequently privy to watching *others* interact around food on television, and that interaction increasingly pivots around a poor relationship with food (or a thriving relationship with poor food), be it an inability to cook, to follow a diet, to eat according to that highly elastic term: health. The appeal of these shows can best be described as *schadenfreude,* or as Krishnendu Ray put it while questioning the pornographic labeling of much current food TV, the "real problem may be with seeing and watching something that used to be intimate."[45]

Exposure to something that used to be private does not have to be a problem. It can be the source of aesthetic pleasure, such as reading someone's memoirs, or even educational, such as watching someone on TV managing preparations for a dinner party. However, when it comes to food, the increasingly ambiguous line between public and private, which is a feature of modern media generally, also ties in strongly with prevailing off-screen representations of some foods as toxic, unsafe, and unhealthy. When food is in the news in any of these contexts—often now in the broader context of obesity—discourses typically revolve around controversial issues of risk and responsibility, or who (is) to blame. Government? Industry (manufacturers and purveyors of junk food)? The consumer? Tied to the question of blame is the one of whose responsibility it is to fix the perceived problem. Should public institutions such as government agencies intervene in people's private lives by telling them what they can and cannot eat (as they have been doing for well over a century already)? Should they interfere with industry by forcing restaurants to post calorie listings on their menus in an effort to discourage overconsumption? Ban non-nutritious food in schools? Ban homemade cupcakes at school bake sales because they have no nutritional labeling? Or is it up to the individual to take responsibility for themselves and for their families? These questions, unanswerable in a way that satisfies all parties, belong to the dietary cacophony, and contribute to perpetuating apprehensions around how and what to eat.

Throughout the century people have had good reason to harbor insecurities about food, thanks to societal transformations (loss of servants through urbanization, wars) and the introduction of unfamiliar products, whether rationed or convenience foods. This is where food personalities have played an important moderating role, as Marguerite Patten did, for example, by teaching British people to cook with rationed ingredients during World War II. Although not the first cook on British television (she featured on the BBC's inaugural magazine show, *Designed for Women*, on screens from 1947 till the early 1960s), Patten is cited by some as the original celebrity chef for the widespread impact she had. She would be followed by many throughout the decades, including Julia Child, Graham Kerr, Keith Floyd, Delia Smith, Emeril Lagasse, Mario Batali, Rachael Ray, and Jamie Oliver. While they each have different approaches to food, what these personalities share is what accounts for their respective successes: public recognition as authorities on food. Not public authorities such as government agencies, but private people who are comfortable with food, and who endeavor to make their viewing publics equally comfortable with food. Celebrity chefs are the representatives of food that is safe, fun, and easy—and some of their achievements include Emmy Awards (Julia Child, Rachael Ray), being recognized by *Time* 100 (Mario Batali, Rachael Ray), and inspiring national cranberry shortages, as Delia Smith famously did with one of the recipes from her 1995 *Winter Collection*.[46]

For his part in trying to improve school nutrition, Jamie Oliver received the prestigious TED (Technology, Entertainment, Design) Prize in 2010—also the first time it was awarded to a chef. Apart from the opportunity to address some of the world's movers and shakers, the award comprises $100,000 to be spent on realizing Oliver's stated wish to "create a strong, sustainable movement to educate every child about food, inspire families to cook again and empower people everywhere to fight obesity." It is an ambitious task and Jamie Oliver is patently not the first to have such a wish. Nor, can we conclude, is the lack of the situation he wishes for due to a lack of available information about food. Indeed, if the history of food representations and of the effect of those representations in the modern era is anything to go by, the outlook is bleak. As Bill Buford concluded after watching seventy-two hours of continuous food programming in 2006, "Never in our history as a species have we been so ignorant about our food."[47] These comments re-cite German critic Siegfried Kracauer's views in an essay not on food, but on photography: "Never before has an age been so informed about itself, *if being informed means having an image of objects that resembles them in a photographic sense*...Never before has a period known so little about itself. In the hands of the ruling society, the invention of illustrated magazines is one of the most powerful means of *organizing a strike against understanding*" (my emphases).[48] Those words were written in 1927.

FOOD IN THE FUTURE

There have been stories about food (or lack thereof) in the future for centuries, notably the Malthusian prediction of population growth outstripping food supply.[49] The modern era's imaginings have included futuristic visions of replacing food with pills (perhaps made of human corpses, as the 1973 film *Soylent Green* portrays it), utopian hankerings for a return to a pre-modern past,[50] and more recently, titles such as *The End of Food* (2008), in which author Paul Roberts warns against the "coming crisis in the world food industry."

The history of (unfulfilled) predictions should make us wary of making predictions, except for one: people will continue to tell stories about—and through—food, because it is a natural conduit for thinking about and nego-tiating life. Without food, there is no life—which means we can confidently expect future representations of food in all its guises: as pure sustenance, as comforting nourishment, as ideology (organic, sustainable, ethical, local), as good, bad, indulgent, junk, and functional.

Sometimes the futuristic steps into the present, as at the Moto restau-rant in Chicago, where diners could be expected to consume the (edible) menu after ordering from it, and after dinner, to eat the fortune inside the cookie. Or at London's Inamo, where an interactive touch pad on the table allows patrons to order at the click of a finger, and to pick a table cloth of their choice. Transgenically modified foods are controversial because they challenge the distinctions between natural and synthetic foods. Still, whether it is a steak grown in a lab, a piece of edible paper, or a meal of cin-namon chicken ordered through a table, if it is fit for human consumption, then it is simply food—though perhaps worthy of a more interesting story.

CHAPTER TEN

World Developments

FABIO PARASECOLI

The previous chapters in this volume have illustrated various aspects of food culture from the 1920s to the new millennium. This chapter does not claim to offer new insights based on original material, but it is rather an overview of developments, dynamics, products, food-related behaviors, social structures, and concepts in cultural environments that often found themselves at the margins of Western modernity, but that a growing attention on issues such as post-colonialism, development, and globalization has brought to the forefront not only of scholarly research, but also of public debates in civil society. This chapter will focus on the expansion of imperialism, World War II, the process of postwar reconstruction and decolonization, the complex dynamics of economic growth and its connections with globalization, as well as some contemporary trends.

IMPERIALISM AND WAR

During the nineteenth century, improved communication and transportation technologies, the increased demand for commercial crops following the explosion of consumer markets, fast-paced urbanization, and the industrialization of food production in most Western European countries, the United States, and Japan, as well as the intensification of international trade, provided the basis for the complex system of cultural, political, and economic relationships that constituted imperialism. From the beginning of the twentieth century, the growth of industrialized nation-states, the mounting requirements for the raw materials necessary to their productive systems, and the need for markets to export their added-value goods led Western powers to expand their direct control, often through military occupation, many areas of the globe. A world system structured around unequal economic and political interactions between core and peripheral areas reached its zenith. For instance, foreign farmers largely controlled the most lucrative cash crops in African territories, such as coffee in Cameroun or tea in Kenya, while bureaucracy and colonial policies often prevented local peasants from participating in the profits.[1] The same exclusionary dynamics that favored foreign investors were common also in other food sectors, such as fishing in Malawi.[2] Elsewhere, such as in the rice areas of Burma, Thailand, and the Mekong Delta, local smallholders took advantage of the irrigation, transportation, and trade infrastructures put into place by the foreign powers, thus producing enough crops to feed workers in other colonial enterprises in South East Asia, including mines and rubber plantations.[3]

After the global economic and financial slump triggered by the Great Depression, colonies had to deal with what seemed to be a structural oversupply of cash crops, which caused international prices and farmers' incomes to decrease.[4] In the African territories where exports of commercial crops such as coffee, cocoa, or tea were the main sources of revenue, public governmental agencies were established to serve as sole buyers of the commodities, entitled to fix domestic prices and to negotiate on the international markets.[5] In other areas, the colonial authorities pushed for the diffusion of crops such as maize, which could ensure food security for the local population while guaranteeing large-scale yields to the advantage of the colonial powers, especially in the period immediately before World War II.[6]

The extraction of raw material and food resources, rice above all, was particularly harsh within Japan's Asian empire. With the declared goal of liberating Asia from European colonialism, Japan occupied territories once held by the French, the British, and the Dutch, at times installing native leaders as part of puppet governments. By 1940, Japan's Greater East Asia Co-Prosperity Sphere included parts of China, Taiwan, Korea, and during the war it would extend its influence over much of South East Asia and the islands of the Pacific. While the exploitation was often ruthless and destroyed pre-existing social and productive structures, Japan's presence introduced elements of modernization in terms of agricultural techniques and infrastructures, which nevertheless suffered greatly during the war.

However, at the same time, Japan's neighbors were exerting a certain influence on its cuisine, despite the nationalistic tones often used to praise domestic customs. From the 1920s, Chinese cuisine became popular in Japan as military and civilian personnel stationed in the colonies wanted to experience the flavors they had got familiar with abroad once they got back to Japan. Chinese specialties, such as *gyoza* and noodles, were also introduced into military menus: since they contained meat and fat, they were suited to the wartime diet, as rice became increasingly harder to find. However, charged with cultural and social values, rice constituted an important, if small, part of war rations, spreading also among portions of the populations that were more used to less-refined grains such as barley. Other foods, such as bread, noodles, and items produced for the military such as ship biscuits, curry powder, tinned food, and cooking oils, became common, reducing the differences between rural and urban diets. Due to war scarcity, the Japanese even appreciated tripe and offal sold at Korean food stalls; after the war, these lesser meats were replaced with beef, evolving into the grilled dishes known as *yakiniku*. Women were also involved in the war effort, ensuring social reproduction thanks to their abilities to reconcile nutrition, hygiene, and economy.[7]

World War II was a period of food scarcity and hardship in many areas of Africa, Asia, and Latin America. The first years of war brought requisitions of cash crops by the colonial powers, together with difficulties in transportation and distribution that caused shortages of imported goods, both essential and luxury items, leading to rationing in urban areas. The consequences of the conflict were less evident in areas that had traditionally practiced subsistence agriculture and local barter.[8]

POSTWAR RECONSTRUCTION

The years following the end of the war witnessed a worldwide effort to jumpstart reconstruction and development, together with calls for political self-determination that eventually gave way to dynamics of decolonization, as former territories that were part of global empires acquired independence, at times through traumatic transactions. However, many countries, especially in Africa, felt that the former colonial powers still controlled them through indirect political means and economic dependency, exploiting them under a new set of relationships that came to be known as *neocolonialism*. This situation prompted some countries to tighten their ties with the communist block, while others formed the Non-Aligned Movement, meant to establish a third, independent force on the geopolitical scene. Food security became one of the priorities for the leaderships of the young nation states, which considered it as a fundamental source of political legitimacy. For instance, Ethiopian leader Haile Selassie used it to strengthen his internal and international position, providing food for the Middle Eastern markets and receiving, for this reason, the praise of the American President Roosevelt.[9] National elites found themselves at the helm of new countries in need of urgent economic development, where agriculture played a paramount role. The responses varied. In many new African states, governments took control of the national marketing boards to extract revenue from the rural sectors and invest it into more so-called modern activities, especially industries and manufacturing, with the goal of producing substitutes for high-added-value imports to increase self-reliance.[10]

The debates about development and neocolonialism took place while the Soviet Union and China adopted radical politics of agricultural collectivization, which offered alternative models for growth and social change. Between 1928 and 1940, Stalin pursued a rural policy aimed at establishing collective (*kolkhoz*) and state (*sovkhoz*) farms to increase production of export crops, raw materials, and reliable food supplies for the industrial (and mostly urban) sectors of the country. The human and cultural impact of these policies is hard to gauge, but it is now widely accepted that they took a huge toll on large sections of the rural population. Fertile Ukraine, for instance, was struck by a tremendous famine in 1932–1933, which affected millions of people. Private plots, which were completely banned only at the height of collectivization, ensured the survival of the population in rural areas, with production of meat, milk, eggs, and vegetables also allowing the continuation of local food customs. With their traditional social structures threatened and their standards of life worsening, farmers often opposed collectivization, resorting to sabotage, strikes, and destruction of property.[11] These acts of resistance caused innumerable arrests, confinements in labor-camps, and executions. Farmers were tied to the land, which has led many to consider their condition as a new kind of serfdom. However, collectivization allowed the introduction of large-scale economies, mechanization, and modern techniques of fertilization. Despite the generalized low level of efficiency in the agricultural sector, the Soviet Union became one of the biggest exporters of wheat, potatoes, and sugar beets.[12] At the same time, the government experimented with the production of luxury items such as caviar, champagne, chocolate, and liquor, with the goal of laying the foundations for a socialist consumer culture.[13] A few restaurants thrived in large cities like Moscow and Leningrad, highlighting and maintaining Russian food traditions. However, if in principle these places were open to everybody, only the highest echelons of the party and their circles had actual access to them.

While the Soviet Union gave priority to the growth of its industrial and more modern sectors, China embraced a different model of development that took into account the reality of its immense rural population and its limited industrial structure. Right after taking power in 1949, the communist party led by Mao Zedong launched a major reform, aimed at redistributing land ownership among the whole population while creating a system of mutual aid in terms of labor and tools. In 1954, the first cooperatives were introduced, based on permanent sharing of agricultural inputs, which constituted the first step towards full collectivization. Between 1958 and 1960, with the set of policies known as the Great Leap Forward, the government created the people's communes, which marked the end of private land property. To increase efficiency in food consumption, farmers were often required to stop cooking in their homes and eat in collective canteens. This move delivered a heavy blow to rural food traditions that were hard to maintain except on special occasions. When in 1955 bad harvests were made worse by the request of the party to use all available metal in order to increase industrial production, agriculture faced enormous difficulties, leading to a famine that peaked in 1961 and whose victims are incalculable (to this day, the party officially defines this period as "three years of natural disasters"). Despite the hordes of young students sent to the countryside to share the life of the peasants, the rural sector was not affected by the

Cultural Revolution as much as the urban and industrial structures.[14] In the late 1970s, Deng Xiaoping introduced a series of reforms that allowed farmers to grow crops to sell on the free market, albeit after meeting the quota assigned by the central planning authorities. In the 1980s, agriculture turned into the engine of economic development in China, only to be later supplanted by the fast growth of industries, especially in the coastal areas.[15]

During the Cold War, some countries became disputed territories, with heavy consequences on productive structures and on cultural attitudes toward food. Korea and later Vietnam probably constitute the best examples of these dynamics. In Korea, land reforms redistributed revenue among the population, often at the expense of the landlords that had collaborated with the Japanese. However, following the Korean War, in the South the reforms led to agricultural modernization and to the participation in global markets, while in the North they gave way to collectivization under Kim Il Sung. Culturally, while maintaining appreciation for its traditions and its Asian roots, as the popularity of *naengmyen* cold noodles (originally a Northern dish), *kimchi,* and the traditional soybean and red-chili pastes show, the South embraced a globalized diet where fast, if not instant food now plays an important role. Furthermore, Korea has shown a clear shift from a rice-based diet to growing consumption of meat—a phenomenon that has been observed in many developing countries all over the world. *Bulgogi* (barbecue beef) and *kalbi* (beef ribs) are no longer reserved for special occasions.[16]

AGRICULTURAL CHANGES

Other countries, especially in Asia, embraced what became known as the Green Revolution. The term was coined in 1968 by William Gaud, director of the U.S. Agency for International Development, to indicate a set of measures aimed at increasing agricultural yields to eliminate hunger, by using new crop varieties, fertilizers, pesticides, irrigation, and mechanization. The efforts behind these policies, funded by developing countries, together with the Rockefeller Foundation and the Ford Foundation, started with the introduction of new wheat varieties in Mexico right after the war, which turned the country into a wheat exporter in twenty years.

The new agricultural techniques were soon adopted by many South East Asian countries and India, which implemented ambitious measures including the exploitation of ground water resources, the introduction of new land management techniques, and electrification to ensure food security for its booming population.[17]

Attempts at introducing the Green Revolution in Africa were less successful, due to factors including corruption, lack of infrastructure, and environmental features, such as water scarcity and soil fragility. As a matter of fact, desertification in the Sahel area of Sub-Saharan Africa caused famines of immense impact. The Green Revolution, hailed by many as a success, particularly in terms of yields, often proved to be non-sustainable in the long term, causing loss of biodiversity, scarcity of water, environmental problems due to chemicals, soil impoverishment, and dominant positions guaranteed to the producers of seeds and other inputs.[18]

In the 1980s, following the end of the Cold War and the global wave of neoliberal policies, many developing countries adopted various measures toward the opening of agricultural markets, such as the privatization of public enterprises, marking the end of government agencies being in charge of crop exports, trade and internal deregulation, and international negotiations aimed at reducing, and eventually eliminating, protectionism, subsidies, and tariffs.[19]

In many areas of the world, both in rural and urban environments, large portions of the population still experience crises in food security and, at times, famine, due to problems requiring long-term interventions on issues such as climate change, political instability, structural socioeconomic processes, lack of investment, and environmental disasters.[20] At times, the reasons behind famine are also political: in the case of North Korea, for instance, the limited arable land, the breakdown of the mechanized agricultural system subsidized by the Soviet Union, and the ideologically motivated embrace of self-sufficiency has generated a situation of chronic food shortage that the regime has so far refused to acknowledge, and that its tentative reforms have only made worse.[21]

Production, distribution, and consumption of food have been changing due to economic and social factors, such as rapid rates of urbanization, migrations—both domestic and international—the growing presence of women in the workforce, increasing inequalities, and the overall transformation of food systems.[22] A relevant trend is the growing portion of food that is processed, preserved, and industrially mass-produced by transnational corporations using raw materials, ingredients, and labor from a varied provenance and in diverse locations. Durable, cheap, mostly safe, and dense in calories (although frequently not the best kind), this food is advertised, marketed, and distributed everywhere, from the most remote rural communities in developing countries to the hypermarkets of the richest countries. These epochal transformations go together with the diffusion of technological innovations such as canning, freezing, and the improvement of storage and worldwide transportation. While these processed foods are often indicated as one of the main causes of the obesity epidemics that have struck large groups of the poorest in industrialized and developing countries, it cannot be denied that they play an important role in freeing relevant portions of human kind from worries about conservation, affordability, and availability.[23]

CURRENT TRENDS

These changes in food systems are part of a larger phenomenon often referred to as globalization, usually indicating the increasingly (and apparently) unfettered mobility of ideas, information, goods, money, and people from one corner of the globe to the next. The demands of food corporations, which often invest directly in developing countries, play an enormous role in determining the agricultural choices as well as the planting, picking, and packing techniques adopted by rural communities worldwide, while determining what foods will be available and promoted all over the globe.[24] Food, as a commodity, has become the object of international trade negotiations, especially after the establishment of the World Trade Organization in 1994.

However, globalization does not merely relate to the circulation of mass-produced food or the popularity of fast food all over the world.[25] It also refers to the diffusion of cuisines from one country to another, especially in urban environments where immigrant communities are more numerous. Ethnic restaurants have become a fixture in urban landscapes all over the world, with Italian, French, Japanese, Chinese, Indian, and Mexican at the forefront, and with Thai, Ethiopian, Moroccan, and Lebanese following right behind, each of them occupying various segments of the food scene in terms of prestige and price.[26]

The rekindled interest in wine and food, and especially in culinary traditions, local products, and artisanal delicacies, which is reaching new heights in Western Europe and in the United States, also constitutes an important trend in Japan, where urban dwellers order rural foods by mail or over the Internet, and where *furusato* (hometown) products are very popular travel souvenirs.[27] In developing countries, until a few years ago, traditional ingredients and dishes would have been considered embarrassing and uncouth, being uncomfortably close to the rural realities and the ethnic groups that had often been at the margin of national projects. Growing numbers of consumers are learning to appreciate the role of local communities and their traditions, the manual skills and the know-how of food producers, and their ties with historically determined material cultures and specific places. Urban China dwellers, especially in Hong Kong and other coastal areas, display a nostalgic interest toward the rustic food of the countryside and ethnic-minority traditions.[28] Other countries are moving in the same direction, such as Brazil, Mexico, and even Costa Rica, where limited but growing upper classes with disposable incomes have recently shown shifting sensitivity about the cultural relevance of food traditions.[29]

Traditional foodways, however, are not excluded from the dynamics of globalization that involve many aspects of material culture. While the international exposure can bring new life to, or even save a disappearing ingredient or dish, the participation in the global flows of people, money, goods, and information can also bring disruption and tensions. For instance, it is increasingly harder for non-sedentary populations to maintain their food customs. Pastoralists such as the Maasai of Kenya see the territories related to their traditional productions shrinking due to the expansion of farming, urban growth, and even the presence of natural parks.[30] In Inner Mongolia, collectivization, initially during the Maoist era and more recently with the privatization of lands, has worsened the pastoralists' life standards, reduced their mobility, and has damaged the pastures; similar dynamics are taking place in other areas of Central Asia.[31]

While traditional lifestyles and foodways are disappearing, the populations of post-colonial countries are showing a growing interest in food and cooking as constitutive elements of their national identities—often used to overcome class and regional tensions.[32] National governments in Africa and the Caribbean, increasingly aware of the relevance of food for their tourist industry, are trying to create a marketable national cuisine almost by bureaucratic decree.[33] This approach is just one aspect of the often ambivalent approach of developing countries toward tourism: on one hand it has the potential to ensure jobs and to valorize local culinary traditions, and on the other hand it can succumb to commercial interests, with the result that in many resorts it is almost impossible to find local food, while ingredients, as well as staff, are brought from abroad to satisfy international patrons.[34] Furthermore, local staff frequently leave their communities of origin for long periods, bringing back unfamiliar food-related values, and customs that can cause tensions and instability.[35]

NOTES

Introduction

1. Yeats 2010.
2. Marchand 1985; Ewen 1976; Lears 1994.
3. Curtis 1957.
4. Freiberg 2009.
5. Bentley 1988, 143–44. Portions of this section are taken from chapter 5 of *Eating for Victory.*
6. These numbers are not the actual amount people consumed, but the number in the food supply available for consumption. Because of inevitable wastage in processing and transporting food, it is assumed that the numbers actually consumed are fewer.
7. Bentley 1988, 144–45.
8. Quoted in Bentley 1988, 168.
9. Bentley 1988, 169.
10. Bentley 1988, 168.
11. Later CARE packages became more culturally diverse and eventually the packages were discontinued in favor of agricultural surpluses, and non-food items such as carpentry tools, medicines, and blankets.
12. Bentley 1988, 170.
13. Mustard 2003, 42.
14. *New York Times* 1956.
15. *New York Times* 1953.
16. Lancaster 1956.
17. Wehrwein 1959.
18. Gold 1957.

19. Smith 1957.
20. *Christian Science Monitor* 1957.
21. Love 1986.
22. Watson 2006.
23. Peters 1922.
24. Guthman 2004.
25. Belasco 2006a.
26. Otter 2010, 1.
27. Otter 2010, 2.
28. Patel 2008, 315.
29. Roberts 2008, 232.
30. Flammang 2010.
31. Lears 1981.
32. Pollan 2006.
33. Guthman 2007; Flanagan 2010.

Chapter 1

1. Belasco 2006a.
2. Belasco and Horowitz 2009.
3. Smil 2001.
4. Fitzgerald 2003.
5. Medvedev 1987; Pilcher 2006.
6. Worster 1979.
7. Hewitt de Alcántara 1976.
8. Olmstead and Rhode 2008.
9. Charles 2001.
10. Anderson 2008.
11. Weir and Shapiro 1981.
12. Cotter 2003.
13. Bayliss-Smith and Wanmali 1984; Gupta 1998.
14. Raikes 1988; Perkins 1997.
15. Bonnano 1994; Rothenberg 2000; Henke 2008; Petrick n.d.
16. Goldfrank 1994.
17. McNeill 2001.
18. Crutchfield 1991.
19. Wilson 1999; Valenzuela-Zapata and Nabham 2003.
20. Belasco [1989] 2006b; Guthman 2004.
21. Guthman 2004; Fromartz 2006.
22. Giedion 1948.
23. Pilcher 2004.
24. Barrett 1987; Halperin 1997; Horowitz 1997.

25. Horowitz 2006.
26. MacLachlan 2001; DuPuis 2002; Stull and Broadway 2004; Warren 2007.
27. Watts 2004; Horowitz 2006.
28. Stull and Broadway 2004.
29. Sanderson 1986; Perren 2006.
30. Manchester 1992; Fischler 1999; Perren 2006.
31. Josephson 2002.
32. Bonnano and Constance 1996.
33. Myers and Worm 2003.
34. Stickney 1996.
35. Taylor 1999.
36. *The Economist* 2009.
37. Winston 2002; Annear 2004
38. Winston 2002; Paarlberg 2005.
39. Doyle 1985; Altieri 2001; McAfee 2003; Neuman and Pollack 2010.
40. Warren 1997; Jacoby 2001.
41. La Pradelle 2006.
42. Gilbert 1996.
43. Horowitz 2006; Freidberg 2009.
44. Levenstein [1993] 2003; Josephson 2002, Hamilton 2003.
45. Stull and Broadway 2004; Horowitz 2006.

Chapter 2

1. Roberts 2008, 11.
2. Feenstra 2002, 100.
3. See, for example, Ross 1925.
4. See for example, Duddy 1929.
5. See for example, Durand 1967, 1964, and 1940.
6. Friedland et al. 1981.
7. Friedland 1984.
8. Buttel and Goodman 1989, 87–88.
9. Jarosz 2000; FitzSimmons 1986.
10. Freidberg 2004
11. Duval-Diop and Grimes 2005.
12. Blay-Palmer and Donald 2006; Fine and Leopold 2002, and Fine et al. 1996.
13. Block, Chavez, and Birgen 2008; Stevenson and Pirog 2008.
14. Peterson 2002.
15. Kaplinsky 2004, 80.
16. Friedmann 1993, 30.
17. Burch and Lawrence 2009.

18. Friedmann and McMichael 1989.
19. Burch and Lawrence 2009; Pritchard 1998; Le Heron and Roche 1996; Le Heron 1993.
20. Page 1996; Goodman and Watts 1994.
21. Campbell and Dixon 2009; McMichael 2009.
22. Pothukuchi and Kaufman 2000, 118.
23. Glanz 2009; Diez Roux 2001.
24. Block 2009; Duffy 1990.
25. Donofrio 2007.
26. USDA 1959.
27. Dixon 2009.
28. Dixon 2009, 325.
29. Levenstein 1988.
30. Block 2009.
31. Block 2009.
32. USDA 1959.
33. Cochrane 1979, 205.
34. Block 2004.
35. Cochrane [1979] 1993.
36. Paarlberg 1980, 22.
37. Block 2009; Paarlberg 1980.
38. U.S. Census Bureau 1933, 528, 637.
39. National Commission on Food Marketing [1966] 1976, 70–72.
40. Marion 1986, 296.
41. Friedmann 1982.
42. Friedmann 1982, S249.
43. Friedmann 1982.
44. Dickens and Moore 1981, 15.
45. Friedmann 1982, S262.
46. McMichael 1994.
47. Davis 1959, 684.
48. Davis 1959, 685.
49. Friedmann 1982, S264.
50. Friedmann 1982, S266.
51. Kasaba and Tabak 1995.
52. McMichael 1994, 2.
53. Schlosser 2001; Friedmann 1982.
54. Friedmann 1982, S271.
55. Clapp 2009, 131.
56. McMichael and Kim 1994, 24.
57. Raynolds 1997.
58. Burch and Lawrence 2009; Le Heron and Roche 1996.
59. Burch and Lawrence 2009, 268.
60. Konefal, Mascarenhas, and Hatanaka 2005.

61. Fuchs, Kalfagianni, and Arentsen 2009.
62. Deusche 2006; Seth and Randall 2005.
63. Food Marketing Institute 2009.
64. Food Marketing Institute 2009.
65. Block, Chavez, and Birgen 2008.
66. Fuchs, Kalfagianni, and Arentsen 2009.
67. Guptill and Wilkins 2002.
68. Friedland 1994.
69. Guptill and Wilkins 2002.
70. Mansfield 2003, 6.
71. McMichael 2009; Schwartz and Lyson 2007.
72. Schwartz and Lyson 2007.
73. Friedberg 2004.
74. Friedberg 2004, 113–114.
75. Fuchs, Kalfagianna, and Arentsen 2009, 46.
76. Guptill and Wilkins 2002, 48.
77. Burch and Lawrence 2009.
78. McMichael 2009.
79. McMichael 2009; Holt-Giménez 2008.
80. Black and Mackinko 2008.
81. Moore and Diez Roux 2006.
82. Raja, Changxing, and Yadav 2008.
83. Morland and Filomena 2007.
84. Block and Kouba 2006.
85. Bustillos et al. 2009.
86. For a similar discussion, see Block 2010.
87. eFoodAlert.com 2010.
88. Pepitone 2009.
89. Pepitone 2009.
90. Blay-Palmer and Donald 2006; Guthman 2004.

Chapter 3

1. Vaughan 1987, 1.
2. Devereux 2000.
3. Devereux 2009a.
4. Nestle 1999.
5. Webster 1982; Oddy 2003.
6. Mayhew 1988, 452.
7. Kingsford 1982.
8. Nord, Andrews, and Carlson 2008.
9. Whitbeck, Chan and Johnson 2006; Li, Dachner, and Tarasuk 2009; Tarasuk et al. 2009.

10. Weiser et al. 2009.
11. Amistani and Terrolle 2008.
12. Booth 2006.
13. Cummins and Macintyre 2006.
14. Smith and Cummins 2009.
15. Macrae and Zwi 1994.
16. Holmes 2003.
17. Guidonet 2008.
18. Guidonet 2009.
19. Nussbaumer and Exenberger 2009, 23.
20. League of Nations 1946.
21. Milward 1977.
22. Oddy, Atkins, and Amilien 2009.
23. Trienekens 2000.
24. Horowitz 1997.
25. Sloan 1958.
26. Hionidou 2006.
27. Milward 1977.
28. Nissen 2006.
29. Mouré and Schwartz 2007.
30. Bueltzingsloewen 2005, 2007.
31. Oddy 2003.
32. Dwork 1987.
33. Schmidt 2007, 69.
34. Steege 2007.
35. Zweiniger-Bargielowska 2000.
36. Roodhouse 2006.
37. Messer and Cohen 2006.
38. FAO 2000; Teodosijevi 2003.
39. Scanlan and Jenkins 2001.
40. Vernon 2007.
41. Mahood and Satzewich 2009.
42. Vernon 2007, 35.
43. Buerk 2004, 1.
44. Campbell 2007, 361.
45. Moeller 1999.
46. Kraus 2004.
47. Mallory 1926.
48. Li 2007.
49. Becker 1996.
50. Thaxton 2008.
51. Chang 1991.
52. Sen 1981.

53. Devereux 2009b.
54. Atkins 2009.
55. Banik 2007.
56. Devereux 2009b, 71.
57. Watts 1983.
58. Tauger 2001.
59. Perks 1993; Merridale 2000.
60. de Waal 2005, 7–8.
61. Marcus 2003.
62. Keen 1994.
63. Edkins 2009; de Waal 1997.
64. Nally 2008.
65. Rimmer 1981.
66. Aiken and Lafollette 1995; Chatterjee 2004; Cohen and Brown 2008.
67. Atkins 2010.
68. Stanziani 2003.
69. Trentmann 2006.
70. Atkins 2008.
71. Beck 1992.
72. Caldwell 2004; Holtzman 2006.
73. Misselhorn 2005; McLaughlin and Dietz 2008.
74. Devereux 2009c.
75. Macrae and Zwi 1994.
76. de Waal 2009.
77. Gazdar 2007.

Chapter 4

1. Dahl 1961; Frieden and Lake 2000, 1.
2. Scott 1990.
3. Kiple and Ornelas 2000.
4. Hutt and Hutt 1984.
5. Nestle [2002] 2010.
6. Salin and Hooker 2001.
7. Roe 2004; Roberts 2007.
8. Eisner 2000.
9. Food and Drug Administration 2007.
10. Food and Drug Administration 2009.
11. Becker 2009.
12. Nestle 2008.
13. Ingelfinger 2008.
14. GAO 2005.

15. Thompson 2007.
16. Kass 1997.
17. Thompson 2007.
18. Nestle [2002] 2010.
19. Miller 1997.
20. Shiva 2005.
21. Bernauer 2003, 165.
22. Ioffe, Nefedova, and Zastavsky 2006.
23. Ioffe, Nefedova, and Zastavsky 2006, 10.
24. Davies and Wheatcroft 2004.
25. Riasanovsky 1993, 496–97.
26. Riasanovsky 1993, 496.
27. Davies and Wheatcroft 2004.
28. Davies and Wheatcroft 2004, 412.
29. Lin 1996.
30. Aston et al. 1984.
31. Dimitri, Effland, and Conklin 2005.
32. Skocpol and Finegold 1982.
33. Hurt 2002, 94–95.
34. Hurt 2002, 99.
35. Cochrane [1979] 1993.
36. Lowi 1979.
37. Garzon 2006.
38. Wilson and Wilson 2001, 38–39.
39. Wilson and Wilson 2001, 38–39.
40. Ackrill 2000.
41. Garzon 2006, 21–23.
42. Mahant 2004.
43. Ackrill 2000; Ludlow 2005.
44. Ackrill 2000.
45. Patel 2008.
46. Friedmann 1982.
47. Helfand 1999; Patel 2008.
48. Friedmann 1982.
49. Friedmann 1982.
50. Nestle [2002] 2007.
51. Nestle 2000.
52. United States Department of Agriculture and U.S. Department of Health and Human Services 2005.
53. Cannon 1992.
54. WHO Regional Office for Europe 2003.
55. FAO n.d.
56. World Health Organization 2003.
57. World Health Organization 2004.

58. Steigher 2007.
59. Kahn 2003.
60. Waxman 2002.
61. United States Department of Agriculture 2010.
62. United States Department of Agriculture and United States Department of Health and Human Services 2010.
63. Young 1989.
64. White House Conference on Food, Nutrition, and Health 1969.
65. Levy and Stokes 1987.
66. Kellogg Company 1985.
67. Brandt, Moss, and Ellwood 2010.
68. Consumer Reports 2010.
69. Institute of Medicine 2010.
70. Clapp 2010.
71. Thompson 1992.
72. World Trade Organization 1994.
73. General Agreement on Tariffs and Trade 1947.
74. Anderson 2001.
75. Finger and Schuknecht 2001.
76. Putnam 1988.
77. Elbehri, Umstaetter, and Kelch 2008.
78. World Trade Organization 2005.
79. Elbehri, Umstaetter, and Kelch 2008, 17.
80. Avery 1993.
81. General Agreement on Tariffs and Trade 1994b.
82. United Nations 2010.
83. Johnson and Hanrahan 2009.
84. Cho 2009.

Chapter 5

1. Stewart, Blisard, and Joliffe 2006, 1.
2. Millstone and Lang 2008, 92–93. Figures are for 2005.
3. Albert de la Bruhèze and Otterloo 2003, 320.
4. Amilien 2003. However, much behind other European countries in its culinary sophistication, Norway caught up fast: the Norwegian entrant won the first *Bocuse d'or* international culinary competition in 1987 and three times since, most recently in 2009.
5. Flandrin (2007) tracks the times of meals in France from the Middle Ages through the nineteenth century.
6. Douglas ([1972] 1975) begins her elaborate structuralist analysis of Hebrew dietary laws with a simpler, but by no means simple, analysis of the meal structure of her own (middle-class British) family, over the day, the week, the year

and lives of family members. What strikes the reader is how deeply embedded the meal identifications are without being articulated.

7. Spang 2000.

8. Brillat-Savarin [1826] 1839, 168. "However refined the food, however sumptuous the setting, there is no pleasure at table if the wine is bad, the guests brought together with no care, the faces gloomy and the meal eaten in haste." Meditation XIV, "On Pleasure at table." Cf. Pampille [1913] 2008.

9. Simmel [1910] 1997.

10. Elias [1969] 1994.

11. Bourdieu [1979] 1984.

12. Brillat-Savarin [1826] 1839, 168, Meditation XI, "On gourmandise."

13. Thiébaut 1994, following the lead of Elias (1994), documents the ever-greater elaboration of cutlery and dinnerware over the nineteenth and into the twentieth century. See also Girveau 2001.

14. See Ferguson 2008; Beaugé and Demorand 2009.

15. For a wonderful illustration of the significance of plating, see the highly aestheticized photographs in Bartelsman 2008. Increasingly vivid photographs in magazines such as *Gastronomica* and *Saveur,* both aimed at the general food-philic public, seek to convey distinctive taste experiences visually. Close-ups of food seek to convey their texture. It is worth noting that the emphasis on the construction of a dish in aesthetic terms harks back to the grand tradition of French cuisine in the seventeenth century and articulated most forcefully in the nineteenth by M-A. Carême, who viewed pastry making as a branch of architecture. Today's conception of presentation reaches beyond pastry to every dish.

16. Moskin 2009 references a *real* home-cooked version of the paradigmatic stew (*Je sais cuisiner* by Ginette Mathiot, closer to Irma Rombauer's classic *Joy of Cooking* [1931] 1976 than Child et al. 1961, *Mastering the Art of French Cooking*).

17. DBDG Kitchen and Bar, the recent (2009) venture of French-New York restaurateur Daniel Boulud, serves hot dogs along with several different kinds of sausage, his takes on matzoh ball soup and hamburgers (the "Frenchie" comes with confitted pork belly, arugula, tomato-onion compote and a slab of Morbier cheese, in a peppered brioche bun with cornichons and mustard on the side). The decidedly French menu context (lots of offal) as well as the extravagant preparations defamiliarizes the familiar that the cuisine incorporates.

18. On the tensions between the charismatic chef, the *community of cuisine,* and communities of diners, see Fine [1996] 2009, xiii.

Chapter 6

1. Flandrin and Montanari [1996] 1999; Jacobs and Scholliers 2003a.

2. Jacobs and Scholliers 2003a, 1.

 3. Flandrin and Montanari [1996] 1999, 2.
 4. Wrangham 2009.
 5. Ibid.
 6. Lhuissier 2003, 341.
 7. Hines, Marshall, and Weaver 1987, 84.
 8. Carter et al. 2006, 2–150.
 9. Ferguson 2007, 567.
10. Chaucer 1975, 137.
11. Carter et al. 2006.
12. Drouard 2003, 216.
13. Pilcher 2000, 127.
14. Browne 1998, 9.
15. Millston and Lang 2008, 94.
16. Pilcher 2000, 130.
17. Drouard 2003, 222–24.
18. Orwell 1961, 57.
19. See Wheaton 1983; Ferguson 2004.
20. Rombauer [1936] 1946, xiii.
21. Ibid. [1936] 1946, xxx.
22. Rombauer Papers, MC 449, MC 450.
23. Rombauer and Rombauer Becker [1931] 1976, xxx.
24. See www.jamieoliver.com/campaigns/jamies-food-revolution.

Chapter 7

 1. Richards 1932.
 2. Gubrium and Holstein 1990.
 3. Rich 1976; Rapp 1982.
 4. DeVault 1991, 15.
 5. For elaboration, see Meiselman 2000.
 6. Examples include: Douglas 1984; Sobal 1999; Jenson 2008.
 7. See Glenn 1985.
 8. See Kessler-Harris 1990; Clark 2000; Osawa 2006; Dhara et al. 1995.
 9. For examples see Jones 1985; Boydston 1990; Kessler-Harris 1990; Ruiz 1998.
10. Cowan 1983; Strasser1982.
11. See contemporary examples in Aukrust and Snow 1998; Blum-Kulka 1994;
    Hupkens et al. 1998.
12. Bentley 2005, 71.
13. Kessler-Harris 1990.
14. Overacker 1998.
15. Glenn 1985.
16. Theophano and Curtin 1991; Williams 1984; Counihan 2004.

17. Ibid. See also McIntosh and Zey 1989.
18. Dash 2006; Beoku Betts 1995.
19. Cancian 1986.
20. Mintz and Kellogg 1989.
21. Jones 1985.
22. Bentley 1998; Biltekoff 2002.
23. Block 2005.
24. Morton 1995.
25. Endrijonas 2001, 157.
26. Coontz 1992.
27. Avakian 1992.
28. D'Emilio, 2002.
29. Belasco 2006b.
30. Stack 1974; Boyd 1989. See also White 2000.
31. Witt 1999.
32. Elias N 1969 [1994]. See also: Mennell [1985] 1996
33. Leavitt 2002
34. Friedan 1963.
35. For the history of kitchens see Freeman 2004; Hayden 1982; Harrison 2005; Paradis 2008.
36. Organization for Economic and Cooperative Development 2010.
37. Smith 1993. See also Coontz 1992.
38. Murcott 1997. See also Otnes 1991.
39. Murcott 1997, 46.
40. Belasco 2006a.
41. DeVault 1991, 206.

Chapter 8

1. McClelland 1997; Kiple 2007.
2. Armstrong 1996; Brumberg 1997; Larsen 2000.
3. Korsmeyer 1999.
4. Egerton 1994, 281.
5. Adams 1990; Fiddes 1991; Probyn 2000; Orland 2004.
6. Diner 2001.
7. Sontag 1977; Banner 1983; Schwartz 1986.
8. Bynum 1988; Brumberg 1989.
9. Green 1986; Stearns 1997.
10. Kulick and Meneley 2005.
11. Levenstein 1988; Mudry 2009.
12. Belasco 2006a, 28, 77.

13. Bruegel 2002.
14. Amato 2000, 108.
15. Meikle 1979.
16. Belasco 2006a, 47.
17. Belasco 2006a, 230–35.
18. Brownell and Horgen 2004; Dalton 2004.
19. Stearns 1997.
20. Wansink 2006.
21. Gard and Wright 2005; Dixon and Broom 2007.
22. Belasco 2006a, 119–46.
23. Lears 2009, 1.
24. Kundera 1999.
25. Korsmeyer 1999, 11–37.
26. Liebs 1995; Langdon 1986.
27. Belasco 2008, 58. Similar percentages applied throughout the modern industrial world.
28. Berry 1970; Logsdon 1994.
29. Belasco 2006b.
30. Petrini 2001; Pollan 2006.
31. E.g. Ehrlich 1998; Kingsolver 2007; Wizenberg 2009.
32. Stern and Stern 1984.
33. Meiselman 2009.
34. Strasser 1982; Cowan 1983.
35. Freidberg 2009.
36. Murcott 1983; DeVault 1991.
37. Williams 1984.
38. Witt 1999.
39. Belasco 2006a, 221–2.
40. Belasco 1979.
41. Allen 2002.
42. Belasco 2006b.
43. Martyn 1701.
44. Dalby 2000, 11.
45. Belasco 2006a, 75.
46. Mintz 1986.
47. Whorton 1982.
48. Orr 1994, 172.
49. Belasco 2006a, 10.
50. Levenstein 1988.
51. Sinclair 1906; McWilliams 1939; Steinbeck 1939.
52. *Black Washingtonians* 2005, 189–90, 238.
53. Wackernagel and Rees 1996; Trubek 2008.

Chapter 9

1. Child, Beck, and Berthold 1961; *Julie & Julia* 2009.
2. de Certeau 1984, 186.
3. Levenstein 1988, 191.
4. Ibid. 46.
5. For the rise of domestic science, see Shapiro [1986] 2008. For histories of the calorie, see Hargrove 2006 and Cullather 2007.
6. For a history of the USDA's Food Guide, see Welsh, Davis, and Shaw 1993.
7. Nestle [2002] 2007, 298–337. For more on nutritionism, see Pollan 2007.
8. Glassner 2007, xi.
9. The term derives from French sociologist Claude Fischler. Cit. Levenstein [1993] 2003, 212.
10. While obesity has been in evidence for most of the century, though with significant escalations in the 1980s, it was not until the turn of the century that its representation as a global epidemic took hold. See, for instance, WHO 2000.
11. Co-written by Jacqueline Verrett and Jean Carper, the subject of their book was food additives, and a critique of the FDA for putting economic considerations before consumer safety (Belasco 1989, 140).
12. Brownell and Horgen (2004) coined the term *toxic environment* with specific reference to increasing rates of obesity (here, toxicity refers both to the availability of cheap junk food and to an environment—computers, television, transport—that discourages physical activity), but the term can as well describe anxieties about artificial additives in food (the subject of Verrett's book, op cit), and more lately, regular food scares resulting in recalls of contaminated products.
13. A 1950 *Time* article ("Foreign News, The Pause That Arouses") reported on the French Communist Press warning against the *Coca-Colonization* that would follow if France began importing Coca-Cola. The term has since been used more broadly to refer to colonization by American products. *McDonaldization* was coined by sociologist George Ritzer ([1993] 1996) to describe a society dominated by the characteristics of a fast-food industry (efficiency, calculability, predictability, and control). The term is analogous, rather than explicitly related to food.
14. Although the array of prepared foods on the market in 1900 suggested to one group of Boston women that "'home cooking as we now know it' would soon be a thing of the past" (Shapiro [1986] 2008, 199), by the 1920s the woman as domestic scientist was beginning to be reconfigured as *homemaker* (ibid. 209).
15. For more on U.S. cookbooks in the 1950s, see Neuhaus 1999.
16. Cit. Chaney 1998, 217.
17. In the words of Clarissa Dickson-Wright, of *Two Fat Ladies* fame, "It is this vision of a land that existed solely in Elizabeth David's imagination which has shaped our food, our dreams, and our thinking over the past fifty years. Those

who rush to buy holiday homes in France or Chiantishire (as Tuscany has now been renamed) or those endless books that have only to mention purple lavender fields or baskets of lemons to make the best-seller lists, all are searching for a place that isn't there except in the heart of this great food writer" (2002, iii). For more on culinary tourism, see Long 2004.

18. Collins 2009, 79.
19. Child, Beck, and Berthold 1961; Fisher [1968] 1970.
20. Schrambling 2004.
21. Lovegren 2005, 227.
22. Beard and Calvert 1959.
23. Superchefs are chef-entrepreneurs whose media profiles and business acumen surpass normal celebrity chefs. See Rossant 2004.
24. Puck 2004; Eddy and Clark 2002; Food Network Kitchens 2006.
25. Belasco [1989] 2006b, 247.
26. Ibid. 22. Alice Waters continues to campaign for a "delicious revolution" with her "edible schoolyards." Her long-standing dream of a vegetable garden on the White House lawn was finally realized in 2009.
27. Bhide 2010.
28. O'Neill 2003.
29. Cit. Lopate 1995, 545.
30. Schrambling 2005.
31. Cockburn 1977.
32. On the vicarious consumption of food television, see Adema 2000.
33. Lowe and Butryn 2007.
34. Fisher 1990, 273.
35. Fagone 2006, 206. For answers to questions such as "where do 50 hardboiled eggs go if you eat them in six minutes?", see Dan Cesareo's documentary *The Science of Speed Eating* (National Geographic, 2007). Lawrence C. Rubin (2008, 8) suggests that these spectacles of "organized debauchery and sanctioned bulimia" provide further evidence of what Michael Pollan has called a *national eating disorder*.
36. See Golan 2003.
37. For more on Rosler's work, which includes *A Budding Gourmet* (1974), and *Semiotics of the Kitchen* (1975), see de Zegher 1998.
38. Cit. Davidson 1999, 542.
39. On why molecular gastronomy is a misnomer, see Adrià et al. 2006, McBride 2006.
40. Available online: http://www.nypl.org/audiovideo/day-elbulli-ferran-adria-conversation-corby-kummer-harold-mcgee. (Accessed May 4, 2010.)
41. "Tested and Approved Recipes" 1917.
42. Shapiro 2004.
43. Barthes [1957] 2000, 79.
44. For histories of food television, see Buford 2006; Hansen 2008; Collins 2009.

45. Ray 2007, 26. On why the term food porn is boring, see Probyn 2000. On technical similarities between food television and pornography, see Kaufman 2005.
46. Humble 2005, 236. For a similar Jamie Oliver effect, see Smith 2008, 122.
47. Buford 2006.
48. Kracauer [1927] 1993, 432.
49. For a history of the future of food, see Belasco 2006a.
50. For more on culinary luddism, see Laudan 1999.

Chapter 10

1. Mbapndah 1994; Moxham 2004.
2. McCracken 1987.
3. Elson 2004.
4. Daviron and Daponte 2005, 12–15.
5. Alence 2001.
6. Fourshey 2008.
7. Cwiertka 2006.
8. Boahen 1985; Mazrui 1993.
9. Bekele 2009.
10. Bates 2005.
11. Fitzpatrick 1994.
12. Davies 1998.
13. Gronow 2003.
14. Selden and Lippit 1982.
15. Powell 1992.
16. Pettid 2008.
17. Perkins 1997.
18. Shiva 1991; Conway 1998.
19. Buckland 2004.
20. Baro and Deubel 2006; Drakakis-Smith 1991; Maxwell 1999.
21. Haggart, Sen, and Nolan 2009.
22. FAO Food and Nutrition Division 2004.
23. Laudan 2001.
24. Phillips 2006.
25. Watson and Caldwell 2005; Wilk 2006a.
26. Wu and Cheung 2002; Issenberg 2007.
27. Knight 1998; Cwiertka 2006, 167–74.
28. Wu 2004; Cheung 2005.
29. Cafferada and Pomareda 2009; Granados and Alvarez 2002.
30. Fratkin 2001.

31. Humphrey and Sneath 1999.
32. Appadurai 1998; Wilk 2006b.
33. Cusack 2000.
34. Guerròn-Montero 2004; Sheller 2003.
35. Re Cruz 2003.

BIBLIOGRAPHY

Ackrill, Robert. 2000. *The Common Agricultural Policy*. Sheffield: Sheffield Academic Press.

Adams, Carol J. 1990. *The Sexual Politics of Meat: A Feminist-Vegetarian Critical Theory*. New York: Continuum.

Adema, Pauline. 2000. "Food, Television and the Ambiguity of Modernity." *Journal of American Culture* 23 (1): 113–23.

Adrià, Ferran, Heston Blumenthal, Thomas Keller, and Harold McGee. 2006. "Statement on the 'New Cookery.'" *The Observer* (December 10). http://observer.guardian.co.uk/foodmonthly/story/0,1968666,00.html.

Aiken, W., and H. Lafollette, eds. 1995. *World Hunger and Morality*. New York: Prentice-Hall.

de la Bruhèze, Adri, and Anneke H. van Otterloo. 2003. "Snacks and Snack Culture and the Rise of Eating Out in the Netherlands in the Twentieth Century." In *Eating out in Europe: Picnics, Gourmet Dining and Snacks since the Late Eighteenth Century*, eds. Marc Jacobs and Peter Scholliers. Oxford: Berg.

Alence, Rod. 2001. "Colonial Government, Social Conflict and State Involvement in Africa's Open Economies: The Origins of the Ghana Cocoa Marketing Board, 1939–46." *The Journal of African History* 42 (3): 397–416.

Allen, Keith. 2002. "Berlin in the *belle époque*: A Fast Food History." In *Food Nations: Selling Taste in Consumer Societies*, eds. Warren Belasco and Philip Scranton, 240–57. New York: Routledge.

Altieri, Miguel A. 2001. *Genetic Engineering in Agriculture: The Myths, Environmental Risks, and Alternatives: Food First Special Report no. 1*. Oakland: Food First.

Amato, Joseph. 2000. *Dust: A History of the Small and the Invisible*. Berkeley: University of California Press.

Amilien, Virginie. 2003. "The Rise of Restaurants in Norway in the Twentieth Century." In *Eating Out in Europe: Picnics, Gourmet Dining and Snacks Since the Late Eighteenth Century*, eds. Marc Jacobs and Peter Scholliers. Oxford: Berg.

Amistani, C., and D. Terrolle. 2008. "L'Alimentation des Sans-Abri." *Anthropology of Food* 6. http://aof.revues.org/index4952.html.

Anderson, J. L. 2008. *Industrializing the Corn Belt: Agriculture, Technology, and Environment, 1945–1972.* De Kalb: Northern Illinois University Press.

Anderson, Kym. 2001. "Bringing Discipline to Agricultural Policy via the WTO." In *Developing Countries and the WTO: A Pro-active Agenda,* eds. Bernard Hoekman and Will Martin. Oxford: Blackwell Publishers.

Annear, C. M. 2004. "'GM or Death': Food and Choice in Zambia." *Gastronomica* 4 (2): 16–23.

Appadurai, Arjun. 1988. "How to Make a National Cuisine: Cookbooks in Contemporary India." *Comparative Studies in Society and History* 30 (1): 3–24.

Armstrong, Tim, ed. 1996. *American Bodies: Cultural Histories of the Physique.* New York: New York University Press.

Aston, Basil, Kenneth Hill, Allan Piazza, and Robin Zeitz. 1984. "Famine in China, 1958–1961." *Population and Development Review* 10 (4): 613–45.

Atkins, P. J. 2008. "Fear of Animal Foods: a Century of Zoonotics." *Appetite* 51: 18–21.

Atkins, P. J. 2009. "Famine." In *International Encyclopedia of Human Geography,* eds. R. Kitchin and N. Thrift, vol. 1. Oxford: Elsevier.

Atkins, P. J. 2010. *Liquid Materialities: A History of Milk, Science and the Law.* Farnham: Ashgate.

Aukrust, V. G., and C. E. Snow. 1998. "Narratives and Explanations during Mealtime Conversations in Norway and the U.S." *Language in Society* 27.

Avakian, Arlene Voski. 1992. *Lion Woman's Legacy: An Armenian–American Memoir.* New York: Feminist Press.

Avakian, A., and B. Haber. 2005. *From Betty Crocker to Feminist Food Studies: Critical Perspectives on Women and Food.* Amherst: University of Massachusetts Press.

Avakian, A. 2006. *Through the Kitchen Window: Women Explore the Intimate Meanings of Food and Eating.* London: Berg Publishers.

Avery, William, ed. 1993. "Agriculture and Free Trade." In *World Agriculture and the GATT.* Boulder: Lynne Rienner Publishers.

Banik, D. 2007. *Starvation and India's Democracy.* London: Routledge.

Banner, Lois W. 1983. *American Beauty.* Chicago: University of Chicago Press.

Baro, Mamadou, and Tara F. Deubel. 2006. "Persistent Hunger: Perspectives on Vulnerability, Famine, and Food Security in Sub-Saharan Africa." *Annual Revue of Anthropology* 35: 521–38.

Barr, Ann, and Levy, Paul. 1984. *The Official Foodie Handbook,* London: Ebury.

Barrett, James R. 1987. *Work and Community in the Jungle: Chicago's Packinghouse Workers, 1894–1922.* Urbana: University of Illinois Press.

Bartelsman, Jan. 2008. *Dining in New York City.* The Netherlands: Fotostudio Jan Bartelsman.

Barthes, Roland. [1957] 2000. "Ornamental Cookery." In *Mythologies.* London: Vintage.

Bates, Robert H. 2005. *Markets and States in Tropical Africa*. Berkeley: University of California Press.

Bayliss-Smith, Tim P., and Sudhir Wanmali, eds. 1984. *Understanding Green Revolutions: Agrarian Change and Development Planning in South Asia. Essays in Honour of B. H. Farmer*. Cambridge: Cambridge University Press.

Beard, James, and Isabel E. Calvert. 1959. *The James Beard Cookbook*. New York: Angle.

Beaugé, Bénédict, and Sébastien Demorand. 2009. *Les cuisines de la critique gastronomique*. Paris: Sciences Po.

Beck, U. 1992. *Risk Society: Towards a New Modernity*. London: Sage.

Becker, Geoffrey. 2009. *U.S. Food and Agricultural Imports: Safeguards and Selected Issues*. Washington, DC: Congressional Research Service.

Becker, J. 1996. *Hungry Ghosts: Mao's Secret Famine*. London: Murray.

Bekele, Getnet. 2009. "Food Matters: The Place of Development in Building the Postwar Ethiopian State, 1941–1974." *International Journal of African Historical Studies* 42 (1): 29–54.

Belasco, Warren J. 1979. "Toward a Culinary Common Denominator: The Rise of Howard Johnson's, 1925–1940." *Journal of American Culture* 2 (3): 503–18.

Belasco, Warren J. 2006a. *Meals to Come: A History of the Future of Food*. Berkeley: University of California Press.

Belasco, Warren J. [1989] 2006b. *Appetite for Change: How the Counterculture Took on the Food Industry*. Ithaca: Cornell University Press.

Belasco, Warren J. 2008. *Food: The Key Concepts*. Oxford: Berg Publishers.

Belasco, Warren J., and Roger Horowitz, eds. 2009. *Food Chains: From Farmyard to Shopping Cart*. Philadelphia: University of Pennsylvania Press.

Bentley, Amy. 1998. *Eating for Victory: Food Rationing and the Politics of Domesticity*. Urbana: University of Illinois Press.

Bentley, Amy. 2005. "Feeding Baby, Teaching Mother: Gerber and the Evolution of Infant Food and Feeding Practices." In *From Betty Crocker to Feminist Food Studies: Critical Perspectives on Women and Food,* eds. A. Avakian and B. Haber. Amherst: University of Massachusetts Press.

Beoku Betts, J. 1995. "We Got Our Way of Cooking Things: Women, Food, and Preservation of Cultural Identity among the Gullah." *Signs* 9 (5).

Bernauer, Thomas. 2003. *Genes, Trade, and Regulation: The Seeds of Conflict in Food Biotechnology*. Princeton, NJ: Princeton University Press.

Berry, Wendell. 1970. *A Continuous Harmony: Essays Cultural and Agricultural*. New York: Harcourt Brace Jovanovich.

Bhide, Monica. 2010. "Q & A: Sanjeev Kapoor, India's Chef to Millions." *Washington Post* (February 24). http://www.washingtonpost.com/wp-dyn/content/story/2010/02/23/ST2010022302196.html.

Biltekoff, C. 2002. "'Strong Men and Women Are Not Products of Improper Food': Domestic Science and The History of Eating and Identity." *Journal for the Study of Food and Society* 6 (1).

Bittman, Mark. 2008. *Food Matters: A Guide to Conscious Eating.* New York: Simon and Schuster.

Black, J. L., and J. Macinko. 2008. "Neighborhoods and Obesity." *Nutrition Reviews* 66 (1): 2–20.

Black Washingtonians: 300 Years of African American History. 2005. Hoboken: Wiley.

Blay-Palmer, A., and B. Donald. 2006. "A Tale of Three Tomatoes: The New Food Economy in Toronto, Canada." *Economic Geography* 82 (4): 383–99.

Block, D. R. 2004. "Dairy Industry." In *Oxford Encyclopedia of Food and Drink in America*, ed. A. Smith. New York: Oxford University Press.

Block, D. 2005. "Saving Milk through Masculinity: Public Health Officers and Pure milk, 1880–1930." *Food and Foodways* 13 (1–2).

Block, D., and J. Kouba. 2006. "A Comparison of the Availability and Affordability of a Market Basket in two Chicago Communities." *Public Health Nutrition* 9: 837–45.

Block D., N. Chavez, and J. Birgen. 2008. *Finding Food in Chicago and the Suburbs: The Report of the Northeastern Illinois Community Food Security Assessment.* http://www.csu.edu/nac/documents/reporttothepublic060308.pdf.

Block, D. R., M. Thompson, J. Euken, T. Liquori, F. Fear, and S. Baldwin. 2008. "Engagement for Transformation: Value Webs for Local Food System Development." *Agriculture and Human Values* 25: 379–88.

Block, D. R. 2009. "Public Health, Cooperatives, Local Regulation, and the Development of Modern Milk Policy: The Chicago Milkshed, 1900–1940." *Journal of Historical Geography* 35: 128–53.

Bock, D. R. 2010. "Taking Food and Agricultural Studies to the Streets: Community Engagement, Working Across Disciplines, and Community Change. *Agricultural and Human Values* 27: 519–24.

Blum-Kulka, S. 1994. "The Dynamics of Family Dinner Talk: Cultural Contexts for Children's Passages to Adult Discourse." *Research on Language and Social Interaction* 27 (1).

Boahen, Albert Adu. 1985. *Africa under Colonial Domination 1880–1935.* Paris: UNESCO.

Bonnano, Alessandro, and Douglas Constance. 1996. *Caught in the Net: The Global Tuna Industry, Environmentalism, and the State.* Lawrence: University Press of Kansas.

Bonnano, Alessandro, Lawrence Busch, William Frieland, Lourdes Gouveia, and Enzo Mingione, eds. 1994. *From Columbus to ConAgra: The Globalization of Agriculture and Food.* Lawrence: University of Kansas Press.

Booth, S. 2006. "Eating Rough: Food Sources and Acquisition Practices of Homeless Young People in Adelaide, South Australia." *Public Health Nutrition* 9: 212–18.

Bourdieu, Pierre. [1979] 1984. *Distinction. A Social Critique of the Judgement of Taste.* Cambridge: Harvard University Press.

Boyd, M. 1989. "Family and Personal Networks in International Migration: Recent Developments and New Agendas." [Special issue on international migration and assessment for the 90s.] *International Migration Review* 23 (3).

Boydston, Jeanne. 1990. *Home and Work: Housework, Wages, and the Ideology of Labor in the Early Republic*. New York: Oxford University Press.

Bracken, Peg. 1960. *The I Hate to Cook Book*. New York: Harcourt, Brace & World.

Bracken, Peg. 1962. *The I Hate to Housekeep Book*. New York: Harcourt, Brace & World.

Bracken, Peg. 1967. *The I Still Hate to Cook Book*. London: Arlington Books.

Brandt, M. B., J. Moss, K. Ellwood, M. Ferguson, and A. Asefa. 2010. "Tracking Label Claims." *Food Technology* 64 (1): 35–40.

Brillat-Savarin, Jean Anthelme. [1826] 1839. *Physiologie du goût, ou Méditations de gastronomie transcendante*. Paris: Charpentier.

Brown, Dona. 1997. *Inventing New England: Regional Tourism in the Nineteenth Century*. Hanover: University of New England Press.

Browne, William. 1988. *Private Interests, Public Policy, and American Agriculture*. Lawrence: The University Press of Kansas.

Brownell, Kelly D., and Katherine Battle Horgen. 2004. *Food Fight: The Inside Story of the Food Industry, America's Obesity Crisis, and What We Can Do About It*. Chicago: Contemporary Books.

Bruegel, Martin. 2002. "How the French Learned to Eat Canned Food." In *Food Nations: Selling Taste in Consumer Societies*, eds. Warren Belasco and Philip Scranton, 113–30. New York: Routledge.

Brumberg, Joan Jacobs. 1989. *Fasting Girls: The History of Anorexia Nervosa*. New York: Plume.

Brumberg, Joan Jacobs. 1997. *The Body Project. An Intimate History of American Girls*. New York: Random House.

Bueltzingsloewen, I. von, ed. 2005. *Morts d'Inanition: Famine et Exclusions en France sous l'Occupation*. Rennes: Presses Universitaires de Rennes.

Bueltzingsloewen, I. von. 2007. *L'Hécatombe des Fous: la Famine dans les Hôpitaux Psychiatriques Français sous l'Occupation*. Paris: Editions Aubier.

Buerk, M. 2004. *The Road Taken*. London: Hutchinson.

Buford, Bill. 2006. "TV Dinners: The Rise of Food Television." *The New Yorker* (October 2). http://www.newyorker.com/printables/fact/061002fa_fact.

Buckland, Jerry. 2004. *Ploughing Up the Farm: Neoliberalism, Modern Technology and the State of the World's Farmers*. London: Zed Books.

Burch, D., and G. Lawrence. 2009. "Towards a Third Food Regime: Behind the Transformation." *Agriculture and Human Values* 26: 267–79.

Burnett, John. 2003. "Eating in the Open Air in England." In *Eating Out in Europe: Picnics, Gourmet Dining and Snacks Since the Late Eighteenth Century*, eds. Marc Jacobs and Peter Scholliers. London: Berg Press.

Bustillos, B., J. R. Sharkey, J. Anding, and A. McIntosh. 2009. "Availability of More Healthful Food Alternatives in Traditional, Convenience, and Nontraditional Types of Food Stores in Two Rural Texas Counties." *Journal of the American Dietetic Association* 109 (5): 883–89.

Buttel, F. H., and D. Goodman. 1989. "Class, State, Technology and International Food Regimes." *Sociologia Ruralis* 33 (2): 86–92.

Bynum, Caroline Walker. 1988. *Holy Feast and Holy Fast: The Religious Significance of Food to Medieval Women*. Berkeley: University of California Press.

Cafferada, Julio Paz, and Carlos Pomareda. 2009. *Indicaciones geográficas y denominaciones de origen en Centroamérica: situación y perspectivas*. Geneva: ICTSD.

Caldwell, M. L. 2004. *Not by Bread Alone: Social Support in the New Russia*. Berkeley: University of California Press.

Campbell, D. 2007. "Geopolitics and Visuality: Sighting the Darfur Conflict." *Political Geography* 26: 357–82.

Campbell, D., D. Clark, and K. Manzo, eds. 2005. *Imaging Famine*. http://www.imaging-famine.org.

Campbell, H., and J. Dixon. 2009. "Introduction to the Special Symposium: Reflecting on Twenty Years of the Food Regimes Approach in Agri-food Studies." *Agriculture and Human Values* 26 (4): 261–65.

Cancian, F. 1986. "The Feminization of Love." *Signs* 11 (4).

Cannon, Geoffrey. 1992. *Food and Health: The Experts Agree*. London: Consumers' Association.

Carrington, C. 1999. *No Place Like Home: Relationships and Family Life Among Lesbians and Gay Men*. Chicago: University of Chicago Press.

Carter, Susan B., Scott S. Gartner, Michael R. Haines, Alan L. Olmstead, Richard Sutch, and Gavin Wright, eds. 2006. *Historical Statistics of the United States*. Cambridge: Cambridge University Press.

Cesereo, Dan, producer. 2007. *The Science of Speed Eating*. Big Fish Entertainment. Distributor, National Geographic.

Charles, Daniel. 2001. *Lords of the Harvest: Biotech, Big Money, and the Future of Food*. Cambridge, MA: Perseus Publishing.

Chaney, Lisa. 1998. *Elizabeth David*. London: Pan.

Chang, J. 1991. *Wild Swans*. London: HarperCollins.

Chatterjee, D. K. 2004. *The Ethics of Assistance: Morality and the Distant Needy*. Cambridge: Cambridge University Press.

Chaucer, Geoffrey. 1975. *The Canterbury Tales*. London: Penguin.

Cheung, Sidney C. H. 2005. "Consuming 'Low' Cuisine after Hong Kong's Handover: Village Banquets and Private Kitchens." *Asian Studies Review* 29 (3): 259–73.

Child, Julia, Simone Beck, and Louisette Berthold. 1961. *Mastering the Art of French Cooking*. New York: Knopf.

Cho, Sungjoon. 2009. "United States: Continued Suspension of Obligations in the EC-Hormones Dispute. WT/DS320/AB/R." *The American Journal of International Law* 103 (2): 299–305.

Christian Science Monitor. 1957. "Supermarket to Dazzle Zagreb Eyes." (September 7).

Cieerad, I. 1999. *At Home: An Anthropology of Domestic Space*. Syracuse: Syracuse University Press.

Clapp, J. 2009. "Corporate Interests in US Food Aid Policy: Global Implications of Resistance to Reform." In *Corporate Power in Global Agrifood Governance*, eds. J. Clapp and D. Fuchs. Cambridge, MA: The MIT Press.

Clapp, Stephen. 2010. "Front-of-Pack Labelling Stirs Controversy on Both Sides of Atlantic." *Food Chemical News* (March 22).

Clark, A. 2000. "The New Poor Law And The Breadwinner Wage: Contrasting Assumptions." *Journal of Social History* 34 (2).

Cochrane, W. W. [1979] 1993. *The Development of American Agriculture: A Historical Analysis*. Reprint, Minneapolis: University of Minnesota Press.

Cockburn, Alexander. 1977. "Gastro-Porn." *New York Review of Books* (December 8): 20. http://www.nybooks.com/articles/8309.

Cohen, M. J., and M. A. Brown, 2008. "Legal Empowerment and the Right to Food." In *Rights and Legal Empowerment in Eradicating Poverty*, ed. D. Banik. Farnham: Ashgate.

Collins, Kathleen. 2009. *Watching What We Eat: The Evolution of Television Cooking Shows*. New York: Continuum.

Consumer Reports. 2010. *Greener Choices: Products for a Better Planet*. http://www.greenerchoices.org/eco-labels/productArea.cfm?ProductCategoryID=174.

Conway, Gordon. 1998. *The Doubly Green Revolution: Food for All in the Twenty-first Century*. Ithaca: Cornell University Press.

Coontz, S. 1992. *The Way We Never Were: American Families and the Nostalgia Trap*. New York: Basic Books.

Cotter, Joseph. 2003. *Troubled Harvest: Agronomy and Revolution in Mexico, 1880–2002*. New York: Praeger.

Counihan, C. 2004. *Around the Tuscan Table Food, Family, and Gender in Twentieth Century Florence*. New York: Routledge.

Cowan, Ruth Schwartz. 1983. *More Work for Mother: The Ironies of Household Technology from the Open Hearth to the Microwave*. New York: Basic Books.

Critser, Greg. 2003. *Fat Land: How Americans Became the Fattest People in the World*. New York: Houghton Mifflin.

Cullather, Nick. 2007. "The Foreign Policy of the Calorie." *American Historical Review* 112 (2): 337–64.

Cummins, S., and S. Macintyre. 2006. "Food Environments and Obesity: Neighbourhood or Nation?" *International Journal of Epidemiology* 35: 100–104.

Curtis, Olga. 1957. "Time-Saving Modern Kitchen Miracles." *Washington Post and Times Herald* (April 22).

Cusack, Igor. 2000. "African Cuisines: Recipes for Nation-Building?" *Journal of African Cultural Studies* 13 (2): 207–25.

Crutchfield, Steve. 1991. "Agriculture and Water Quality Conflicts." *Food Review* 14 (2): 12–15.

Cwiertka, Katarzyna J. 2006. *Modern Japanese Ccuisine: Food, Power, and National Identity*. London: Reaktion Books.

Dahl, Robert. 1961. *Who Governs?* New Haven, CT: Yale University Press.

Dalby, Andrew. 2000. *Dangerous Tastes: The Story of Spices.* Berkeley: University of California Press.

Dalton, Sharron. 2004. *Our Overweight Children: What Parents, Schools, and Communities Can Do to Control the Fatness Epidemic.* Berkeley: University of California Press.

Daniels, A. K. 1987. "Invisible work." *Social Problems* 34 (5).

Dash, J. 2006. "Rice Culture." In *Through the Kitchen Window: Women Explore the Intimate Meanings of Food and Eating,* ed. A. Avakian. London: Berg Publishers.

David, Elizabeth. [1950] 1958. *Mediterranean Food.* London: Penguin.

Davidson, Alan. 1999. *The Oxford Companion to Food.* Oxford: Oxford University Press.

Davies, R. W. 1998. *Soviet Economic Development from Lenin to Khrushchev.* Cambridge: Cambridge University Press.

Davies, R. W., and Stephen G. Wheatcroft. 2004. *The Years of Hunger: Soviet Agriculture, 1931–1933.* New York: Palgrave Macmillan.

Daviron, Benoit, and Stefano, Daponte. 2005. *The Coffee Paradox: Global Markets, Commodity Trade, and the Elusive Promise of Development.* London: Zed Books.

Davis, H. F. 1959. "Sharing Our Bounty." In *Food: The Yearbook of Agriculture, 1959.* U.S. Department of Agriculture, 86th Congress, 1st session, House document no. 29.

de Certeau, Michel. 1984. *The Practice of Everyday Life,* trans. Steven F. Rendall. Berkeley: University of California Press.

D'Emilio, John. 2002. *The World Turned: Essays on Gay History, Politics, and Culture.* Durham, NC: Duke University Press.

Deusche Welle. 2006. *World's Biggest Retailer Closes up Shop in Germany.* http://www.dw-world.de/dw/article/0,2112746,00.html.

DeVault, Marjorie L. 1991. *Feeding the Family: The Social Organization of Caring as Gendered Work.* Chicago: University of Chicago Press.

Devereux, S. 2000. "Famine in the Twentieth Century." *IDS Working Paper* 105. Brighton: Institute of Development Studies, University of Sussex.

Devereux, S., ed. 2009a. "Introduction: from 'Old Famines' to 'New Famines.'" In *The New Famines.* London: Routledge.

Devereux, S., ed. 2009b. "Sen's Entitlement Approach: Critiques and Counter-critiques." In *The New Famines.* London: Routledge.

Devereux, S., ed. 2009c. *The New Famines.* London: Routledge.

Devereux, S., P. Howe, and L. B. Deng. 2002 "Introduction: The New Famines." *IDS Bulletin* 33 (4): 1–11.

de Waal, A. 1997. *Famine Crimes: Politics and the Disaster Relief Industry in Africa.* Oxford: James Currey.

de Waal, A. 2005. "Defining Genocide." *Index on Censorship* 1: 6–13.

de Waal, A. 2009. "AIDS, Hunger and Destitution: Theory and Evidence for the 'New Variant Famines' Hypothesis in Africa." In *The New Famines,* ed. S. Devereux. London: Routledge.

de Zegher, Catherine, ed. 1998. *Martha Rosler: Positions in the Life World.* Birmingham: Ikon Gallery.

Dickens, R. E., and R. K. Moore. 1981. "Food Policy in North America: The Bread Basket." In *Food Politics: The Regional Context,* eds. D. N. Balaam and M. J. Carey. London: Allanheid, Osmun, Croom, and Helm.

Dickson Wright, Clarissa. 2002. "Foreword." In *Mediterranean Food,* ed. Elizabeth David. New York: New York Review of Books.

Diez-Roux, A. V. 2001. "Investigating Neighborhood and Area Effects on Health." *American Journal of Public Health* 91 (11): 1783–89.

Dimitri, Carolyn, Anne Effland, and Neilson Conklin. 2005. *The Twentieth Century Transformation of US Agriculture and Farm Policy.* Washington, DC: United States Department of Agriculture.

Diner, Hasia. 2001. *Hungering for America: Italian, Irish, and Jewish Foodways in the Age of Migration.* Cambridge, MA: Harvard University Press.

Dixon, J. 2009. "From the Imperial to the Empty Calorie: How Nutrition Relations Underpin Food Regime Transitions." *Agriculture and Human Values* 26 (4): 321–33.

Dixon, Jane, and Dorothy H. Broom, eds. 2007. *The 7 Deadly Sins of Obesity: How the Modern World is Making Us Fat.* Sydney: UNSW Press.

Dodd, G. 1856. *The Food of London.* London: Longman, Brown, Green, and Longmans.

Donofrio, G. A. 2007. "Feeding the City." *Gastronomica* 7 (4): 30–41.

Douglas, Mary. [1972] 1975. "Deciphering a Meal." In *Implicit Meanings: Essays in Anthropology.* London: Routledge and Kegan Paul.

Douglas, M., and N. Nicod. 1974. "Taking the Biscuit: The Structure of British Meals." *New Society* 34.

Douglas, M., ed. 1984. *Food in the Social Order: Studies of Food and Festivities in Three American Communities.* New York: Russell Sage Foundation.

Doyle, Jack. 1985. *Altered Harvest: Agriculture, Genetics, and the Fate of the World's Food Supply.* New York: Viking.

Drakakis-Smith, David. 1991. "Urban Food Distribution in Asia and Africa." *The Geographical Journal* 157 (1): 51–61.

Drouard, Alain. 2003. "Escoffier, Bocuse et (surtout) les autres…" In *Eating Out in Europe: Picnics, Gourmet Dining and Snacks Since the Late Eighteenth Century,* eds. M. Jacobs and P. Scholliers. London: Berg Press.

Duddy, E. A. 1929. "Agriculture in the Chicago Region." *Social Sciences Studies* 15. Chicago: University of Chicago Press.

Duffy, J. 1990. *The Sanitarians: A History of American Public Health.* Urbana, IL: University of Illinois Press.

DuPuis, E. Melanie. 2002. *Nature's Perfect Food: How Milk Became America's Drink*. New York: New York University Press.

Durand, L. 1940. "Dairy Regional of Southeastern Wisconsin and Northeastern Illinois." *Economic Geography* 16 (4): 416–28.

Durand, L. 1964. "The Major Milksheds of the Northeastern Quarter of the United States." *Economic Geography* 40 (1): 9–33.

Durand, L. 1967. "The Historical and Economic Geography of Dairying in the North Country of New York State." *The Geographical Review* 57 (1): 24–47.

Duval-Diop, D., and J. M. Grimes. 2005. "Tales from Two Deltas: Catfish Fillets, High-value Foods, and Globalization." *Economic Geography* 81: 177–200.

Dwork, D. 1987. *War is Good for Babies and Other Young Children*. London: Tavistock.

Economist, The. 2009. "Fishy Tales." (April 25): 58.

Eddy, Jackie, and Eleanor Clark. 2002. *The Absolute Beginner's Cookbook: Or, How Long Do I Cook a 3-Minute Egg?* New York: Clarkson Potter.

Edkins, J. 2009. "The Criminalization of Mass Starvations: from Natural Disaster to Crime against Humanity." In *The New Famines*, ed. S. Devereux. London: Routledge.

eFoodAlert.com. 2010. http://efoodalert.blogspot.com/2010/02/fda-to-kellogg-company-leggo-your.html.

Egerton, March, ed. 1994. *Since Eve Ate Apples*. Portland, OR: Tsunami Press.

Ehrlich, Elizabeth. 1998. *Miriam's Kitchen*. New York: Penguin.

Ehrlich, Paul. 1968. *The Population Bomb*. New York: Ballantine Books.

Eisner, Marc Allen. 2000. *Regulatory Politics in Transition*. Rev. ed. Baltimore: The Johns Hopkins University Press.

Elbehri, Aziz, Johannes Umstaetter, and David Kelch. 2008. *The EU Sugar Policy-Regime and Implications of Reform: Economic Research Report Number 59*. Washington, DC: United States Department of Agriculture, Economic Research Service.

Elias, Norbert. [1939] 1994. *The Civilising Process*, trans. Edmund Jephcott. Oxford: Blackwell.

Elson, Robert. 2004. "Reinventing a Region: Southeast Asia and the Colonial Experience." In *Contemporary Southeast Asia,* ed. Mark Beeson. Basingstoke: Palgrave Macmillan.

Endrijonas, E. 2001. "Processed Foods from Scratch: Cooking for a Family in the 1950s." In *Kitchen Culture in America: Popular Representations of Food, Gender, and Rrace,* ed. S. Inness. Philadelphia: University of Pennsylvania Press.

Ewen, Stuart. 1976. *Captains of Consciousness: Advertising and the Social Roots of Consumer Culture*. New York: McGraw-Hill.

Fagone, Jason. 2006. *Horsemen of the Esophagus: Competitive Eating and the Big Fat American Dream*. New York: Crown.

Federico, Giovanni. 2005. *Feeding the World: An Economic History of World Agriculture, 1800–2000*. Princeton, NJ: Princeton University Press.

Feenstra, Gail. 2002. "Creating Space for Sustainable Food Systems: Lessons from the Field." *Agriculture and Human Values* 19 (2): 99–106.

Ferguson, Priscilla Parkhurst. 2004. *Accounting for Taste: The Triumph of French Cuisine*. Chicago: University of Chicago Press.

Ferguson, Priscilla Parkhurst. 2007. "Food." In *Encyclopedia of Sex and Gender*, ed. F. Malti-Douglas, 565–70. Detroit: Macmillan.

Ferguson, Priscilla Parkhurst. 2008. "Michelin Comes to America." *Gastronomica* 8 (1): 49–55.

Ferguson, Priscilla Parkhurst. 2010. "Culinary Nationalism." *Gastronomica* 10 (1): 102–9.

Fiddes, Nick. 1991. *Meat: A Natural Symbol*. London: Routledge.

Fine, Ben, Michael Heasman, and Judith Wright. 1996. *Consumption in The Age of Affluence: The World of Food*. London: Routledge.

Fine, Ben, and E. Leopold. 2002. *The World of Consumption*. London: Routledge.

Fine, Gary Alan. [1996] 2009. *Kitchens: The Culture of Restaurant Work*. Berkeley: University of California Press.

Finger, J. Michael, and Ludger Schuknecht. 2001. "Market Advances: The Uruguay Round." In *Developing Countries and the WTO: A Pro-Active Agenda*, eds. Bernard Hoekman and Will Martin. Oxford: Blackwell Publishers.

Fischler, Claude. 1999. "The 'Mad Cow' Crisis: A Global Perspective." In *Food in Global History*, ed. Raymond Grew. Boulder: Westview Press.

Fischler, Claude, and Estelle Masson, eds. 2007. *Manger: Français, Européens et Américains face à l'alimentation*. Paris: Odile Jacob.

Fisher, M.F.K. [1968] 1970. *The Cooking of Provincial France*. New York: Time, Inc.

Fisher, M.F.K. 1990. "As the Lingo Languishes." In *The State of Language*, eds. Christopher Ricks and Leonard Michaels. Berkeley: University of California Press.

Fitzgerald, Deborah K. 2003. *Every Farm a Factory: The Industrial Ideal in American Agriculture*. New Haven, CT: Yale University Press.

Fitzpatrick, Sheila. 1994. *Stalin's Peasants: Resistance and Survival in the Russian Village after Collectivization*. Oxford: Oxford University Press.

FitzSimmons, M. 1986. "The New Industrial Agriculture: The Regional Integration of Specialty Crop Production." *Economic Geography* 62: 334–53.

Flammang, Janet A. 2010. *The Taste for Civilization: Food, Food Politics, and Civil Society*. Urbana: University of Illinois Press.

Flanagan, Caitlin. 2010. "Cultivating Failure: How Our School Gardens are Cheating Our Most Vulnerable Students." *The Atlantic Online* (January/February). http://www.theatlantic.com/doc/print/201001/school-yard-garden.

Flandrin, Jean-Louis, and Massimo Montanari, eds. [1996] 1999. *Food: A Culinary History*. New York: Columbia University Press.

Flandrin, Jean-Louis. 2007. *Arranging the Meal: A History of Table Service in France*, trans. Julie E. Johnson. Berkeley: University of California Press.

Food and Agriculture Organization. n.d. *Food-Based Dietary Guidelines*. http:// www.fao.org/ag/humannutrition/nutritioneducation/fbdg/en/.

Food and Agriculture Organization of the United Nations. 2000. *The State of Food and Agriculture 2000*. Rome: FAO.

Food and Agriculture Organization, Food and Nutrition Division. 2004. *Globalization of Food Systems in Developing Countries: Impact on Food Security and Nutrition*. Rome: FAO.

Food and Drug Administration. 2007. *FDA Science and Mission at Risk*. http:// www.fda.gov/ohrms/dockets/AC/07/briefing/2007–4329b_02_01_FDA Report on Science and Technology.pdf.

Food and Drug Administration. 2009. *2009 Recalls, Market Withdrawals, and SAFETY alerts*. http://www.fda.gov/safety/recalls/default.htm.

Food Marketing Institute. 2009. *Median Average Store Size-square Feet*. www.fmi.org.

Food Network Kitchens, 2006. *How to Boil Water: Life Beyond Takeout*. New York: Wiley.

"Foreign News: The Pause That Arouses." *Time* (March 13). http://www.time. com/time/magazine/article/0,9171,812138–1,00.html.

Fourshey, Catherine Cymone. 2008. "'The Remedy for Hunger is Bending the Back': Maize and British Agricultural Policy in Southwestern Tanzania 1920– 1960." *International Journal of African Historical Studies* 41 (2): 223–61.

Fratkin, Elliot. 2001. "East African Pastoralism in Transition: Maasai, Boran, and Rendille Cases." *African Studies Review* 44 (3): 1–25.

Freeman, J. 2004. *The Making of the Modern Kitchen: A Cultural History*. London: Berg Publishers.

Friedan, B. 1963. *The Feminine Mystique*. London: Gollancz.

Friedberg, Suzanne. 2004. *French Beans and Food Scares: Culture and Commerce in an Anxious Age*. New York: Oxford University Press.

Friedberg, Suzanne. 2009. *Fresh: A Perishable History*. Cambridge, MA: Harvard University Press.

Frieden, Jeffrey, and David Lake. 2000. *International Political Economy: Perspective on Global Power and Wealth*. Boston: St. Martin's.

Friedland, W. H., A. Barton, and R. Thomas. 1981. *Manufacturing Green Gold*. New York: Cambridge University Press.

Friedland, W. H. 1984. "Commodity Systems Analysis: An Approach to the Sociology of Agriculture." In *Research in the Rural Sociology of Agriculture*, ed. H. Schwarzweller. Greenwich, CT: JAI Press.

Friedland, W. H. 1994. "The Global Fresh Fruit and Vegetable System: An Industrial Organization Analysis." In *The Global Restructuring of Agro-Food Systems*, ed. P. McMichael. Ithaca, NY: Cornell University Press.

Friedmann, Harriet. 1982. "The Political Economy of Food: The Rise and Fall of the Postwar International Food Order." *The American Journal of Sociology* 88: S248–S286.

Friedmann, Harriet. 1993. "The Political Economy of Food: A Global Crisis." *New Left Review* 197 (1): 29–57.

Friedmann, H., and P. McMichael. 1989. "Agriculture and The State System: The Rise and Decline of National Agricultures, 1870 to the Present." *Sociologia Ruralis* 29 (2): 93–117.

Fromartz, Samuel. 2006. *Organic, Inc.: Natural Foods and How They Grew.* New York: Harcourt.

Fuchs, D., A. Kalfagianni, and M. Arentsen. 2009. "Retail Power, Private Standards, and Sustainability in The Global Food System." In *Corporate Power in Global Agrifood Governance*, eds. J. Clapp and D. Fuchs. Cambridge, MA: MIT Press.

Gabaccia, Donna R. 1998. *We Are What We Eat: Ethnic Food and the Making of Americans.* Cambridge, MA: Harvard University Press.

Gard, Michael, and Jan Wright. 2005. *The Obesity Epidemic: Science, Morality and Ideology.* London: Routledge.

Garzon, Isabelle. 2006. *Reforming the Common Agricultural Policy: History of a Paradigm Change.* New York: Palgrave Macmillan.

Gazdar, H. 2007. "Pre-modern, Modern and Post-modern Famine in Iraq, 1990–2003." In *The New Famines,* ed. S. Devereux. London: Routledge.

General Agreement on Tariffs and Trade. 1947. http://www.wto.org/english/docs_e/legal_e/gatt47_01_e.htm.

General Agreement on Tariffs and Trade (Uruguay Round Protocol). 1994a. *Agreement on Agriculture.* http://www.wto.org/english/docs_e/legal_e/14-ag_01_e.htm.

General Agreement on Tariffs and Trade (Uruguay Round Protocol). 1994b. *Agreement on the Application of Sanitary and Phytosanitary Measures.* http://www.wto.org/english/docs_e/legal_e/15sps_01_e.htm.

Giedion, Siegfried. 1948. *Mechanization Takes Command: A Contribution to Anonymous History.* New York: Oxford University Press.

Gilbert, Alan, ed. 1996. *The Mega City in Latin America.* New York: United Nations Press.

Gill, Dhara. S., and Bennett Matthews. 1995. "Changes in the Breadwinner Role: Punjabi Families in Transition." *Journal of Comparative Family Studies* 26.

Girveau, Bruno, ed. 2001. *A table au XIXe siècle.* Paris: Flammarion.

Glanz, K. 2009. "Measuring Food Environments: A Historical Perspective." *American Journal of Preventive Medicine* 36 (4): S93–S98.

Glassner, Barry. 2007. *The Gospel of Food: Why We Should Stop Worrying and Enjoy What We Eat.* New York: Ecco.

Glenn, E. Nakano. 1985. "Racial Ethnic Women's Labor: The Intersection of Race, Gender, and Class Oppression." *Review of Radical Political Economics* 17.

Golan, Romy. 2003. "Ingestion/Anti-Pasta." *Cabinet* (Spring). http://www.cabinetmagazine.org/issues/10/anti-pasta.php.

Gold, Bill. 1957. "The District Line." *Washington Post and Times Herald* (October 22).

Goldfrank, Walter L. 1994. "Fresh Demand: The Consumption of Chilean Produce in the United States." In *Commodity Chains and Global Capitalism,* eds. Gary Gereffi and Miguel Korzeniewicz. Westport, CT: Greenwood Publishing.

Goodman, D., and M. Watts. 1994. "Reconfiguring the Rural or Fording the Divide?: Capitalist Restructuring and the Global Agro-food System." *Journal of Peasant Studies* 22 (1): 1–49.

Government Accountability Office. 2005. *Food Safety: Experiences of Seven Countries in Consolidating Their Food Safety Systems* [GAO-05–212]. February 22.

Granados, Leonardo, and Carlos Alvarez. 2002. "Viabilidad de establecer el sistema de denominaciones de origen de los productos agroalimentarios en Costa Rica." *Agronomía Costarricense* 26 (1): 63–72.

Green, Harvey. 1986. *Fit for America.* New York: Pantheon.

Gronow, Jukka. 2003. *Caviar with Champagne: Common Luxury and the Ideals of the Good Life in Stalin's Russia.* Oxford: Berg.

Gubrium, J. F., and J. A. Holstein, 1990. *What is Family?* Mountain View, CA: Mayfield.

Guerròn-Montero, Carla. 2004. "Afro-Antillean Cuisine and Global Tourism." *Food, Culture and Society* 7 (2): 29–47.

Guidonet, A. 2008. "La Réciprocité Comme Stratégie." *Anthropology of Food* 6. http://aof.revues.org/index4562.html.

Guidonet, A. 2009. "The Spanish Civil War and Post-war Period: Social Change and Strategies for Eating." Paper presented at *Food and War in Europe in the Nineteenth and Twentieth Centuries,* 11th Symposium of the International Commission for Research into European Food History, University of Paris-Sorbonne, September 8–11.

Gupta, Akhil. 1998. *Postcolonial Developments: Agriculture in the Making of Modern India.* Durham: Duke University Press.

Guptill, A., and J. L. Wilkins. 2002. "Buying into the Food System: Trends in Food Retailing in the US and Implications for Local Foods." *Agriculture and Human Values* 19 (1): 39–51.

Guthman, Julie. 2004. *Agrarian Dreams: The Paradox of Organic Farming in California.* Berkeley: University of California Press.

Guthman, Julie. 2007. "Can't Stomach It: How Michael Pollan et al. Made Me Want to Eat Cheetos." *Gastronomica* 7 (2): 75–79.

Haggart, Stephan, Amartya Sen, and Marcus Nolan. 2009. *Famine in North Korea: Markets, Aid, and Reform.* New York: Columbia University Press.

Halperin, Rick. 1997. *Down on the Killing Floor: Black and White Workers in Chicago's Packinghouses, 1904–1954.* Urbana: University of Illinois Press.

Hamilton, Shane. 2003. "Cold Capitalism: The Political Ecology of Frozen Concentrated Orange Juice." *Agricultural History* 77 (4): 557–81.

Hansen, Signe. 2008. "Television." In *The Business of Food: Encyclopedia of the Food and Drink Industries,* eds. Ken Albala and Gary Allen. Westport, CT: Greenwood.

Hareven, T. K. 1987. "Historical Analysis of the Family." In *Handbook of Marriage and the Family*, eds. B. Sussman and S. K. Steinmetz. New York: Plenum Press.

Hargrove, James L. 2006. "History of the Calorie in Nutrition." *The Journal of Nutrition* 136 (12): 2957–61.

Harrison, D. 2005. *Encyclopedia of Kitchen History*. Bradford, UK: Emerald Group Publishing.

Hauck-Lawson, Annie. 1992. "Hearing the Food Voice: An Epiphany for a Researcher." *Digest* 12 (1–2): 26–27.

Hayden, D. 1982. *The Grand Domestic Revolution: A History of Feminist Designs for American Homes, Neighborhoods, and Cities*. Cambridge: MIT Press.

Helfand, Steven M. 1999. "The Political Economy of Agricultural Policy in Brazil: Decision Making and Influence from 1964 to 1992." *Latin American Research Review* 34 (2): 3–41.

Henke, Christopher. 2008. *Cultivating Science, Harvesting Power: Science and Industrial Agriculture in California*. Cambridge, MA: MIT Press.

Hewitt de Alcántara, Cynthia. 1976. *Modernizing Mexican Agriculture: Socioeconomic Implications of Technological Change, 1940–1970*. Geneva: United Nations Research Institute for Social Development.

Hines, Mary Anne, Gordon Marshall, and William Woys Weaver. 1987. *The Larder Invaded: Reflections on Three Centuries of Philadelphia Food and Drink*. Philadelpha: Library Company of Philadelphia.

Hionidou, V. 2006. *Famine and Death in Occupied Greece, 1941–1944*. Cambridge: Cambridge University Press.

Holmes, H. 2003. "Food from the Hedgerows: Collecting Wild Fruits and Plants in Scotland During the Second World War and its Aftermath." In *The Landscape of Food*, eds. M. Hietala and T. Vahtikari. Helsinki: Finnish Literature Society.

Holt-Giménez, E. 2008. *The World Food Crisis: What's Behind it and What We Can Do About It*. Policy Brief 16. October 2008. Oakland, CA: Institute for Food and Development Policy.

Holtzman, J. D. 2006. "Food and Memory." *Annual Review of Anthropology* 35: 361–78.

Horowitz, Roger. 1997. *"Negro and White, Unite and Fight!" A Social History of Industrial Unionism in Meatpacking, 1930–1990*. Urbana: University of Illinois Press.

Horowitz, Roger. 2006. *Putting Meat on the American Table: Taste, Technology, Transformation*. Baltimore: Johns Hopkins University Press.

Horowitz, S. R. 1997. *Voicing the Void: Muteness and Memory in Holocaust Fiction*. Albany: State University of New York Press.

Humble, Nicola. 2005. *Culinary Pleasures: Cookbooks and the Transformation of British Food*. London: Faber and Faber.

Humphrey, Caroline, and David Sneath. 1999. *The End of Nomadism? Society, State, and the Environment in Inner Asia*. Durham, NC: Duke University Press.

Hupkens, C.L.H., R. A. Knibbe, A. H. Van Otterloo, and M. J. Drop. 1998. "Class Differences in the Food Rules Mothers Impose on Their Children: A Cross-national Study." *Social Science and Medicine* 47 (9).

Hurt, R. Douglas. 2002. *Problems of Plenty: The American Farmer in the Twentieth Century*. Chicago: Ivan R. Dee.

Hutt, Peter Barton, and Peter Barton Hutt II. 1984. "A History of Government Regulation of Adulteration and Misbranding of Food." *Food, Drug and Cosmetic Law Journal* 39: 2–73.

Ingelfinger, Julie. 2008. "Melamine and the Global Implications of Food Contamination." *New England Journal of Medicine* 359 (26): 2745–48.

Institute of Medicine. 2010. *Examination of Front-of-Package Nutrition Rating Systems and Symbols, Phase I Report*. Washington, DC: National Academies Press.

Ioffe, Grigory, Tatyana Nefedova, and Ilya Zaslavsky. 2006. *The End of Peasantry? The Disintegration of Rural Russia*. Pittsburgh: The University of Pittsburgh Press.

Issenberg, Sasha. 2007. *The Sushi Economy: Globalization and the Making of a Modern Delicacy*. New York: Gotham Books.

Jacobs, Marc, and Peter Scholliers. 2003. *Eating Out in Europe: Picnics, Gourmet Dining and Snacks Since the Late Eighteenth Century*. London: Berg.

Jacobs, Marc, and Peter Scholliers, eds. 2003. "Vaut ou ne vaut pas le détour: Conviviality, Custom(er)s and Public Places of New Taste Since the Late Eighteenth Century." In *Eating Out in Europe: Picnics, Gourmet Dining and Snacks Since the Late Eighteenth Century*. Oxford and New York: Berg.

Jacoby, Karl. 2001. *Crimes against Nature: Squatters, Poachers, Thieves, and the Hidden History of American Conservation*. Berkeley: University of California Press.

Jarosz, Lucy, 2000. "Understanding Agri-Food Networks as Social Relations." *Agriculture and Human Values* 7 (3): 279–83.

Johnson, Renee, and Charles E. Hanrahan. 2009. *The US–EU Beef Hormone Dispute*. Washington, DC: Congressional Research Service.

Jones, J. 1985. *Labor of Love, Labor of Sorrow: Black Women, Work, and the Family From Slavery to the Present*. New York: Basic Books.

Josephson, Paul R. 2002. *Industrialized Nature: Brute Force Technology and the Transformation of the Natural World*. Washington, DC: Shearwater Books.

Julie & Julia. 2009. Director Nora Ephron, Producer, Scott Rudin Productions, Distributor, Columbia Pictures.

Kahn, R. 2003. "Letter to Gro Harlem Brundtland, Director General, World Health Organization." [Letter]. World Sugar Research Organization. www.who.int/dietphysicalactivity/media/en/gsfao_cmr_030325.pdf.

Kaplinsky, R. 2004. "Spreading the Gains from Globalization." *Problems of Economic Transition* 47: 74–115.

Kasaba, R., and F. Tabak. 1995. "Fatal Conjuncture: The Decline and Fall of the Modern Agrarian Order during the Bretton Woods Era." In *Food and the Agrarian Orders in the World Economy,* ed. P. McMichael. Westport, MA: Greenwood Press.

Kass, Leon. 1997. "The Wisdom of Repugnance." *New Republic* 216 (22).

Katzen, Molly. 1977. *The Moosewood Cookbook: Recipes from Moosewood Restaurant.* Ithaca, NY: Ten Speed Press.

Kaufman, Frederick. 2005. "Debbie Does Salad: The Food Network at the Frontiers of Pornography." *Harpers* (October). http://www.barbaranitke.com/harpersmag.html.

Keen, D. 1994. *The Benefits of Famine: A Political Economy of Famine and Famine Relief in South-western Sudan, 1983–1989.* Princeton, NJ: Princeton University Press.

Keller Brown, L., and K. Mussell, eds. 1984. *Ethnic and Regional Foodways in the United States: The Performance of Group Identity.* Knoxville: University of Tennessee Press.

Kellogg Company. 1985. *A Citizen's Petition: The Relationship Between Diet and Health.* Submitted May 22, 1985 to Dockets Branch, United States Food and Drug Administration.

Kessler, David. 2009. *The End of Overeating: Taking Control of the Insatiable American Appetite.* Emmaus, PA: Rodale Books.

Kessler-Harris, A. 1990. "The Wage Conceived: Value and Need as Measures of a Woman's Worth." In *A Woman's Wage: Historical Meanings and Social Consequences.* Lexington: University Press of Kentucky.

Kingsford, P. 1982. *The Hunger Marchers in Britain, 1920–1939.* London: Lawrence and Wishart.

Kingsolver, Barbara. 2007. *Animal, Vegetable, Miracle.* New York: HarperCollins.

Kiple, Kenneth, and Kriemhild Ornelas, eds. 2000. *The Cambridge World History of Food and Nutrition.* Cambridge: Cambridge University Press.

Kiple, Kenneth F. 2007. *A Moveable Feast: Ten Millennia of Food Globalization.* New York: Cambridge University Press.

Knight, John. 1998. "Selling Mother's Love?: Mail Order Village Food in Japan." *Journal of Material Culture* 3 (2): 153–73.

Konefal, J., M. Mascarenhas, and M. Hatanaka. 2005. "Governance in the Global Agro-food System: Backlighting the Role of Transnational Supermarket Claims." *Agriculture and Human Values* 22 (3): 291–302.

Korsmeyer, Carolyn. 1999. *Making Sense of Taste: Food and Philosophy.* Ithaca, NY: Cornell University Press.

Kracauer, Siegfried. [1927] 1993. "Photography." Reprint, *Critical Inquiry* 19 (3): 421–36.

Kraus, D. 2004. *The Death of Kevin Carter: Casualty of the Bang Bang Club.* Documentary film. http://www.imdb.com/title/tt0439676/.

Kulick, Don, and Anne Meneley, eds. 2005. *Fat: The Anthropology of an Obses-sion.* New York: Tarcher.

Kundera, Milan. 1999. *The Unbearable Lightness of Being.* New York: Perennial.

Kurlansky, Mark, ed. 2002. *Choice Cuts: A Savory Selection of Food Writing from Around the World and Throughout History.* London: Penguin.

Lancaster, Gertrude P. 1956. "Emphasis on Food Quality: New Products Savor Old Standards." *Christian Science Monitor* (October 26).

Langdon, Philip. 1986. *Orange Roofs, Golden Arches.* New York: Knopf.

La Pradelle, Michèle de. 2006. *Market Day in Provence,* trans. Amy Jacobs. Chi-cago: University of Chicago Press.

Lappé, Frances Moore. 1971. *Diet for a Small Planet.* New York: Ballantine.

Larsen, Bernard. 2000. "Height and Nutrition." In *The Cambridge World History of Food,* eds. Kenneth E. Kiple and Kriemhild Coneé Ornelas, vol. 2, 1427–39. New York: Cambridge University Press.

Laudan, Rachael. 1999. "A World of Inauthentic Cuisine: Against Culinary Lud-dism." In *Cultural and Historical Aspects of Foods,* eds. Mary Wallace Kelsey and ZoeAnn Holmes. Oregon: Oregon State University.

Laudan, Rachel. 2001. "A Plea for Culinary Modernism: Why We Should Love New, Fast, Processed Food." *Gastronomica* 1 (1): 36–44.

League of Nations, Economic, Financial and Transit Department. 1946. *Food, Famine and Relief 1940–1946.* Geneva: League of Nations.

Lears, T. Jackson. 1981. *No Place of Grace: Antimodernism and the Transforma-tion of American Culture, 1880–1920.* New York: Pantheon.

Lears, T. Jackson. 1994. *Fables of Abundance: A Cultural History of Advertising in America.* New York: Basic Books.

Lears, T. Jackson. 2009. *Rebirth of a Nation.* New York: HarperCollins.

Leavitt, S. 2002. *From Catharine Beecher to Martha Stewart: A Cultural History of Domestic Advice.* Chapel Hill: University of North Carolina Press.

Le Heron, R. 1993. *Globalized Agriculture: Political Choice.* New York: Pergamon.

Le Heron, R., and M. Roche. 1996. "Globalization, Sustainability, and Apple Or-charding, Hawke's Bay, New Zealand." *Economic Geography* 72 (4): 416–32.

Levenstein, Harvey A. 1988. *Revolution at the Table: The Transformation of the American Diet.* New York: Oxford University Press.

Levenstein, Harvey A. [1993] 2003. *Paradox of Plenty: A Social History of Eating in America.* New York: Oxford University Press/University of California Press.

Levy A., and R. Stokes. 1987. "Effects of a Health Promotion Advertising Cam-paign on Sales of Ready-to-Eat Cereals." *Public Health Reports* 102: 398–403.

Lhuissier, Anne. 2003. "Eating out During the Workday: Consumption and Work-ing Habits among Urban Labourers in France in the Second Half of the Nine-teenth Century." In *Eating Out in Europe: Picnics, Gourmet Dining and Snacks,* eds. Marc Jacobs and Peter Scholliers. London: Berg Press.

Li, A., N. Dachner, and V. Tarasuk. 2009. "Food Intake Patterns of Homeless Youth in Toronto." *Canadian Journal of Public Health* 100: 36–40.

Li, L. M. 2007. *Fighting Famine in North China.* Stanford, CA: Stanford University Press.

Liebs, Chester. 1995. *Main Street to Miracle Mile: American Roadside Architecture.* Baltimore: Johns Hopkins University Press.

Lin, Justin Yifu. 1996. "Success in Early Reform: Setting the Stage." In *The Third Revolution in the Chinese Countryside,* eds. Ross Garnaut, Guo Shutian, and Mao Guonan, 13–26. New York: Cambridge University Press.

Logsdon, Gene. 1994. *At Nature's Pace: Farming and the American Dream.* New York: Pantheon.

Long, Lucy M., ed. 2004. *Culinary Tourism.* Kentucky: The University of Kentucky Press.

Lopate, Philip, ed. 1995. *The Art of the Personal Essay: An Anthology from the Classical Era to the Present.* New York: Anchor.

Love, John F. 1986. *McDonald's: Behind the Arches.* New York: Bantam.

Lovegren, Sylvia. 2005. *Fashionable Foods, Seven Decades of Food Fads.* Chicago: University of Chicago Press.

Lowe, M. R., and M. L Butryn. 2007. "Hedonic Hunger: A New Dimension of Appetite." *Physiology and Behavior* 91: 432–39.

Lowi, Theodore. 1979. *The End of Liberalism: The Second Republic of the United States.* New York: W. W. Norton and Company.

Ludlow, N. Piers. 2005. "The Making of the CAP: Towards a Historical Analysis of the EU's First Major Policy." *Contemporary European History* 14 (3): 347–71.

MacLachlan, Ian. 2001. *Kill and Chill: Restructuring Canada's Beef Commodity Chain.* Toronto: University of Toronto Press.

Mathiot, Ginette, and H. Delage, eds. 1932. *Je sais cuisiner.* Paris: Albin Michel.

McAfee, Kathleen. 2003. "Corn Culture and Dangerous DNA: Real and Imagined Consequences of Maize Transgene Flow in Oaxaca." *Journal of Latin American Geography* 2 (1): 18–42.

McBride, Anne E. 2006. "The New Chef's Whites: A Lab Coat?" *Institute of Culinary Education.* http://www.iceculinary.com/news/articles/article_37.shtml.

McClelland, Peter D. 1997. *Sowing Modernity: America's First Agricultural Revolution.* Ithaca, NY: Cornell University Press.

McCracken, John. 1987. "Fishing and the Colonial Economy: The Case of Malawi." *The Journal of African History* 28 (3): 413–29.

McIntosh, W. A., and S. Evers. 1982. "The Role of Women in the Production of Food and Nutrition in Less Developed Countries." In *Women in International Development,* ed. P. Horne. Texas A&M University, The President's World University Series, No. 2.

McIntosh, W. A., and M. Zey. 1989. "Women as Gatekeepers of Food Consumption: A Sociological Critique." *Food and Foodways* 3 (4).

McIntosh, Wm. Alex. 1999. "The Family Meal and Its Significance in Global Times." In *Food in Global History,* ed. Raymond Grew. Boulder: Westview Press.

McLaughlin, P., and T. Dietz. 2008. "Structure, Agency and Environment: Toward an Integrated Perspective on Vulnerability." *Global Environmental Change* 18: 99–111.

McMichael, P., ed. 1994. "Introduction: Agro-food System Restructuring–Unity in Diversity." In *The Global Restructuring of Agro-food Systems*. Ithaca, NY: Cornell University Press.

McMichael, P., and C. K. Kim. 1994. "Japanese and South Korean Agricultural Restructuring in Comparative and Global Perspective." In *The Global Restructuring of Agro-food Systems*, ed. P. McMichael. Ithaca, NY: Cornell University Press.

McMichael, P. 2009. "A Food Regime Analysis of the 'World Food Crisis.'" *Agriculture and Human Values* 26 (4): 281–95.

McNeill, J. R. 2001. *Something New Under the Sun: An Environmental History of the Twentieth-Century World*. New York: W. W. Norton and Company.

McWilliams, Carey. 1939. *Factories in the Field*. New York: Little and Brown.

Macrae, J., and A. Zwi, eds. 1994. "Famine, Complex Emergencies and International Policy in Africa: an Overview." In *War and Hunger*. London: Zed Books.

Mahant, Edelgard. 2004. *Birthmarks of Europe: The Origins of the European-Community Reconsidered*. Burlington, VT: Ashgate Publishing Company.

Mahood, L., and V. Satzewich. 2009. "The Save the Children Fund and the Russian Famine of 1921–23: Claims and Counter-claims about Feeding 'Bolshevik' Children." *Journal of Historical Sociology* 22: 55–83.

Mallory, W. H. 1926. *China: Land of Famine*. New York: American Geographical Society.

Manchester, Alden. 1992. *Rearranging the Economic Landscape: The Food Marketing Revolution, 1950–1981*. Economic report 660. Washington, DC: USDA.

Mansfield, B. 2003. "Spatializing Globalization: A 'Geography of Quality' in the Seafood Industry." *Economic Geography* 79 (1): 1–16.

Marchand, Roland. 1985. *Advertising the American Dream: Making Way for Modernity, 1920–1940*. Berkeley: University of California Press.

Marcus, D. 2003. "Famine Crimes in International Law." *American Journal of International Law* 97: 245–81.

Martyn, Henry. 1701. *Considerations on the East India Trade*. London: np.

Marion, B. W. 1986. *The Organization and Performance of the U.S. Food System*. Written with the NC 117 committee. Lexington, MA and Toronto: Lexington Books.

Maxwell, Daniel. 1999. "The Political Economy of Urban Food Security in Sub-Saharan Africa." *World Development* 27 (11): 1939–53.

Mayhew, M. 1988. "The 1930s Nutrition Controversy." *Journal of Contemporary History* 23: 445–64.

Mazrui, A. Ali. 1993. *Africa Since 1935*. Paris: UNESCO.

Mbapndah, Ndobegang M. 1994. "French Colonial Agricultural Policy, African Chiefs, and Coffee Growing in the Cameroun Grassfields, 1920–1960." *The International Journal of African Historical Studies* 27 (1): 41–58.

Medvedev, Z. 1987. *Soviet Agriculture*. New York: W. W. Norton and Company.

Meikle, Jeffrey L. 1979. *Twentieth Century Limited: Industrial Design in America, 1925–1939*. Philadelphia: Temple University Press.

Meiselman, H., ed. 2000. *Dimensions of the Meal: Science, Culture, Business, Art*. Colorado: Aspen Publishers.

Meiselman, Herbert L. 2009. *Meals in Science and Practice: Interdisciplinary Research and Business Applications*. Cambridge: Woodhead Publishing.

Mennell, Stephen. [1985] 1996. *All Manners of Food: Eating and Taste in England and France from the Middle Ages to the Present*. Urbana: University of Illinois Press.

Merridale, C. 2000. *Night of Stone: Death and Memory in Russia*. London: Granta.

Messer, E., M. J. Cohen, and J. D'Costa. 1998. *Food from Peace: Breaking the Links between Conflict and Hunger*. Washington, DC: International Food Policy Research Institute.

Messer, E., and M. J. Cohen. 2006. "Conflict, Food Insecurity, and Globalization." *Food Consumption and Nutrition Division Discussion Paper* 206. Washington, DC: International Food Policy Research Institute.

Miller, Henry. 1997. *Policy Controversy in Biotechnology: An Insider's View*. Austin, TX: R. G. Landes Company.

Millstone, Erik, and Tim Lang. 2008. *The Atlas of Food. Who Eats What, Where, and Why*. Berkeley: University of California Press.

Milward, A. S. 1977. *War, Economy and Society, 1939–1945*. London: Allen Lane.

Mintz, Sidney. 1986. *Sweetness and Power: The Place of Sugar in Modern History*. New York: Penguin.

Mintz, S., and S. Kellogg. 1989. *Domestic Revolutions: A Social History Of American Family Life*. New York: Free Press.

Misselhorn, A. A. 2005. "What Drives Food Insecurity in Southern Africa? A Meta-analysis of Household Economy Studies." *Global Environmental Change* 15: 33–43.

Moeller, S. D. 1999. *Compassion Fatigue: How the Media Sell Disease, Famine, War and Death*. London: Routledge.

Moore, L. V., and A. V. Diez Roux. 2006. "Associations of Neighborhood Characteristics With the Location and Type of Food Stores." *American Journal of Public Health* 96 (2): 325–31.

Morland, K., and S. Filomena. 2007. "Disparities in the Availability of Fruits and Vegetables between Racially Segregated Urban Neighbourhoods." *Public Health Nutrition* 10: 1481–89.

Morton, S. 1995. *Ideal Surroundings: Domestic Life in a Working-class Suburb in the 1920s*. Toronto: University of Toronto Press.

Moskin, Julia. 2009. "A Boeuf Bourguignon In (Gasp!) Five Steps." *New York Times* (August 26). http://query.nytimes.com/gst/fullpage.html?res=9B07E2D C1638F935A1575BC0A96F9C8B63&sec=&spon=&pagewanted=print.

Mouré, K., and P. Schwartz. 2007. "On Vit Mal: Food Shortages and Popular Culture in Occupied France, 1940–1944." *Food, Culture and Society* 10: 261–95.

Moxham, Roy. 2004. *Tea: Addiction, Exploitation, and Empire.* New York: Carroll and Graf.

Mudry, Jessica J. 2009. *Measured Meals: Nutrition in America.* Albany: SUNY Press.

Murcott, A. 1982. "On the Social Significance of the 'Cooked Dinner' in South Wales." *Social Science Information* 21 (4–5): 677–96.

Murcott, Anne. 1983. "'It's a Pleasure to Cook for Him': Food, Mealtimes, and Gender in Some South Wales Households." In *The Public and Private,* eds. E. Garmarnikow, D. Morgan, J. Purvis, and D. Taylorson. London: Heinemann.

Murcott, Anne. 1997. "The Nation's Diet: An Overview of Early Results." *British Food Journal* 99 (3): 89–96.

Mustard, Allen. 2003. "An Unauthorized History of FAS." *Foreign Service Journal* (May): 36–43.

Myers, Ransom A., and Boris Worm. 2003. "Rapid Worldwide Depletion of Predatory Fish Communities." *Nature* 423: 280–83.

Nally, D. 2008. "'That Coming Storm': The Irish Poor Law, Colonial Biopolitics, and the Great Famine." *Annals of the Association of American Geographers* 98: 714–41.

National Commission on Food Marketing. [1966] 1976. *Food From Farmer to Consumer: Report of the National Commission on Food Marketing.* Reprint, New York: Arno.

Nestle, M. 1999. "Hunger in America: A Matter of Policy." *Social Research* 66: 257–82.

Nestle, Marion. 2000. "Ethical Dilemmas in Choosing a Healthful Diet: Vote with Your Fork!" *Proceedings of the Nutrition Society (UK)* 59: 619–29.

Nestle, Marion. [2002] 2007. *Food Politics: How the Food Industry Influences Nutrition and Health.* Berkeley: University of California Press.

Nestle, Marion. 2008. *Pet Food Politics: The Chihuahua in the Coal Mine.* Berkeley: The University of California Press.

Nestle, Marion. [2002] 2010. *Safe Food: The Politics of Food Safety.* Berkeley: University of California Press.

Neuhaus, Jessamyn. 1999. "The Way to a Man's Heart: Gender Roles, Domestic Ideology, and Cookbooks in the 1950s." *Journal of Social History* 32 (3): 529–55.

Neuman, W., and A. Pollack. 2010. "Rise of the Superweeds." *New York Times* (May 4): B1.

New York Times. 1953. "State's Canned Food Exceeds all Russia's." (October 31).

New York Times. 1956. "World Crops 120% of Pre-war Rate: Output Keeping Up with Rise in Population, US Reports–Free World Lead Reds." (April 14).

Nissen, M. R. 2006. "Danish Food Production in the German War Economy." In *Food and Conflict in the Age of the Two World Wars*, eds. F. Trentmann and F. Just. Basingstoke: Palgrave Macmillan.

Nord, M., M. Andrews, and S. Carlson. 2008. *Household Food Security in the United States, 2007*. Washington, DC: United States Department of Agriculture, Economic Research Service.

Nussbaumer, J., and A. Exenberger. 2009. "Century of Hunger, Century of Plenty: How Abundance Arrived in Alpine Valleys." In *The Rise of Obesity on Europe*, eds. D. J. Oddy, P. J. Atkins, and V. Amilien. Farnham: Ashgate.

Oddy, D. J. 2003. *From Plain Fare to Fusion Food: British Diet from the 1890s to the 1990s*. Woodbridge: Boydell.

Oddy, D. J., P. J. Atkins, and V. Amilien, eds. 2009. *The Rise of Obesity on Europe*. Farnham: Ashgate.

Oliver, Jamie. *Jamie's Food Revolution*. www.jamieoliver.com/campaigns/jamies-food-revolution.

Olmstead, Alan L., and Paul W. Rhode. 2008. *Creating Abundance: Biological Innovation and American Agricultural Development*. New York: Cambridge University Press.

O'Neill, Molly. 2003. "Food Porn." *Columbia Journalism Review* (September/October). http://cjrarchives.org/issues/2003/5/foodporn-oneill.asp.

Organization for Economic and Cooperative Development; US Census Bureau International Facts. 2010. http://www.census.gov/compendia/statab/cats/international_statistics.html.

Orland, Barbara. 2004. "Turbo-Cows: Producing a Competitive Animal in the Nineteenth and Early Twentieth Centuries." In *Industrializing Organisms: Introducing Evolutionary History*, eds. Susan R. Schrepfer and Philip Scranton, 167–90. New York: Routledge.

Orr, David. 1994. *Earth in Mind: On Education, Environment, and the Human Prospect*. Washington D.C.: Island Press.

Orwell, George. 1961. *Down and Out in Paris and London*. New York: Harcourt Brace.

Osawa, M. 2006. "The Vicious Cycle of the 'Male Breadwinner' Model of Livelihood Security." *Women's Asia: Voices from Japan* 16.

Otnes, P. 1991. "What Do Meals Do?" In *Palatable Worlds: Sociocultural Food Studies*, eds. E. L. Furst, R. Prattala, M. Ekstrom, L. Holm, and U. Kjaernes. Oslo: Solum Forlag.

Otter, Chris. 2010. "Feast and Famine: The Global Food Crisis." *Origins* 3 (6). http://ehistory.osu.edu/osu/origins/article.cfm?articleid=38.

Overacker, I. 1998. *The African American Church Community in Rochester, New York, 1900–1940*. Rochester, NY: University of Rochester Press.

Paarlberg, D. 1980. *Farm and Food Policy: Issues of the 1980's.* Lincoln: University of Nebraska Press.

Paarlberg, Robert. 2005. "The Global Food Fight." In *The Cultural Politics of Food and Eating*, eds. James L. Watson and Melissa L. Caldwell. Oxford: Blackwell Publishing.

Pader, E. J. 1993. "Spatiality and Social Change: Domestic Space-use in Mexico and the United States." *American Ethnologist* 20 (1).

Pader, E. J. 1994. "Sociospacial Relations of Change: Rural Mexican Women in Urban California." In *Women and the Environment*, eds. I. Altman and A. Churchman. New York: Plenum Press.

Page, B. 1996. "Across the Great Divide: Agriculture and Industrial Geography." *Economic Geography* 72 (4): 376–97.

Pampille [Marthe Daudet]. [1913] 2008. "The Awful Meal." In *Les Bons Plats de France-Cuisine régionale.* Paris: CNRS Éditions.

Paradis, T. 2008. *The Greenwood Encyclopedia of Homes Through American History: 1821–1900.* Westport, CT: Greenwood Press.

Patel, Raj. 2008. *Stuffed and Starved: The Hidden Battle for the Food System.* New York: Melville House.

Pepitone, J. 2009. *Leggo Your Eggo: There's a Waffle Shortage.* CNNMoney.com. November 18. http://finance.yahoo.com/family-home/article/108191/leggo-your-eggo-theres-a-waffle-shortage.

Perkins, John H. 1997. *Geopolitics and the Green Revolution: Wheat, Genes, and the Cold War.* New York: Oxford University Press.

Perks, R. 1993. "Ukraine's Forbidden History: Memory and Nationalism." *Oral History* 21: 43–53.

Perren, Richard. 2006. *Taste, Trade, and Technology: The Development of the International Meat Industry since 1840.* Aldershot: Ashgate.

Peters, Lulu Hunt. 1922. *Diet and Health, with a Key to Counting Calories.* Chicago: Reilly and Lee.

Peterson, H. C. 2002. "The 'Learning Supply Chain': Pipeline or Pipedream?" *American Journal of Agricultural Economics* 84: 1329–36.

Petrick, Gabriella M. n.d. *Industrializing Taste: Food Processing and the Transformation of the American Diet, 1900–1965.* Baltimore: Johns Hopkins University Press.

Petrini, Carlo. 2001. *Slow Food: The Case for Taste.* New York: Columbia University Press.

Pettid, Michael J. 2008. *Korean Cuisine: An Illustrated History.* London: Reaktion Books.

Phillips, Lynne. 2006. "Food and Globalization." *Annual Revue of Anthropology* 35: 37–57.

Pilcher, Jeffrey. 2000. "Many Chefs in the National Kitchen: Cookbooks and Identity in Nineteenth Century Mexico." *Latin American Popular Culture: An*

Introduction, eds. William Beezley and Linda Curcia-Nagy. Oxford: Rowan-Littlefield.

Pilcher, Jeffrey M. 2004. "Empire of the 'Jungle': The Rise of an Atlantic Refrigerated Beef Industry, 1880–1920." *Food, Culture and Society* 7 (1): 63–78.

Pilcher, Jeffrey M. 2006. *Food in World History*. New York: Routledge.

Pitte, Jean-Robert, ed. 1990. *Les Restaurants dans le monde et à travers les âges*. Grenoble: Glénat.

Pizzey, Erin. 1981. *Slut's Cookbook*. Missouru: McDonald.

Pollan, Michael. 2006. *The Omnivore's Dilemma: A Natural History of Four Meals*. New York: Penguin Press.

Pollan, Michael. 2007. "Unhappy Meals." *New York Times* (January 28). http://www.nytimes.com/2007/01/28/magazine/28nutritionism.t.html.

Pollan, Michael. 2008. *In Defense of Food: An Eater's Manifesto*. New York: Penguin Press.

Pollan, Michael. 2009. *Food Rules: An Eater's Manual*. New York: Penguin Press.

Pontecorvo, C., and A. Fasulo. 1999. "Planning a Typical Italian Meal: A Family Reflection on Culture." *Culture and Psychology* 5 (3): 313–36.

Post, E. 1922. *Etiquette in Society, in Business, in Politics, and at Home*. New York: Funk and Wagnalls.

Pothukuchi, K., and J. L. Kaufman. 2000. "The Food System: A Stranger to the Planning Field." *Journal of the American Planning Association* 66 (2): 113–24.

Powell, Simon. 1992. *Agricultural Reform in China: From Communes to Commodity Economy, 1978–1990*. Manchester: Manchester University Press.

Pringle, Peter. 2005. *Food, Inc.: From Mendel to Monsanto—The Promises and Perils of the Biotech Harvest*. New York: Simon and Schuster.

Pritchard, W. N. 1998. "The Emerging Contours of the Third Food Regime: Evidence from Australian Dairy and Wheat Sectors." *Economic Geography* 74 (1): 64–74.

Probyn, Elspeth. 2000. *Carnal Appetites: Foodsexidentities*. London: Routledge.

Puck, Wolfgang, et al. 2004. *Cooking Basics for Dummies*. New York: For Dummies, Inc.

Putnam, Robert. 1988. "Diplomacy and Domestic Politics: The Logic of Two-Level Games." *International Organization* 42: 427–60.

Raikes, Philip. 1988. *Modernising Hunger: Famine, Food Surplus and Farm Policy in the EEC and Africa*. London: Catholic Institute for International Relations.

Raja, S., M. Changxing, and P. Yadav. 2008. "Beyond Food Deserts: Measuring and Mapping Racial Disparities in Neighborhood Food Environments." *Journal of Planning Education and Research* 27 (4): 469–82.

Rapp, Rayna. 1982. "Family and Class in Contemporary America: Notes toward an Understanding of Ideology." *Science and Society* 42 (3): 278–300.

Ray, Krishnendu. 2007. "Domesticating Cuisine: Food and Aesthetics on American Television." *Gastronomica* 7 (1): 50–63.

Raynolds, L. 1997. "Restructuring National Agriculture, Agro-food Trade, and Agrarian Livelihoods in the Caribbean." In *Globalising Food,* eds. D. Goodman and M. Watts. London: Routledge.

Re Cruz, Alicia. 2003. "Milpa As an Ideological Weapon: Tourism and Maya Migration to Cancún." *Ethnohistory* 50 (3): 489–502.

Riasanovsky, Nicholas V. 1993. *A History of Russia.* 5th ed. New York: Oxford University Press.

Rich, Adrienne. 1976. *Of Woman Born: Motherhood as Experience and Institution.* New York: Norton.

Richards, A. [1932] 2004. *Hunger and Work in a Savage Tribe: A Functional Study of Nutrition Among the Southern Bantu.* London: Routledge.

Rimmer, D. 1981. "'Basic Needs' and the Origins of the Development Ethos." *Journal of Developing Areas* 15: 215–38.

Ritzer, George. [1993] 1996. *The McDonaldization of Society: An Investigation into the Changing Character of Contemporary Social Life.* California: Pine Forge Press.

Roberts, Paul. 2008. *The End of Food.* New York: Houghton Mifflin Harcourt.

Roberts, Tanya. 2007. "WTP Estimates of the Societal Costs of U.S. Food-Borne Illness." *American Journal of Agricultural Economics* 89 (5): 1183–88.

Roe, Brian. 2004. "Optimal Sharing of Foodborne Illness Prevention Between Consumers and Industry: The Effect of Regulation and Liability." *American Journal of Agricultural Economics* 86 (2): 359–74.

Rombauer, Irma S. 1931. *The Joy of Cooking: A Compilation of Reliable Recipes with an Occasional Culinary Chat.* Missouri: A.C. Clayton.

Rombauer, Irma. [1936] 1946. *The Joy of Cooking.* Indianapolis: Bobbs Merrill.

Rombauer, Irma, and Marion Rombauer Becker. [1931] 1976. *The Joy of Cooking.* Indianapolis: Bobbs Merrill.

Rombauer Papers. Schlesinger Library, Cambridge MA.

Roodhouse, M. 2006. "Popular Morality and the Black Market in Britain, 1939–1955." In *Food and Conflict in the Age of the Two World Wars,* eds. F. Trentmann and F. Just. Basingstoke: Palgrave Macmillan.

Rothenberg, Daniel. 2000. *With These Hands: The Hidden World of Migrant Farmworkers Today.* Berkeley: University of California Press.

Roberts, Wayne. 2008. *The No-Nonsense Guide to World Food.* Oxford: New Internationalist Publications.

Ross, H. A. 1925. "Marketing of Milk in the Chicago Dairy District." *University of Illinois Agricultural Experiment Station Bulletin* 269.

Rossant, Juliette. 2004. *Super Chef: The Making of the Great Modern Restaurant Empires.* New York: Simon and Schuster.

Rubin, Lawrence C. 2008. *Food for Thought: Essays on Eating and Culture.* Jefferson: McFarland.

Ruiz, V. 1998. *From Out of the Shadow: Mexican American Women in Twentieth-Century America.* New York: Oxford University Press.

Salin, Victoria, and Neal Hooker. 2001. "Stock Market Reaction to Food Recalls." *Review of Agricultural Economics* 23 (1): 33–46.

Sanderson, Steven E. 1986. *The Transformation of Mexican Agriculture: International Structure and the Politics of Rural Change.* Princeton: Princeton University Press.

Scanlan, S. J., and J. C. Jenkins. 2001. "Military Power and Food Security." *International Studies Quarterly* 45: 159–87.

Schlosser, Eric. 2001. *Fast Food Nation: The Dark Side of the All-American Meal.* New York: Harcourt Mifflin Company.

Schmidt, J. 2007. "How to Feed Three Million Inhabitants: Berlin in the First Years after the Second World War, 1945–1948." In *Food and the City in Europe Since 1800,* eds. P. J. Atkins, P. Lummel, and D. J. Oddy. Aldershot: Ashgate.

Schneph, Randy, and Jasper Womach. 2008. *Potential Challenges to U.S. Farm Subsidies in the WTO.* New York: Nova Science Publishers.

Schrambling, Regina. 2004. "Julia Child, the French Chef for a Jell-O Nation, Dies at 91." *New York Times* (August 13). http://www.nytimes.com/2004/08/13/dining/13CND-CHILD.html.

Schrambling, Regina. 2005. "The Hungry Mind." *Los Angeles Times* (May 11). http://articles.latimes.com/2005/may/11/food/fo-dish11.

Schran, Peter. 1969. *The Development of Chinese Agriculture, 1950–1959.* Urbana, Illinois: University of Chicago Press.

Schwartz, Hillel.1986. *Never Satisfied: A Cultural History of Diets, Fantasies, and Fat.* New York: Free Press.

Schwartz, R. A., and T. A. Lyson. 2007. "Retail Relations: An Interlocking Directorate Analysis of Food Retailing Corporations in the United States." *Agriculture and Human Values* 24 (4): 489–98.

Schwartz, Ruth Cowan. 1983. *More Work for Mother: The Ironies of Household Technology from the Open Hearth to the Microwave.* New York: Basic Books.

Scott, James. 1990. *Domination and the Arts of Resistance: Hidden Transcripts.* Yale: Yale University Press.

Selden, Mark, and Victor D. Lippit, eds. 1982. *The Transition to Socialism in China.* London: Taylor and Francis.

Sen, A. 1981. *Poverty and Famines.* Oxford: Oxford University Press.

Seth, A., and G. Randall. 2005. *Supermarket Wars: Global Strategies for Food Retailers.* Houndsmills: Palgrave Macmillan.

Shapiro, Laura. 2004. "How Frugal is Gourmet?" *Slate* (September 29). http://www.slate.com/id/2107364/.

Shapiro, Laura. 2007. *Julia Child.* New York: Penguin.

Shapiro, Laura. [1986] 2008. *Perfection Salad: Women and Cooking at the Turn of the Century.* California: University of California Press.

Shaw, D. J. 2007. *World Food Security: A History Since 1945.* Basingstoke: Palgrave.

Sheller, Mimi. 2003. *Consuming the Caribbean.* London: Routledge.

Shipton, P. 1990. "African Famines and Food Security: Anthropological Perspectives." *Annual Review of Anthropology* 19: 353–94.

Shiva, Vandada. 1991. *The Violence of the Green Revolution: Third World Agri-culture, Ecology, and Politics.* London: Zed Books.

Shiva, Vandana. 2005. *Earth Democracy: Justice, Sustainability, and Peace.* Cambridge, MA: South End Press.

Simmel, Georg. [1910] 1997. "The Sociology of the Meal." In *Simmel on Culture,* eds. David Frisby and Mike Featherstone, trans. M. Ritter and D. Frisby. London: Sage.

Sinclair, Upton. 1906. *The Jungle.* New York: Doubleday.

Skocpol, Theda, and Kenneth Finegold. 1982. "State Capacity and Economic Intervention in the Early New Deal." *Political Science Quarterly* 97: 255–78.

Sloan, J., ed. 1958. *Notes from the Warsaw Ghetto: The Journal of Emmanuel Ringleblum.* New York: McGraw-Hill.

Smil, Vaclav. 2001. *Enriching the Earth: Fritz Haber, Carl Bosch, and the Transformation of World Food Production.* Cambridge: MIT Press.

Smith, Andrew. 2007. *The Oxford Encyclopedia of Food and Drink in America.* Oxford: Oxford University Press.

Smith, D., and S. Cummins. 2009. "Obese Cities: How our Environment Shapes Overweight." *Geography Compass* 3: 518–35.

Smith, Delia. [1971] 2008. *How to Cheat at Cooking.* London: Ebury.

Smith, Delia, and Flo Bailey. 1995. *Delia Smith's Winter Collection.* London: BBC Books.

Smith, Dorothy. 1993. "The Standard North American Family: SNAF as an Ideological Code." In *Writing the Social: Critique, Theory, and Investigations.* Toronto: University of Toronto Press.

Smith, Everett M. 1957. "Yugoslavs to See US Supermarket." *Christian Science Monitor* (July 2).

Smith, Gilly. 2008. *The Jamie Oliver Effect.* London: André Deutsch.

Sobal, J. 1999. "Food System Globalization, Eating Transformations, and Nutrition Transformations." In *Food in Global History,* ed. R. Grew. Colorado: Westview Press.

Sontag, Susan. 1977. *Illness as Metaphor.* New York: Vintage.

Spang, Rebecca L. 2000. *Invention of the Restaurant: Paris and Modern Gastronomic Culture.* Cambridge: Harvard University Press.

Stacey, J. 1990. *Brave New Families.* New York: Basic Books.

Stack, Carol. 1974. *All Our Kin: Strategies for Survival in a Black Community.* New York: Harper.

Stanziani, A. 2003. *La Qualité des Produits en France, XVIIIe–XXe Siècles.* Paris: Belin.

Stearns, Peter N. 1997. *Fat History: Bodies and Beauty in the Modern West.* New York: New York University Press.

Steege, P. 2007. *Black Market, Cold War: Everyday Life in Berlin, 1946–1949.* New York: Cambridge University Press.

Steigher, W. R. 2002. "To Gro Harlem Brundtland, Director General, WHO (World Health Organization)" [letter]. Washington, DC: United States Department

of Health and Human Services Office of International Affairs. www.who.int/
dietphysicalactivity/media/en/gsfao_cmo_096.pdf.

Steinbeck, John. 1939. *Grapes of Wrath.* New York: Viking.

Stern, Jane, and Michael Stern. 1984. *Square Meals.* New York: Knopf.

Stevenson, G. W., and R. Pirog. 2008. "Values-based supply chains: Strategies for
agrifood enterprises of the middle." In *Food and the Mid-level Farm,* eds. T. A.
Lyson, G. W. Stevenson, and R. Welch. Cambridge, MA: MIT Press.

Stewart, Hayden, Noel Blisard, and Dean Jolliffe. 2006. *Let's Eat Out. Americans
Weigh Taste, Convenience, and Nutrition.* United States Department of Agriculture Economic Research Service Economic Information Bulletin 19 (October). http://www.ers.usda.gov/Publications/EIB19/.

Stickney, Robert R. 1996. *Aquaculture in the United States: A Historical Survey.*
New York: John Wiley and Sons.

Strasser, Susan. 1982. *Never Done: A History of American Housework.* New York:
Pantheon Books.

Stull, Donald, and Michael Broadway. 2004. *Slaughterhouse Blues: The Meat and
Poultry Industry in North America.* Belmont, CA: Wadsworth.

Tarasuk, V., N. Dachner, B. Poland, and S. Gaetz. 2009. "Food Deprivation is
Integral to the 'Hand to Mouth' Existence of Homeless Youths in Toronto."
Public Health Nutrition 12: 1437–42.

Tasch, Woody. 2010. *Inquiries into the Nature of Slow Money: Investing as if
Food, Farms, and Fertility Mattered.* White River Junction, VT: Chelsea Green
Publishing.

Tauger, M. B. 2001. *Natural Disaster and Human Action in the Soviet Famine of
1931–1933.* Pittsburgh: University of Pittsburgh.

Taylor, Joseph E., III. 1999. *Making Salmon: An Environmental History of the
Northwest Fisheries Crisis.* Seattle: University of Washington Press.

Temple, B. 2001. "Polish Families: A Narrative Approach." *Journal of Family Issues* 22.

Teodosijevi, S. B. 2003. "Armed Conflicts and Food Security." *ESA Working Paper*
3–11. Rome: FAO.

"Tested and Approved Recipes." 1917. *Good Housekeeping* (August). http://history
matters.gmu.edu/d/5055/.

Thaxton, R. 2008. *Catastrophe and Contention in Rural China: Mao's Great Leap
Forward Famine and the Origins of Righteous Resistance in Da Fo Village.*
Cambridge: Cambridge University Press.

Theophano, J., and K. Curtin. 1991. "Sisters, Mothers and Daughters: Food Exchange and Reciprocity in an Italian-American Community." In *Diet and Domestic Life in Society,* ed. A. Sharman. Philadelphia: Temple University Press.

Theophano, J. 2003. *Eat My Words: Reading Women's Lives Through the Cookbooks They Wrote.* New York: Palgrave Macmillan.

Thiébaut, Philippe. 1994. "De 1920 à 1990: A la recherche d'un style de vie con-
temporain." In *Histoire de la table-Les arts de la table des origines à nos jours,*
eds. Pierre Ennis, Gérard Mabille, and Philippe Thiébaut. Paris: Flammarion.

Thompson, Paul. 1992. *The Ethics of Aid and Trade: U.S. Food Policy, Foreign Competition, and the Social Contract*. Cambridge: Cambridge University Press.

Thompson, Paul. 2007. *Food Biotechnology in Ethical Perspective*. Dordrecht: Springer.

Trentmann, F. 2006. "Coping with Shortage: the Problem of Food Security and Global Visions of Coordination, c. 1890s–1950." In *Food and Conflict in the Age of the Two World Wars*, eds. F. Trentmann and F. Just. Basingstoke: Palgrave Macmillan.

Trienekens, G. 2000. "The Food Supply in the Netherlands During the Second World War." In *Food, Science, Policy and Regulation in the Twentieth Century*, eds. D. F. Smith and J. Phillips, 117–33. London: Routledge.

Trubek, Amy. 2000. *Haute Cuisine: How the French Invented the Culinary Profession*. Philadelphia: University of Pennsylvania Press.

Trubek, Amy B. 2008. *The Taste of Place: A Cultural Journey into Terroir*. Berkeley: University of California Press.

Trueman, John M. 1905. *Milk Supply of Chicago and Twenty-Six Other Cities*. University of Illinois Experiment Station Bulletin 120.

Turner, Katherine Leonard. 2009. "Tools and Spaces: Food and Cooking in Working-Class Neighborhoods, 1880–1930." In *Food Chains*, eds. W. Belasco and R. Horowitz. Philadelphia: University of Pennsylvania Press.

United Nations. 2010. *Codex Alimentarius: Current Official Standards*. http://www.codexalimentarius.net/web/standard_list.do?lang = en.

United States Census Bureau. 1933. *Census of Distribution: Vol. 1: Retail Distribution, Part 2, Reports by States*.

United States Department of Agriculture. 1959. *Food: The Yearbook of Agriculture, 1959*. 86th Congress, 1st Session, House Document 29.

United States Department of Agriculture. 2010. *Dietary Guidelines for Americans*. http://www.cnpp.usda.gov/dietaryguidelines.htm.

United States Department of Agriculture and United States Department of Health and Human Services. 2005. *Dietary Guidelines for Americans, 2005*. http://www.health.gov/dietaryguidelines/dga2005/document/.

United States Department of Agriculture and United States Department of Health and Human Services. 2010. *Dietary Guidelines for Americans 2010*. 7th ed. Washington, DC: U.S. Government Printing Office. www.dietaryguidelines.gov.

Valenzuela-Zapata, Ana G., and Gary Paul Nabham. 2003. *¡Tequila! A Natural and Cultural History*. Tucson: University of Arizona Press.

Vaughan, M. 1987. *The Story of an African Famine: Gender and Famine in Twentieth Century Malawi*. Cambridge: Cambridge University Press.

Vernon, J. 2007. *Hunger: A Modern History*. Cambridge, MA: Belknap Press.

Visser, M. 1993. *The Rituals of Dinner: The Origins, Evolution, Eccentricities and Meaning of Table Manners*. Harmondsworth: Penguin.

Wackernagel, Mathis, and William Rees. 1996. *Our Ecological Footprint: Reducing Human Impact on the Earth*. Gabriola Island, BC: New Society Publishers.

Wansink, Brian. 2006. *Mindless Eating: Why We Eat More Than We Think.* New York: Bantam.

Warren, Louis. 1997. *The Hunter's Game: Poachers and Conservationists in Twentieth-Century America.* New Haven: Yale University Press.

Warren, Wilson J. 2007. *Tied to the Great Packing Machine: The Midwest and Meatpacking.* Iowa City: University of Iowa Press.

Watson, James L., and Melissa L. Caldwell, eds. 2005. *The Cultural Politics of Food and Eating: A Reader.* Malden, MA: Blackwell.

Watson, James, ed. 2006. *Golden Arches East: McDonald's in East Asia.* Stanford: Stanford University Press.

Watts, M. J. 1983. *Silent Violence: Food, Famine and Peasantry in Northern Nigeria.* Berkeley: University of California Press.

Watts, Michael J. 2004. "Are Hogs like Chickens? Enclosure and Mechanization in Two 'White Feat' Filières." In *Geographies of Commodity Chains,* eds. Alex Hughes and Suzanne Reimer. New York: Routledge.

Waxman, A. 2004. "The WHO Global Strategy on Diet, Physical Activity and Health: The Controversy on Sugar." *Development* 47 (2): 75–82.

Webster, C. 1982 "Healthy or Hungry Thirties?" *History Workshop Journal* 13: 110–29.

Wehrwein, Austin C. 1959. "Premier to Find Iowa Doors Open: Hosts Hope to Show Russian Cross-section View of life Under US Capitalism." *New York Times* (September 11).

Weir, David, and Mark Schapiro. 1981. *Circle of Poison: Pesticides and People in a Hungry World.* Oakland: Food First.

Weiser, S. D., D. R. Bangsberg, S. Kegeles, K. Ragland, M. B. Kushel, and E. A. Frongillo. 2009. "Food Insecurity among Homeless and Marginally Housed Individuals Living with HIV/AIDS in San Francisco." *AIDS and Behaviour* 13: 841–48.

Welsh, Susan O., Carol Davis, and Anne Shaw. 1993. "USDA's Food Guide: Background and Development." *Miscellaneous Publication No 1514* (September). Available at: http://www.cnpp.usda.gov/Publications/MyPyramid/OriginalFood GuidePyramids/FGP/FGPBackgroundAndDevelopment.pdf. Accessed November 3, 2009.

Wheaton, Barbara Ketcham. 1983. *Savoring the Past.* Philadelphia: University of Pennsylvania Press.

Whitaker, George M. 1911. "The Milk Supply of Chicago and Washington." *U.S. Department of Agriculture, Bureau of Animal Industry Bulletin* 438.

Whitaker, J. 2005. "Domesticating the Restaurant." In *From Betty Crocker to Feminist Food Studies: Critical Perspectives on Women and Food,* eds. A. Avakian and B. Haber. Amherst: University of Massachusetts Press.

Whitbeck, L. B., X. Chen, and K. D. Johnson. 2006. "Food Insecurity among Homeless and Runaway Adolescents." *Public Health Nutrition* 9: 47–52.

White House Conference on Food, Nutrition, and Health. 1969. *Final Report.* Washington, DC: United States Government Printing Office. http://www.nns. nih.gov/1969/full_report/PDFcontents.htm#top.

White, J. 2000. "Kinship and Reciprocity and the World Market." In *Dividends of Kinship: Meanings and Uses of Social Relatedness,* ed. P. Schweitzer. New York: Routledge.

Whorton, James C. 1982. *Crusaders for Fitness: The History of American Health Reformers.* Princeton: Princeton University Press.

Wilk, Richard R. 2006a. *Fast Food/Slow Food: The Cultural Economy of the Global Food System.* Lamham, MD: AltaMira Press.

Wilk, Richard R. 2006b. *Home Cooking in the Global Village: Caribbean Food from Buccaneers to Ecotourists.* Oxford: Berg.

Williams, Brett. 1984. "Why Migrant Women Feed Their Husbands Tamales: Foodways as a Basis for as Revisionist View of Tejano Family Life." In *Ethnic and Regional Foodways in the United States: The Performance of Group Identity,* eds. Linda Keller Brown and Kate Mussell, 113–26. Knoxville: University of Tennessee Press.

Williams-Forson, Psyche. 2000. "Suckin' the Chicken Bone Dry: African American Women, History and Food Culture." In *Cooking Lessons: The Politics of Gender and Food,* ed. Sherrie Inness. Lanham, MD: Rowman and Littlefield.

Wills, C. 2001. "Women, Domesticity, and the Family: Recent Feminist Work in Irish Cultural Studies." *Cultural Studies* 15 (1).

Wilson, Edward O. 1999. *The Diversity of Life.* New York: W. W. Norton and Company.

Wilson, Geoff A., and Olivia J. Wilson. 2001. *German Agriculture in Transition: Societies, Policies and Environment in a Changing Europe.* New York: Palgrave Macmillan.

Winston, M. L. 2002. *Travels in the Genetically Modified Zone.* Cambridge: Harvard University Press.

Witt, Doris. 1999. *Black Hunger: Food and the Politics of U.S. Identity.* New York: Oxford University Press.

Wizenberg, Molly. 2009. *A Homemade Life.* New York: Simon and Schuster.

World Health Organization. 2000. "Obesity: Preventing and Managing a Global Epidemic." *World Health Organization Technical Report Series* 894. Geneva. http://apps.who.int/bookorders/anglais/detart1.jsp.

World Health Organization. 2003. "Diet, Nutrition, and the Prevention of Chronic Disease: Report of a Joint WHO/FAO Expert Consultation." *WHO Technical Report Series 916.* http://whqlibdoc.who.int/trs/WHO_TRS_916.pdf.

World Health Organization Regional Office for Europe. 2003. *Food-Based Dietary Guidelines in the WHO European Region.* Copenhagen. http://www.euro.who.int/Document/E79832.pdf.

World Health Organization. 2004. *Global Strategy on Diet, Physical Activity and Health.* www.who.int/entity/dietphysicalactivity/strategy/eb11344/strategy_english_web.pdf.

World Trade Organization. 1994. *Marrakesh agreement establishing the World Trade Organization.* http://www.wto.org/english/docs_e/legal_e/04-wto_e.htm.

World Trade Organization. 2005. *European Communities—Export Subsidies on sugar. AB-2005–2: Report of the Appellate Body.* http://www.wto.org/english/tratop_e/dispu_e/265_266_283abr_e.pdf.

Worster, Donald. 1979. *Dust Bowl: The Southern Plains in the 1930s.* New York: Oxford University Press.

Wrangham, Richard. 2009. *Catching Fire: How Cooking Made Us Human.* New York: Basic Books.

Wriston, John C. Jr. 1991. *Vermont Inns and Taverns, Pre-Revolution to 1925 An Illustrated and Annotated Checklist.* Rutland, VT: Academy Books.

Wu, David Y. H., and Sidney C. H. Cheung. 2002. *The Globalization of Chinese Food.* Honolulu: University of Hawaii Press.

Wu, Xu. 2004. "'Ethnic Foods' and Regional Identity." *Food and Foodways* 12 (4): 225–46.

Yeats, William Butler. 2010. "The Second Coming." In *Poetry by William Butler Yeats: Sailing to Byzantium, Politics, the Second Coming, Blood and the Moon, Easter, 1916, a Prayer for My Daughter.* Memphis, TN: Books, LLC.

Young, James Harvey. 1989. *Pure Food: Securing the Food and Drugs Act of 1906.* Princeton: Princeton University Press.

Zweinger-Bargielowska, I. 2000. *Austerity in Britain: Rationing, Controls, and Consumption 1939–1955.* Oxford: Oxford University Press.

CONTRIBUTORS

Peter J. Atkins is professor of geography at Durham University. Much of his research has been on the history of food and drink, and he has also published on public health, for instance with regard to the current crisis of contaminated ground water in Bangladesh. His most recent book is *Liquid Materialities: A History of Milk, Science and the Law* (2010).

Warren Belasco is Professor Emeritus of American Studies at the University of Maryland, Baltimore County, and a visiting professor of gastronomy at Boston University. He is the author of *Appetite for Change* (1990), *Meals to Come* (2006), and *Food: The Key Concepts* (2008).

Amy Bentley is an associate professor in the Department of Nutrition, Food Studies, and Public Health at New York University. A historian with interests in the social, historical, and cultural contexts of food, she is the author of *Eating for Victory: Food Rationing and the Politics of Domesticity* (1998), and is currently working on a history of infant food and feeding practices. Bentley is cofounder of the Experimental Cuisine Collective, an interdisciplinary group of scientists, food studies folks, and chefs who study the intersection of science and food.

Daniel Block is a professor of geography at Chicago State University, the director of the Fred Blum Neighborhood Assistance Center, and an adjunct assistant professor of preventive medicine at Northwestern University. He has a broad interest in spatial health disparity patterns and community-based research, with a particular interest in inner-city food access issues. He led the Northeastern Illinois Community Food Security Assessment, a large scale food access study of the Chicago region. In an earlier project, he led a large food-access study of the Austin neighborhood of Chicago's west side. Dr. Block is active in the Chicago Food Policy Advisory Council, as well as community commissions on food access issues. Dr. Block has a PhD in geography from UCLA, where he focused on milk, public health, regulation, and the rise of the modern American food system. He is a past president of the Agriculture, Food, and Human Values Society.

Priscilla Parkhurst Ferguson received her PhD in French literature from Columbia University, where she now teaches in the Department of Sociology. Her work on French literary and culinary culture includes *Literary France: The Making of a Culture* (1987), *Paris as Revolution: Reading the 19th-century City* (1994), and *Accounting for Taste: The Triumph of French Cuisine* (2004) as well as articles in sociological, literary, and historical journals. She is currently writing a book on "Food Talk."

Maya Joseph is a PhD candidate in politics at the New School for Social Research, where her dissertation examines how American regulatory agencies address new technologies such as animal cloning. She has taught in the Food Studies Department of the New School University, and currently maintains a rooftop garden in New York City.

Alice Julier is associate professor and director of the graduate program in food studies at Chatham University. She writes and teaches about material life, cultural ideals, social justice, domestic life, race, consumption, men and food, and gender in retail marketing. Her work includes "Mapping Men onto the Menu," a coedited double issue of *Food and Foodways*; "Julia at Smith," in a special issue of *Gastronomica*; "The Political Economy of Obesity: The Fat Pay All," in the most recent edition of *Food and Culture: A Reader*; and "Hiding Race and Class in the Discourse of Commercial Food" in *From Betty Crocker to Feminist Food Studies*. Her book, *Things Taste Better in Small Houses: Food, Friendship, and Inequality,* is forthcoming.

Marion Nestle is Paulette Goddard Professor in the Department of Nutrition, Food Studies, and Public Health at New York University (NYU), which she chaired from 1988–2003. She is also professor of sociology at NYU and visiting professor of nutritional sciences at Cornell. She is the author of *Food Politics: How the Food Industry Influences Nutrition and Health* (revised edition, 2007), *Safe Food: The Politics of Food Safety* (revised edition, 2010), *What to Eat* (2006), *Pet Food Politics: The Chihuahua in the Coal Mine* (2008), and the just released *Feed Your Pet Right* (with Malden Nesheim). Her current project is a book about calories, also with Dr. Nesheim. She writes the "Food Matters" column for the *San Francisco Chronicle,* and blogs daily (almost) at www.foodpolitics.com and for TheAtlantic.com/Life, and twitters @marionnestle.

Fabio Parasecoli is associate professor of food studies at the New School in New York City. His research focuses on the intersections among food, media, and politics. His current projects focus on the history of Italian food and on the sociopolitical aspects of geographical indications. His recent publications include *Food Culture in Italy* (2004), the introduction to *Culinary Cultures in Europe* (The Council of Europe, 2005), and *Bite Me! Food in Popular Culture* (2008).

Jeffrey M. Pilcher is a professor of history at the University of Minnesota, where he teaches classes on the world history of food and drink. His books include the prize-winning volume, *Que vivan los tamales! Food and the Making of Mexican Identity* (1998), *The Sausage Rebellion: Public Health, Private Enterprise, and Meat in Mexico City* (2006), and *Food in World History* (2006). He is editor of the forthcoming *Oxford Handbook of the History of Food.*

Signe Rousseau (née Hansen) teaches critical literacy at the University of Cape Town, where she also completed her doctoral and post-doctoral work. She is a contributing author to *The Business of Food: Encyclopedia of the Food and Drink Industry, Food Cultures of the World, Icons of American Cooking, The Oxford Companion to Food,* and author of the forthcoming *Food Media: Celebrity Chefs and the Politics of Everyday Interference,* also published by Berg.

Amy B. Trubek is an associate professor in the Nutrition and Food Science Department at the University of Vermont. Trained as a cultural anthropologist and chef, her research interests include the history of the culinary profession, globalization of the food supply, the relationship between taste and place, and cooking as a cultural practice. She is the author of *Haute Cuisine: How the French Invented the Culinary Profession* (2000) and *The Taste of Place: A Cultural Journey into Terroir* (2008) as well as numerous articles and book chapters.

INDEX